Many Californias

WESTERN LITERATURE SERIES

Western Trails: A Collection of

Short Stories by Mary Austin

selected and edited by Melody Graulich

Cactus Thorn

by Mary Austin with foreword and

afterword by Melody Graulich

Dan De Quille, the Washoe Giant

A Biography and Anthology

prepared by Richard A. Dwyer

and Richard E. Lingenfelter

Desert Wood: An Anthology of Nevada Poets

edited by Shaun T. Griffin

Many Californias: Literature from the Golden State

edited by Gerald W. Haslam

MANY

CALIFORNIAS

LITERATURE FROM

THE GOLDEN STATE

EDITED BY GERALD W. HASLAM

UNIVERSITY OF NEVADA PRESS ▲▲ RENO, LAS VEGAS, & LONDON

Western Literature Series Editor:
John H. Irsfeld

Special thanks are due Sonoma State
University for a summer research stipend
that aided the editor's work on this project.

The paper used in this book meets the
requirement of American National
Standard for Information Sciences—
ANSI Z39.48-1984. Binding materials were
chosen for strength and durability.

Jacket and cover art:
Alexis Smith
Same Old Paradise (1987)
mixed media installation, 20 × 60 feet
Courtesy of Margo Leavin Gallery,
Los Angeles
Photographer: Peter Muscato

Library of Congress
Cataloging-in-Publication Data
Many Californias : literature from the
Golden State / edited by Gerald W. Haslam.
    p.   cm. — (Western literature series)
  ISBN 0-87417-182-2 (cloth ed. : acid-free
paper). — ISBN 0-87417-183-0 (pbk. :
acid-free paper)
  1. American literature—California.
2. California—Literary collections.
I. Haslam. Gerald W.   II. Series.
PS571.C2M36   1991
810.8′09794—dc20   91-34480
                                              CIP

9 8 7 6 5 4 3 2 1

For my mother,

who read to me,

and for all the

fine California writers

I could not include . . .

Contents

. . . .

*Asterisks indicate excerpts from longer works.
Titles of poems are enclosed in quotation marks.

Acknowledgments

. . . .

Gary Soto, who was an architect of the contemporary writers' section, deserves particular thanks. Without him this task would have been immeasurably more difficult.

A number of folks suggested entries for this volume, or generously offered bibliographies, or both: James D. Houston, Jean Sherrell, David Wilson, Michael Kowalewski, David Madden, Gerald Locklin, Wanda Burzycki, Robert Dantzler, David Fine, James J. Rawls, David Robertson, Marek Brieger, Joyce P. Miller, Lawrence Clark Powell, and Ernesto Trejo. To them I am most grateful.

Introduction

. . . .

Califoria is elusive. That's true largely because so many who look for it think they already know where and what it is. Outsiders are often more certain of their versions than are natives because outsiders are seldom burdened by facts or knowledge of the state's actual diversity. They don't know the many Californias.

For people who yearn to be here, this state seems to be a land of tan, sun-bleached blondes with straight teeth, blondes who don't have to work but who do hurry on roller skates from hot tubs to haute cuisine to the strobe-lit splendor of nightclubs; or, in the last century, a place where gold nuggets could be scooped up by the shovelful and fruit burgeoned year-round. Un-realistic expectations have led to disillusionment: said a homeless man at a San Francisco shelter in 1989, "I thought California was about somethin', but it ain't about nothin'."

How could opinions be less strong? The first mention of the Golden State in literature, *Las sergas de Esplandian* by Garci Ordoñez de Montalvo, which antedated European discovery of the area by two decades, created a California of the mind that still intrigues: "Know ye that on the right hand of the Indies there is an island called California."

There you have it. Illusion preceded reality and this state has rarely been viewed as conventional or common since. While 30 million human beings experience real life here every day, California remains at least as much state of mind as state of the union.

Back at the turn of the twentieth century, Theodore Roosevelt observed, "When I am in California, I am not in the west, I am west of the west." It was clear even then that this state was indeed unique. The terms of that uniqueness, however, remained puzzling. Like many outsiders, Roosevelt failed to recognize that there were—and are—many Californias and that those Californias are constantly changing. At the very time he saw a ver-sion of the state that wasn't western, vaqueros and cowboys herded cattle

I

over much of the state's open territory; shepherds trailed their flocks toward fresh grass; America's last "wild Indian," Ishi, struggled to survive in hills and canyons east of the Sacramento Valley; and miners still haunted this state's deserts and foothills. Those sections were the West, period.

But in Southern California at the same time, a great real-estate boom, wedded to an increasingly romanticized version of the mission past, was churning. Meanwhile, Hollywood was beginning its move from sleepy village to motion-picture capital, producing a society that was indeed west of the West . . . west, perhaps, of anything. In fact the very word "west" in this context took on new and bizarre connotations. Yet those places by no means summarized the reality of the state—there was and is so much more.

Where is California? What is it? It is out there where Californians—including authors—really live, a collection of distinct regions, of unique histories, and varied people gathered under one name: we call all of it California, but it has no homogeneous geographic or cultural core. To paraphrase poet Gary Snyder, the state is a fiction but the region is real. Actual people live in particular places—Huron or Susanville, Watts or Hayfork, Bishop or El Sobrante—no one lives in the mythical golden state . . . except in their imaginations.

Early California

First Voices

. . . .

In the beginning was the land.

Mountain ranges surrounded the marshes and prairies of one of the world's great valleys. Vast deserts lay to the east and the south. Forests of pines, of hemlocks, of firs, and of great redwoods blocked the northwest, where rivers surged toward the sea. The coastline—steep and rocky and rich to the north, gentle and sandy and rich toward the south— was a primordial, life-giving, life-sustaining boundary.

Then came The People—Miwok, Atsugewi, Tubatulabal, Wintun, Yana, and Chumash; Hupa, Cahuilla, Karok, Paiute, and Wappo, along with so many others—cultures that bound their lives to the land, as the following "Yokuts Prayer" illustrates: as they found it.

> Do you see me?
> See me, Tuushiut!
> See me, Pamashiut!
> See me, Yuhait!
> See me, Eshepat!
> See me, Pitsuriut!
> See me, Tsuksit!
> See me, Ukat!
>
> Do you all help me?
> My words are tied in one
> With the great mountains,
> With the great rocks,
> With the great trees,
> In one with my body
> And my heart.
> Do you all help me
> With supernatural power

And you, day,
And you, night,
All of you see me
On with this world!

These were varied cultures, varied types: the Mohave were tall, muscular, and formidable; the Pomo appeared soft, with dark, round faces; the Yuki were the shortest tribe in North America. California's Indians were, in fact, as physically varied as the Europeans who would one day disrupt and overwhelm them. None had written languages, so their tales and poems were oral and were employed to explain and establish both sacred and profane worlds—the domains of the spirit and the body, a distinction they believed was by no means absolute.

They visioned the land, these people, living it in their dreams and words as certainly as they dwelt upon it. In chanted poems and traditional tales, California's native population affirmed the sacrality of not only their own lives, but of all life and of the forces shaping it. To the Wintun, "Earth Diver" is a portentous, necessary account of the beginning:

All was water. A mud hen thought that there must be earth below, so all the mud hens dived but they found nothing. Finally turtle said he would try too. He made himself a waterproof suit to travel in under water. Then he got much rope. He said, "If I jerk on the rope, pull me out. If there is no earth, I'll come to the surface all alone."

Finally they pulled him up. He was helpless when he came to the surface. His mouth and ears were all plugged up with mud. They saw mud under his nails. His eyes were wedged with mud. There was mud in his mouth. They got a little mud this way. They dried it and made an island. It grew and became the world.

The very earth of the Northern Miwok is accounted for by "The Beginning of the World":

In the beginning the world was rock. Every year the rains came and fell on the rock and washed off a little; this made earth. By and by, plants grew on the earth and their leaves fell and made more earth. Then pine trees grew and their needles and cones fell every year and with the other leaves and bark made more earth and covered more of the rock. If you look closely at the ground in the woods you will see how the top is leaves and bark and pine needles and cones, and how a little below the top these are matted together, and a little deeper they are rotting and breaking up into earth. This is the way the world grew—and it is growing still.

Yes, it is growing still. Lest these powerful myths sound implausible, remember that our most revered Biblical creation tale, Genesis, begins not with stone or water, but a spiritual being.

California Indians recognized that language was powerful, so its skilled use was much admired among them. With it, people could create new realities or give order and meaning to events that seemed random or threatening. With it, people could evoke the sacred and project the unknowable future. With it, the past could be explained and feelings could be soothed. Tales— the spoken equivalent of written prose—were used to transmit many sacred or mythic lessons. An old Maidu man told this vivid story, "The Birth of the Sacramento River":

The Maidu who used to live around here were happy and rich. Then a whole lot of water came down here and the whole Sacramento Valley was into an ocean. Most of the people were drowned. Some tried to swim away but the frogs and salmon ate them. Only two people got away safe to the Sierras.

Great Man blessed those Maidu with many children, and all the tribes arose. One wise old chief ruled them all. This chief went to the Coast Range but was disconsolate because the valley was still under water. He stayed there for nine days without any food, thinking about the water that covered the plains of the world.

This thinking and fasting changed him. He was not like a man. No arrow could hurt him. He could never be killed after that. He called out to Great Man and told him to get rid of the flood waters. Great Man tore open the Coast Range and made the waters flow down to the ocean. This flow of water was how the Sacramento River began.

Spoken prose was also employed to transmit more nearly secular lessons— how to hunt and why, where to gather and why, what to cook and why— but even those, in the deepest sense, were sacred: everything in Native life seemed to have meaning beyond itself. What people did on this earth mirrored what spirits did on another plane of existence.

That sacred, portentous worldview most separates Native visions from ours. As anthropologist William Brandon suggests, "The Indian world was, and is, a world more alien, really, than we can even yet quite realize." The most common mistake non-Indians make in assessing earlier American cultures is to judge them on the basis of their own, less-mystical standards.

California's indigenous cultures were profoundly literary, and they viewed the power of language as little short of magical. Another scholar, A. Grove Day, explains that poetry "was used only on certain occasions; it was always rhythmic in form and was chanted or sung, usually to the accompaniment of drums or melodic instruments." It was also reserved for significant, often religious purposes because, according to Day, "poetry was power." The "Yokuts Death Song," for instance, captures the most profound of spiritual enigmas, the very meaning of our existence:

> All my life
> I have been seeking
> Seeking.

As that lean, powerful poem illustrates, repetition was the major poetic device, and virtuosity in employing words was much admired. The "Atsugewi Lovers' Song" seemed to say more than the sum of its text:

> It is above that you and I shall go
> Along the Milky Way you and I shall go
> Along the Flower Trail you and I shall go
> Picking flowers on our way you and I shall go,
>> Where will you and I sleep?
>> At the down-turned jagged rim
>> Of the sky
>> You and I will sleep.

So did "Wintun Lullaby":

> Sleep! Sleep!
> In the Land of Dreams
> Find your Grown-up Self

Your future family.
Sleep! Sleep!

Another important use of language was to promote the recovery of the ill or injured. This "Yuma Shaman's Song" was utilized to aid the infirm, and it poetically offers good advice:

> Your heart is good.
> Shining Darkness will be here.
> You think only of sad unpleasant things.
> You are to think of goodness.
> Lie down and sleep here.
> Shining Darkness will join us.
> You think of this goodness in your dream.
> Goodness will be given to you.
> I will speak for it, and it will come to pass.
> It will happen here.
> I will ask for your good.
> It will happen as I sit by you.
> It will be done as I sit here in this place.

Many white people—their illusions shaped by splendid images of Plains Indians in flowing war bonnets and astride heroic horses—have classified Native California cultures as somehow inferior to Indians elsewhere. Anthropologists Theodora Kroeber and Robert Heizer explain, "In their ignorance and their intolerant racism, the white men called the Californians 'Diggers,' regarding them as scarcely human. Indian killers were tolerated, their profession considered an honorable one by many of their fellows." There were indeed savages in California then, but few were Indians.

Many non-Indians have produced books about California's native inhabitants—Helen Hunt Jackson's *Ramona* is perhaps best known—but none have equaled the grandeur of literary expressions produced by this state's tribes. There is, perhaps, one exception: *Ishi in Two Worlds*, Theodora Kroeber's powerful, unembellished retelling of the story of "the last wild Indian in North America." It is one of California's indispensable books, for it gives readers a sense of what was lost when indigenous cultures were destroyed.

Ishi was the last of his tribe, the Yana, and after surrendering himself at a slaughterhouse near Oroville, he was taken to San Francisco where he lived the rest of his life. Kroeber suggests consequences of this:

> The History of Ishi and his people is, inexorably, part of our own history. We have absorbed their lands into our holdings. Just so must we be the responsible custodians of their tragedy, absorbing it into our tradition and morality.

Prior to the arrival of Europeans, this state boasted a diverse and rich native population. Scholars estimate that 300,000 Indians dwelled in California in A.D. 1500, with the Great Central Valley hosting more than half. By 1910—about the time Ishi emerged from the wilderness—disease, displacement, massacres, and the destruction of their environment had reduced their number to only 16,000. In 1960, following a period of slightly more enlightened treatment by their conquerors, the number had risen to 30,000. It remains relatively constant at that figure today, one-tenth of their original population. And what are the consequences? In *Almost Ancestors*, Kroeber and Heizer recount an observation by Fanny Flounder, a Yurok shaman, as she stood at the mouth of the Klamath River:

> You see what happens. The earth tips so far that the ocean spills into the river. Whales will come up the river!
> And all this is because there are no longer enough Yurok people left.
> When there were many of my people they danced and sang stamping their feet hard on the earth.
> This kept the earth from tipping and the ocean from flowing into the river.

Hispanic California

· ·

The first Spanish explorers and settlers of this region created scant literature. They were too preoccupied with the rigors of survival in an alien, challenging land and with establishing a tenuous society, one that would change in the 1820s when news of Mexican independence arrived. Travel journals and diaries dominate literature from the Spanish period and while not artistically accomplished, they are nevertheless revealing, offering human faces to the European conquest of this region.

Fray Pablo Font and Juan Bautista de Anza, for instance, seem to have been men much concerned with status and dignity, with sacred and secular authority, even when so far away from their native land. Writing in 1776, Font, a priest, revealed something of the difficulty and tension of life on the frontier, as well as of how the frayed nerves of people far from home could lead to petty disputes. Encountering Anza, the local military commander, Font complained that the officer did not share plans with him even though he did inform the servants.

Anza replied, "Well, why do you wish, your Reverence, that I should tell you what I decide? I am under no obligation to do so."

Agreeing that no obligation existed, the priest nonetheless insisted, "it appears to me natural that you should tell me, as a companion, what you decide, in order that I may not be caught unprepared, for I also have to travel."

To further illustrate the human tensions generated among those supposedly stoic soldiers and missionaries, it should be pointed out that even the legendary Franciscan Junipero Serra, father president of the missions, feuded with Lieutenant Pedro Fages, who would become Alta California's first governor. The former, only five feet three inches tall, described Fages as "a ridiculous little fellow," while the soldier asserted that Serra behaved with "great despotic spirit and total indifference." These courageous men, surviving far from home, appear to have been possessive of whatever dignity or authority was granted them in the hinterland.

As unimportant as such exchanges may appear, they capture moment-to-moment existence in what is remembered as a heroic age. But as soldiers and associates throughout time have known, boredom is the great enemy, and the early Spanish conquistadors were no exceptions. As they wrested control of coastal California from its native inhabitants, fleas and dirt and nothing-to-do were their greatest opponents.

They did explore, however, despite petty bickering, and these soldiers and priests opened much of present-day California to European settlement. In 1772, Fages and Fray Juan Crespi became the first Spaniards to discover the Great Central Valley, which the priest described as "a grand plain as level as the palm of the hand." He also calculated that the Sacramento River, which flowed from the valley, was "the largest that has been discovered in New Spain."

Perhaps the most delightful memoir from that period of discovery was written by a priest from Aragon in northern Spain, Francisco Garcés. In 1776, with a mule and two Mohave guides, this adventuresome man trekked across the Mojave Desert, over the Tehachapi Mountains, then arrived at a Yokuts' village on "a great river which made much noise and whose waters were crystalline, bountiful and palatable." Garcés had an unusual affinity for native peoples, and Kern River dwellers seemed to sense that. The priest-explorer was unable to swim, so he stripped to his drawers and was carried across that stream's icy water by four Yokuts, whose village was near the present site of Bakersfield.

Wrote Garcés in his journal:

> The people of the rancheria had a great feast over my arrival, and having regaled me well I reciprocated to them all with tobacco and glass beads, congratulating myself on seeing the people so affable and affectionate. The young men are fine fellows, and the women very comely and clean . . . they take great care of the hair and do it up in a topknot; they wear petticoats of antelope skin and mantas of fur; though they are not very coy.

They were certainly not coy by Spanish standards of that day, at any rate, and too trusting for their own good as it turned out because this visit presaged the end of the Yokuts' world.

But this was not the intention of Francisco Garcés, of whom the ethnocentric Font wrote, "he is so fit to get along with Indians, and go about among them, that he seems just like an Indian himself. He squats cross-legged in a circle with them, or at night around the fire, for two or three hours, or even longer, all absorbed, forgetting aught else, discoursing to them with great serenity and deliberation; and though the food of the Indians is as nasty and disgusting as their dirty selves, the padre eats it with great gusto and says it is appetizing and very nice."

Garcés represents well the paradox of that age of conquest: he appears to have been a good, brave man who genuinely sought to bring enlightenment as he understood it to a people he admired, but who opened the door to the destruction of their cultures in the process. His diary remains a most memorable literary work from that period.

In the years before America's conquest, two momentous events dominated life on what was called "the far coast": in 1822, news of Mexico's independence from Spain reached this backwater province and governance gradually altered; twelve years later, the missions were "secularized"—turned into parish churches rather than outposts of the Spanish church. California became a marginal Mexican province, thinly settled (its non-Indian population in 1845 was approximately 7,000) and loosely controlled, although a cadre of Spanish and *mestizo* men and women—called *Californios*—did indeed build lives for themselves in this distant, dusty realm. Despite that relatively sparse population, it nonetheless constituted one of the largest non-nomadic pastoral societies the world has known. Cowhides and tallow were the region's principal products, although the fur of sea otters and, later, beavers would draw more than a few *extanjeros* (foreigners).

Few periods of California's history have been as clouded in romantic illusions as have "the halcyon days of the dons." Gertrude Atherton portrayed it this way in *The Splendid, Idle Forties*:

Caballeros, with silver on their wide, gray hats and on their saddles of embossed leather, gold and silver embroidery on their velvet serapes, crimson sashes about their slender waists, silver spurs and buckskin botas, stood tensely in their stirrups as the racers flew by. . . .

Beautiful women in silken fluttering gowns, bright flowers holding the mantilla from flushed awakened face, sat their impatient horses as easily as a gull rides a wave. . . .

"It is the gayest, the happiest, the most careless life in the world," thought Pio Pico, shutting his teeth, as he looked around him. "But how long will it last? Curse the Americans! They are coming."

Life had its moments then, of course, but in fact it was not the gayest, not the happiest, not the most careless in the world. Life on that frontier was, for most, rough; to pick one small example, fleas abounded—note how frequently that telltale word *pulgas* appears in Californian place names. And if one happened to be a *peón* rather than a *patrón*—as the overwhelming majority of the population was—hard work that bordered on slavery was the rule. Nonetheless, harsh though existence was, it was mitigated by a sense of purpose and shared cultural values, as journals from the time illustrate. And, as Atherton wrote, the Americans were indeed coming.

Two central facts about Mexican California must not be ignored: ranchos depended upon the work of Indians and mestizos, and European hauteur relegated those with Indian blood to subservient status within the society. "In return for their labors," reports historian James J. Rawls, "the Indians usually received nothing more than shelter, food and clothing." This was, moreover, a society of horses and riders (a local proverb said that no person with even a trace of Spanish blood would do work except on horseback), and well into this century Mexican *vaqueros* remained indispensable to the cattle industry in California.

Then it all ended. As *El Clamor Publico*, a Californio newspaper, proclaimed: "*O! fatalidad!* . . . California is lost to all Spanish-Americans!" It actually took about two decades before the world of the Californios was fully destroyed, but the Treaty of Guadalupe Hidalgo in 1848 and the Gold Rush that immediately followed sealed the fate of Hispanic California. Perhaps the finest literary document from the Mexican period is the journal of Mariano Guadalupe Vallejo, the last military governor of the erstwhile province. In it he noted bitter reality:

> The language now spoken in our country, the laws which govern us, the faces which we encounter daily, are those of the masters of the land and, of course, antagonistic to our interests and rights, but what does that matter to the conqueror? He wishes his own well-being and not ours!—a thing that I consider only natural in individuals, but which I condemn in a government which has promised to respect and make respected our rights, and to treat us as its own sons. But what does it avail us to complain? The thing has happened and there is no remedy.

Less than three centuries after they had come as *conquistadores,* Hispanics found themselves conquered in a land they had seized from Indians.

American Incursion and the Gold Rush

. . . .

In 1796 Ebeneezer Dorr became the first Yankee known to have landed on California's coast. Nine years later, William Shaler landed his ship to trade for sea otter pelts and take on supplies, and wrote a journal that is the earliest report of the state by an Anglo-American. He was astounded at the abundance of wildlife ("there are great numbers of sea elephants . . . of sea otter . . . of whales . . . a great abundance of excellent fish"). He also noted the hospitality of local natives, saying of Santa Catalina, "The Indian inhabitants of this island . . . came and encamped with us, and readily afforded us every aid in their power."

In 1826, the trapper Jedediah Smith and two companions led the first transcontinental journey—across deserts, over mountains, into California—by an Anglo-American, an event that astonished and threatened local Mexican authorities. Smith recognized that authorities controlled only a thin coastal strip, and he and his fellow trappers roamed interior California at will. Fortunately, Smith kept a journal, so we know he was much impressed with the region's native inhabitants: "The indians are numerous honest and peaceable in their dispositions." But what most astounded him was the profligacy of beavers, which he and his fellow trappers most sought to harvest, and of grizzlies, which they feared might seek to harvest trappers—so they shot the great bears indiscriminately.

By 1827, when Smith's party reached the American River near present-day Sacramento, it carried fifteen hundred pounds of beaver pelts. The spelling in his journal was idiosyncratic, but Smith's perceptions seem to have been honest and straightforward. In 1828, for example, he recorded the following:

> 29 the March N 6 Miles and encamp on river. i was obliged to cross many slous of the River that were verry miry and passed great numbers of indians who were engaged in digging Roots. I succeeded in giving to

them some presents. they were small size and apparently verry poor and miserable. The most of them had little Rbit Skin Robes. 11 Beaver taken.

By 1835, when young Richard Henry Dana visited this sparsely settled Mexican province, a pastoral but by no means genteel society had developed in California. "Among the Spaniards," he wrote in *Two Years Before the Mast*, "there is no working class; the Indians being slaves and doing all the hard work." He revealed his own Yankee prejudice when he continued, "The Californians are an idle, thriftless people, and can make nothing for themselves. The country abounds in grapes, yet they buy bad wine made in Boston."

He also observed the classic Mexican race/class system: "Their complexions are various, depending . . . upon their rank; or, in other words, upon the amount of Spanish blood they can lay claim to." The darker the person, the less likely that he or she was upper class. Because of Dana's candor and skill as a writer, *Two Years Before the Mast* marks the beginning of high-quality, English-language literature from and about California.

Well before the Treaty of Guadalupe Hidalgo ceded California to the United States, the province's fate had become clear. In 1846 Manuel Micheltorena, the last Mexican governor of California, declared, "We find ourselves threatened by hordes of Yankee emigrants, who have already begun to flock into our country and whose progress we cannot resist. . . . What are we to do?" As it turned out, they were able to do very little to defend this large, thinly settled realm, and they lost it.

The treaty ending Mexican control was signed on February 2, 1848. Nine days earlier, on January 24, James Marshall had seen something glittering in a tailrace at Captain John Sutter's sawmill in Coloma, and the gold that had for so long inflamed Spanish dreams was found. Ironically, it would lead to rapid American settlement of the province, and to the first surge of English-language writing from these golden shores: William Manly, Louisa Smith Clapp, George Horatio Derby, Alonzo Delano, John Rollin Ridge, and later Bret Harte, Ina Coolbrith, Charles Warren Stoddard, Horace Bell, Helen Hunt Jackson, Mark Twain, and Ambrose Bierce would sweep California not only into the Union but into the Union's literary domain as well. By 1860, San Francisco was the thirteenth-largest city in the nation and an acknowledged literary center.

These first American writers in California were all from elsewhere, of course, so they took little in this state for granted. Dana, for instance, describes California before it was swept into the American republic, revealing the prejudices and rationalizations that would eventually lead to American annexation of the region. Clapp describes a raw, rowdy society that characterized the gold rush, including the beating of "a very gentlemanly young Spaniard," that later appeared in John Rollin Ridge's fictionalized biography, *The Life and Adventures of Joaquin Murieta* [*sic*], the first novel by a person of Native American ancestry. It was also the first novel dealing with a Mexican in the United States. Published in 1854 in San Francisco, Ridge's book profoundly influenced many subsequent treatments of "the Robin Hood of California," a bandit whose heroic reputation seems to have been invented by the Cherokee author. And so it goes, a new society forming itself and presenting new possibilities. A cadre of newcomers exploring California's literary potential as eagerly as miners had probed its sandbars and gullies. In the person of young writers such as these, America had arrived and had begun to reshape the Golden State.

Richard Henry Dana

Richard Henry Dana (1815–82) viewed California the way so many Americans did in the nineteenth century, from offshore gazing landward. He was still a teenager when, in January of 1835, aboard the brig Pilgrim, *he saw Santa Barbara. Five years later his book describing that journey,* Two Years Before the Mast—*a classic that has remained in print ever since—was the first significant Yankee description of this state. In it, he revealed not only the unique society he found in the Mexican province, but also a Yankee's disdain for Hispanics, whom he considered lazy and corrupt. Although Dana wrote other books and became a successful attorney, he was not a satisfied man. He wrote to his son in 1872, "My life has been a failure compared with what I might have done. My great success—my book—was a boy's work, done before I came to the Bar."*

. . . .

CALIFORNIOS

The officers were dressed in the costume which we found prevailed through the country—a broad-brimmed hat, usually of a black or dark brown color, with a gilt or figured band round the crown, and lined inside with silk; a short jacket of silk or figured calico, (the European skirted body-coat is never worn;) the shirt open in the neck; rich waistcoat, if any; pantaloons wide, straight, and long, usually of velvet, velveteen or broadcloth; or else short breeches and white stockings. They wear the deer-skin shoe, which is of a dark brown color, and (being made by Indians) usually a good deal ornamented. They have no suspenders, but always wear a sash round the waist, which is generally red, and varying in quality with the means of the wearer. Add to this the never-failing cloak, and you have the dress of the Californian. This last garment, the cloak, is always a mark of the rank and wealth of the owner. The "gente de razon," or aristocracy, wear cloaks of black or dark blue broadcloth, with as much velvet and trimmings as may be; and from this they go down to the blanket of the Indian, the middle classes wearing something like a large table-cloth, with a hole in the middle for the head to go through. This is often as coarse as a blanket, but being beautifully woven with various colors, is quite showy at a distance. Among the Spaniards there is no working class; (the Indians being slaves and doing all the hard work;) and every rich man looks like a grandee, and every poor scamp like a broken-down gentleman. I have often seen a man with a fine figure and courteous manners, dressed in broadcloth and velvet, with a noble horse completely covered with trappings; without a *real* in his pockets, and absolutely suffering for something to eat. . . .

By being thus continually engaged in transporting passengers with their goods, to and fro, we gained considerable knowledge of the character, dress, and language of the people. The dress of the men was as I have before described it. The women wore gowns of various texture—silks, crape, calicoes, etc.—made after the European style, except that the sleeves were short, leaving the arm bare, and that they were loose about the waist, having no corsets. They wore shoes of kid, or satin, sashes or belts of bright colors, and almost always a necklace and ear-rings. Bonnets they had none. I only saw one on the coast, and that belonged to the wife of an American sea-captain who had settled in San Diego and had imported the chaotic mass of straw and ribbon as a choice present to his new wife. They wear their hair (which is almost invariably black, or a very dark brown) long in their necks, sometimes loose, and sometimes in long braids; though the married women often do it up on a high comb. Their only protection against the sun and weather is a large mantle, which they put over their heads, drawing it close round their faces, when they go out of doors, which is generally only in pleasant weather. When in the house or sitting out in front of it, which they often do in fine weather, they usually wear a small scarf or neckerchief of a rich pattern. A band, also, about the top of the head, with a cross, star, or other ornament in front, is common. Their complexions are various, depending—as well as their dress and manner—upon their rank; or, in other words, upon the amount of Spanish blood they can lay claim to. Those who are of pure Spanish blood, having never intermarried with the aborigines, have clear brunette complexions, and sometimes even as fair as those of English women. There are but few of these families in California, being mostly those in official stations, or who, on the expiration of their offices, have settled here upon property which they have acquired; and others who have been banished for state offences. These form the aristocracy; inter-marrying, and keeping up an exclusive system in every respect. They can be told by their complexions, dress, manner, and also by their speech; for, calling themselves Castilians, they are very ambitious of speaking the pure Castilian language, which is spoken in a somewhat corrupted dialect by the lower classes. From this upper class they go down by regular shades, growing more and more dark and muddy, until you come to the pure Indian, who runs about with nothing upon him but a small piece of cloth, kept up by a wide leather strap drawn round his waist. Generally speaking, each person's caste is decided by the quality of the blood, which shows itself, too plainly to be concealed, at first sight. Yet the least drop of Spanish blood, if it be only of quatroon or octoon, is sufficient to raise them from the rank of slaves, and entitle them to wear a suit of clothes—boots, hat, cloak, spurs, long knife, and all complete, though coarse and dirty as may be,—and to call themselves Españolos, and to hold property, if they can get any.

The fondness for dress among the women is excessive, and is often the ruin of many of them. A present of a fine mantle, or of a necklace or pair of ear-rings gains the favor of the greater part of them. Nothing is more common than to see a woman living in a house of only two rooms, and the ground for a floor, dressed in spangled satin shoes, silk gown, high comb, and gilt, if not gold, ear-rings and necklace. If their husbands do not dress them well enough, they will soon receive presents from others. They used to spend whole days on board our vessel, examining the fine clothes and ornaments, and frequently made purchases at a rate which would have made a seamstress or waiting-maid in Boston open her eyes.

Next to the love of dress, I was most struck with the fineness of the voices and beauty of the intonations of both sexes. Every common ruffian-looking fellow, with a slouched hat, blanket cloak, dirty underdress, and soiled leather leggings, appeared to me to be speaking elegant Spanish. It was a pleasure simply to listen to the sound of the language, before I could attach any meaning to it. They have a good deal of the Creole drawl, but it is varied with an occasional extreme rapidity of utterance in which they seem to skip from consonant to consonant, until, lighting upon a broad, open vowel, they rest upon that to restore the balance of sound. The women carry this peculiarity of speaking to a much greater extreme than the men, who have more evenness and stateliness of utterance. A common bullock-driver, on horseback, delivering a message, seemed to speak like an ambassador at an audience. In fact, they sometimes appeared to me to be people on whom a curse had fallen, and stripped them of everything but their pride, their manners, and their voices.

Another thing that surprised me was the quantity of silver that was in circulation. I certainly never saw so much silver at one time in my life, as during the week that we were at Monterey. The truth is, they have no credit system, no banks, and no way of investing money but in cattle. They have no circulating medium but silver and hides—which the sailors call "California bank notes." Everything that they buy they must pay for in one or the other of these things. The hides they bring down dried and doubled, in clumsy ox-carts, or upon mules' backs, and the money they carry tied up in a handkerchief,—fifty, eighty, or an hundred dollars and half dollars.

Louisa Smith Clapp

Louisa Smith Clapp (1819–1906), who signed her work Dame Shirley, was an experienced writer who also happened to be the wife of a physician practicing his trade at "the diggings." She wrote a series of "letters" while living in a mining camp on the Feather River in 1851–52. They were first gathered into book form in 1922 and have since been recognized as the finest account of life in this state's early mining camps. In an age when many writers employed noms de plume, *Dame Shirley's real name remains a mystery. Various literary scholars offer different versions: Both Franklin Walker (in* San Francisco's Literary Frontier) *and James D. Hart (in* The Oxford Companion to American Literature) *call her Louise Amelia Knapp Smith Clappe; however, Lawrence Clark Powell (in* California Classics) *lists her as Louisa Smith Clapp, explaining "Christened Louisa Amelia Knapp Smith, and adding later the married name of Clapp, no wonder she adopted a pseudonym! Louisa became Louise, and 'e' was added to Clapp." In any case, she left us an important book.*

. . . .

LIFE AT THE MINES

July 5, 1852

About half an hour after the close of the Oration, the ladies from the hill arrived. They made a pretty picture descending the steep, the one with her wealth of floating curls turbaned in a showy nubie, and her white dress set off by a crimson scarf; the other, with a little Pamella hat, placed coquettishly upon her brown, braided tresses, and a magnificent Chinese shawl enveloping her slender figure. So lately arrived from the States, with everything fresh and new, they quite extinguished poor Mrs. B. and myself, trying our best to look fashionable in our antique mode of four years ago.

The dinner was excellent. We had a real, live Captain, a very gentlemanly person, who had actually been in action during the Mexican War for president. Many of the toasts were quite spicy and original; one of the new ladies sang three or four beautiful songs, and everything passed off at Rich Bar quite respectably. To be sure, there was a small fight in the bar-room—which is situated just below the dining-room—during which much speech and a little blood were spouted; whether the latter catastrophe was caused by a blow received, or the large talking of the victim, is not known. Two peacefully inclined citizens who, at the first battle-shout, had rushed manfully to the rescue, returned at the subsiding of hostilities with blood-bespattered shirt-bosoms; at which fearful sight, the pretty wearer of the Pamella hat—one of the delinquents being her husband—chose to go faint, and would not finish her dinner, which, as we saw that her distress was real, somewhat marred our enjoyment. . . .

August 4, 1852

The Committee tried five or six Spaniards, who were proven to have been the ringleaders in the Sabbath-day riot. Two of them were sentenced to be whipped, the remainder to leave the Bar that evening; the property of all to be confiscated to the use of the wounded persons. Oh Mary! imagine my anguish when I heard the first blow fall upon those wretched men. I had never thought that I should be compelled to hear such fearful sounds, and, although I immediately buried my head in a shawl, nothing can efface from memory the disgust and horror of that moment. I had heard of such things, but heretofore had not realized, that in the nineteenth century, men could be beaten like dogs, much less that other men, not only could sentence such barbarism, but could actually stand by and see their own manhood degraded in such disgraceful manner. One of these unhappy persons was a very gentlemanly young Spaniard, who implored for death in the most moving terms. He appealed to his judges in the most eloquent manner—as gentlemen, as men of honor; representing to them that to be deprived of life, was nothing in comparison with the never-to-be-effaced stain of the vilest convict's punishment—to which they had sentenced him. Finding all his entreaties disregarded, he swore a most solemn oath, that he would murder every American that he should chance to meet alone, and as he is a man of the most dauntless courage, and rendered desperate by a burning sense of disgrace, which will cease only with his life, he will doubtless keep his word. . . .

John Rollin Ridge

John Rollin Ridge (1827–67), also known as Yellow Bird, was a San Francisco journalist who wrote the first published novel by a Native American, Life and Adventures of Joaquin Murieta, the Celebrated California Bandit. This fictionalized account of an actual outlaw has been treated as biography in some circles. Rumors that Hispanic Californians were planning to band together to retake the state were common in the 1850s, and Ridge's book played upon them. It also touched archetypical elements common to legends of "honorable" outlaws everywhere. But the deepest sources of Ridge's novel were probably familial: his father and grandfather were chiefs of the Cherokees when they were forced to leave their southern homeland and trek to the Indian Territory along the infamous Trail of Tears; later they were murdered by enemies within the tribe. Vengeance became central to John Rollin Ridge, as it did to the fictional Murrieta.

. . . .

JOAQUÍN

The first that we hear of him in the Golden State is that, in the spring of 1850, he is engaged in the honest occupation of a miner in the Stanislaus placers, then reckoned among the richest portions of the mines. He was then eighteen years of age, a little over the medium height, slenderly but gracefully built, and active as a young tiger. His complexion was neither very dark or very light, but clear and brilliant, and his countenance is pronounced to have been, at that time, exceedingly handsome and attractive. His large black eyes, kindling with the enthusiasm of his earnest nature, his firm and well-formed mouth, his well-shaped head from which the long, glossy, black hair hung down over his shoulders, his silvery voice full of generous utterance, and the frank and cordial bearing which distinguished him made him beloved by all with whom he came in contact. He had the confidence and respect of the whole community around him, and was fast amassing a fortune from his rich mining claim. He had built him a comfortable mining residence in which he had domiciled his heart's treasure— a beautiful Sonorian girl, who had followed the young adventurer in all his wanderings with that devotedness of passion which belongs to the dark-eyed damsels of Mexico. It was at this moment of peace and felicity that a blight came over the young man's prospects. The country was then full of lawless and desperate men, who bore the name of Americans but failed to support the honor and dignity of that title. A feeling was prevalent among this class of contempt for any and all Mexicans, whom they looked upon as no better than conquered subjects of the United States, having no rights which could stand before a haughtier and superior race. They made no exceptions. If the proud blood of the Castilians mounted to the cheek of a partial descendant of the Mexiques, showing that he had inherited the old chivalrous spirit of his Spanish ancestry, they looked upon it as a saucy presumption in one so inferior to them. The prejudice of color, the antipathy of races, which are always stronger and bitterer with the ignorant and unlettered, they could not overcome, or if they could, would not because it afforded them a convenient excuse for their unmanly cruelty and oppression. A band of these lawless men, having the brute power to do as they pleased, visited Joaquín's house and peremptorily bade him leave his claim, as they would allow no Mexicans to work in that region. Upon his remonstrating against such outrageous conduct, they struck him violently over the face, and, being physically superior, compelled him to swallow his wrath. Not content with this, they tied him hand and foot and ravished his mistress before his eyes. They left him, but the soul of the young man was from that moment darkened. It was the first injury he had ever received at the hands of the Americans, whom he had always hitherto respected, and it wrung him to the soul as a deeper and deadlier wrong from that very circumstance. He departed with his weeping and almost heart-broken mistress for a more northern portion of the mines; and the next we hear of him, he is cultivating a little farm on the banks of a beautiful stream that watered a fertile valley, far out in the seclusion of the mountains. Here he might hope for peace— here he might forget the past, and again be happy. But his dream was not destined to last. A company of unprincipled Americans—shame that there should be such bearing the name!—saw his retreat, coveted his little home surrounded by its fertile tract of land, and drove him from it, with no other excuse than that he was "an infernal Mexican intruder!" Joaquín's blood boiled in his veins, but his spirit was still unbroken, nor had the iron so far entered his soul as to sear up the innate sensitiveness to honor and right which reigned in his bosom. Twice broken up in his honest pursuit of fortune, he resolved still to labor on with unflinching brow and with that true *moral* bravery, which throws its redeeming light forward upon his subsequently dark and criminal career. How deep must have been the anguish of that young heart and how strongly rooted the native honesty of his soul, none can know or imagine but they who have been tried in a like manner. He bundled up his little movable property, still accompanied by his faithful bosom-friend, and again started forth to strike once more, like a brave and honest man, for fortune and for happiness.

Bret Harte

Bret Harte (1836–1902) created much of the popular image of the gold rush with his tales and poems. But his career almost didn't evolve because, as a journalist in the small town of Union on Humboldt Bay, he wrote an editorial criticizing locals for massacring Indians. He was forced to flee to San Francisco to avoid being lynched. There he became a prominent literary figure, one of the editors of The Overland Monthly, *and perhaps the first nationally known writer from California—a state he virtually created in the minds of many nineteenth-century readers. "The Society Upon the Stanislaus" and "Dickens in Camp" capture the rowdy reality of mining-camp life, plus a little of the romanticism that Harte loved.*

. . . .

THE SOCIETY UPON THE STANISLAUS

I reside at Table Mountain, and my name is Truthful James;
I am not up to small deceit, or any sinful games;
And I'll tell in simple language what I know about the row
That broke up our Society upon the Stanislow.

But first I would remark, that it is not a proper plan
For any scientific gent to whale his fellow-man,
And, if a member don't agree with his peculiar whim,
To lay for that same member for to "put a head" on him.

Now nothing could be finer or more beautiful to see
Than the first six months' proceedings of that same Society,
Till Brown of Calaveras brought a lot of fossil bones
That he found within a tunnel near the tenement of Jones.

Then Brown he read a paper, and he reconstructed there,
From those same bones, an animal that was extremely rare;
And Jones then asked the Chair for a suspension of the rules,
Till he could prove that those same bones was one of his lost mules.

Then Brown he smiled a bitter smile, and said he was at fault—
It seemed he had been trespassing on Jones' family vault.
He was a most sarcastic man, this quiet Mr. Brown,
And on several occasions he had cleaned out the town.

Now I hold it is not decent for a scientific gent
To say another is an ass—at least, to all intent;
Nor should the individual who happens to be meant
Reply by heaving rocks at him, to any great extent.

Then Abner Dean of Angel's raised a point of order—when
A chunk of old red sandstone took him in the abdomen,
And he smiled a kind of sickly smile, and curled up on the floor,
And the subsequent proceedings interested him no more.

For, in less time than I write it, every member did engage
In a warfare with the remnants of a palæozoic age;
And the way they heaved those fossils in their anger was a sin,
Till the skull of an old mammoth caved the head of Thompson in.

And this is all I have to say of these improper games,
For I live at Table Mountain, and my name is Truthful James;
And I've told in simple language what I know about the row
That broke up our Society upon the Stanislow.

DICKENS IN CAMP

Above the pines the moon was slowly drifting,
   The river sang below;
The dim Sierras, far beyond, uplifting
   Their minarets of snow.

The roaring camp-fire, with rude humor, painted
   The ruddy tints of health
On haggard face and form that drooped and fainted
   In the fierce race for wealth;

Till one arose, and from his pack's scant treasure
   A hoarded volume drew,
And cards were dropped from hands of listless leisure
   To hear the tale anew.

And then, while round them shadows gathered faster,
   And as the firelight fell,
He read aloud the book wherein the Master
   Had writ of "Little Nell."

Perhaps 't was boyish fancy—for the reader
   Was youngest of them all—
But, as he read, from clustering pine and cedar
   A silence seemed to fall;

The fir-trees, gathering closer in the shadows,
   Listened in every spray,
While the whole camp with "Nell" on English meadows
   Wandered and lost their way.

And so in mountain solitudes—o'ertaken
   As by some spell divine—
Their cares dropped from them like the needles shaken
   From out the gusty pine.

Lost is that camp and wasted all its fire,
    And he who wrought that spell?
Ah! towering pine and stately Kentish spire,
    Ye have one tale to tell!

Lost is that camp, but let its fragrant story
    Blend with the breath that thrills
With hop-vine's incense all the pensive glory
    That fills the Kentish hills.

And on that grave where English oak and holly
    And laurel wreaths entwine,
Deem it not all a too presumptuous folly,
    This spray of Western pine!

Samuel Langhorne Clemens

Samuel Langhorne Clemens (Mark Twain, 1835–1910) spent some of his salad days hiding from the Civil War in California. From that sojourn came his most famous short story, "The Celebrated Jumping Frog of Calaveras County," plus many hilarious sketches published in The Overland Monthly. *"Baker's Blue-Jay Yarn," first collected in* A Tramp Abroad *(1865), is another of his narrator-within-the-yarn stories that manages to reveal more about humans than its subject might imply, just as it also reveals the tall-tale tradition so loved by the author. He was an associate of Bret Harte, Ina Coolbrith, and Charles Warren Stoddard at* The Overland Monthly *and a fixture in San Francisco's social life in the 1860s. After he returned to the East and published novels such as* The Adventures of Huckleberry Finn *(1884), the ex-printer, ex-steamboat pilot, and ex-journalist emerged by the end of the nineteenth century as one of this country's greatest writers.*

. . . .

BAKER'S BLUE-JAY YARN

Animals talk to each other, of course. There can be no question about that; but I suppose there are very few people who can understand them. I never knew but one man who could. I knew he could, however, because he told me so himself. He was a middle-aged, simple-hearted miner who had lived in a lonely corner of California, among the woods and mountains, a good many years, and had studied the ways of his only neighbors, the beasts and the birds, until he believed he could accurately translate any remark which they made. This was Jim Baker. According to Jim Baker, some animals have only a limited education, and use only very simple words, and scarcely ever a comparison or a flowery figure; whereas, certain other animals have a large vocabulary, a fine command of language and a ready and fluent delivery; consequently these latter talk a great deal; they like it; they are conscious of their talent, and they enjoy "showing off." Baker said, that after long and careful observation, he had come to the conclusion that the bluejays were the best talkers he had found among birds and beasts. Said he:

"There's more *to* a bluejay than any other creature. He has got more moods, and more different kinds of feelings than other creatures; and, mind you, whatever a bluejay feels, he can put it into language. And no mere commonplace language, either, but rattling, out-and-out book-talk—and bristling with metaphor, too—just bristling! And as for command of language—why *you* never see a bluejay get stuck for a word. No man ever did. They just boil out of him! And another thing: I've noticed a good deal, and there's no bird, or cow, or anything that uses as good grammar as a bluejay. You might say a cat uses good grammar. Well, a cat does—but you let a cat get excited once; you let a cat get to pulling fur with another cat on a shed, nights, and you'll hear grammar that will give you the lockjaw. Ignorant people think it's the *noise* which fighting cats make that is so aggravating, but it ain't so; it's the sickening grammar they use. Now I've never heard a jay use bad grammar but very seldom; and when they do, they are as ashamed as a human; they shut right down and leave.

"You may call a jay a bird. Well, so he is, in a measure—because he's got feathers on him, and don't belong to no church, perhaps; but otherwise he is just as much a human as you be. And I'll tell you for why. A jay's gifts, and instincts, and feelings, and interests, cover the whole ground. A jay hasn't got any more principle than a Congressman. A jay will lie, a jay will steal, a jay will deceive, a jay will betray; and four times out of five, a jay will go back on his solemnest promise. The sacredness of an obligation is a thing which you can't cram into no bluejay's head. Now, on top of all this, there's another thing; a jay can out-swear any gentleman in the mines. You think a cat can swear. Well a cat can; but you give a bluejay a subject that calls for his reserve-powers, and where is your cat? Don't talk to *me*—I know too much about this thing. And there's yet another thing; in the one little particular of scolding—just good, clean, out-and-out scolding—a bluejay can lay over anything, a human or divine. Yes, sir, a jay is everything that a man is. A jay can cry, a jay can laugh, a jay can feel shame, a jay can reason and plan and discuss, a jay likes gossip and scandal, a jay has got a sense of humor, a jay knows when he is an ass just as well as you do—maybe better. If a jay ain't human, he better take in his sign, that's all. Now I'm going to tell you a perfectly true fact about some bluejays.

"When I first begun to understand jay language correctly, there was a little incident happened here. Seven years ago, the last man in this region but me moved away. There stands his house—been empty ever since; a log house, with a plank roof—just one big room, and no more; no ceiling—nothing between the rafters and the floor. Well, one Sunday morning I was sitting out here in front of my cabin, with my cat, taking the sun, and looking at the blue hills, and listening to the leaves rustling so lonely in the trees, and thinking of the home away yonder in the states, that I hadn't heard from in thirteen years, when a bluejay lit on that house, with an acorn in his mouth, and says, 'Hello, I reckon I've struck something.' When he spoke, the acorn dropped out of his mouth and rolled down the roof, of course, but he didn't care; his mind was all on the thing he had struck. It was a knot-hole in the roof. He cocked his head to one side, shut one eye and put the other one to the hole, like a possum looking down a jug; then he glanced up with his bright eyes, gave a wink or two with his wings—which signifies gratification, you understand—and says, 'It looks like a hole, it's located like a hole—blamed if I don't believe it *is* a hole!'

"Then he cocked his head down and took another look; he glances up perfectly joyful, this time; winks his wings and his tail both, and says, 'Oh, no, this ain't no fat thing, I reckon! If I ain't in luck!—why it's a perfectly elegant hole!' So he flew down and got that acorn, and fetched it up and dropped it in, and was just tilting his head back, with the heavenliest smile on his face, when all of a sudden he was paralyzed into a listening attitude and that smile faded gradually out of his countenance like a breath off'n a razor, and the queerest look of surprise took its place. Then he says, 'Why I didn't hear it fall!' He cocked his eye at the hole again, and took a long look; raised up and shook his head; stepped around to the other side of the hole and took another look from that side; shook his head again. He studied a while, then he just went into the *details*—walked round and round the hole and spied into it from every point of the compass. No use. Now he took a thinking attitude on the comb of the roof and scratched the back of his head with his right foot a minute, and finally says, 'Well, it's too many for *me,* that's certain; must be a mighty long hole; however, I ain't got no time to fool around here, I got to 'tend to business; I reckon it's all right—chance it, anyway.'

"So he flew off and fetched another acorn and dropped it in, and tried to flirt his eye to the hole quick enough to see what become of it, but he was too late. He held his eye there as much as a minute; then he raised up and sighed, and says, 'Confound it, I don't seem to understand this thing, no way; however, I'll tackle her again.' He fetched another acorn, and done his level best to see what become of it, but he couldn't. He says, 'Well, *I* never struck no such hole as this before; I'm of the opinion it's a totally new kind of a hole.' Then he begun to get mad. He held in for a spell, walking up and down the comb of the roof and shaking his head and muttering to himself; but his feelings got the upper hand of him, presently, and he broke loose and cussed himself black in the face. I never see a bird take on so about a little thing. When he got through he walks to the hole and looks in again for half a minute; then he says, 'Well, you're a long hole, and a deep hole, and a mighty singular hole altogether—but I've started in to fill you, and I'm d—d if I *don't* fill you, if it takes a hundred years!'

"And with that, away he went. You never see a bird work so since you was born. He laid into his work like a nigger, and the way he hove acorns into that hole for about two hours and a half was one of the most exciting and astonishing spectacles I ever struck. He never stopped to take a look any more—he just hove 'em in and went for more. Well, at last he could hardly flop his wings, he was so tuckered out. He comes a-drooping down, once more, sweating like an ice-pitcher, drops his acorn in and says, '*Now* I guess I've got the bulge on you by this time!' So he bent down for a look. If you'll believe me, when his head come up again he was just pale with rage. He says, 'I've shoveled acorns enough in there to keep the family thirty years, and if I can see a sign of one of 'em I wish I may land in a museum with a belly full of sawdust in two minutes!'

"He just had strength enough to crawl up on to the comb and lean his back agin the chimbly, and then he collected his impressions and begun to free his mind. I see in a second that what I had mistook for profanity in the mines was only just the rudiments, as you may say.

"Another jay was going by, and heard him doing his devotions, and stops to inquire what was up. The sufferer told him the whole circumstance, and says, 'Now yonder's the hole, and if you don't believe me, go and look for yourself.' So this fellow went and looked, and comes back and says, 'How many did you say you put in there?' 'Not any less than two tons,' says the sufferer. The other jay went and looked again. He couldn't seem to make it out, so he raised a yell, and three more jays come. They all made the sufferer tell it over again, then they all discussed it, and got off as many leather-headed opinions about it as an average crowd of humans could have done.

"They called in more jays; then more and more, till pretty soon this whole region 'peared to have a blue flush about it. There must have been five thousand of them; and such another jawing and disputing and ripping and cussing, you never heard. Every jay in the whole lot put his eye to the hole and delivered a more chuckle-headed opinion about the mystery than the jay that went there before him. They examined the house all over, too. The door was standing half open, and at last one old jay happened to go and light on it and look in. Of course, that knocked the mystery galley-west in a second. There lay the acorns, scattered all over the floor. He flopped his wings and raised a whoop. 'Come here!' he says, 'Come here, everybody; hang'd if this fool hasn't been trying to fill up a house with acorns!' They all came a-swooping down like a blue cloud, and as each fellow lit on the door and took a glance, the whole absurdity of the contract that that first jay had tackled hit him home and he fell over backward suffocating with laughter, and the next jay took his place and done the same.

"Well, sir, they roosted around here on the housetops and the trees for an hour, and guffawed over that thing like human beings. It ain't any use to tell me a bluejay hasn't got a sense of humor, because I know better. And memory, too. They brought jays here from all over the United States to look at that hole, every summer for three years. Other birds, too. And they could all see the point, except an owl that come from Nova Scotia to visit the Yo Semite, and he took this thing in on his way back. He said he couldn't see anything funny in it. But then he was a good deal disappointed about Yo Semite, too."

Ambrose Bierce

Ambrose Bierce (1842–1914?) was twenty-four years old and a distinguished veteran of the Civil War when he arrived in San Francisco in 1866. He eventually joined the staff of the San Francisco News Letter, *a satirical journal. Later he became a fixture at the* Examiner *where he was known as "Bitter" Bierce for his fierce satiric voice. To friends such as Ina Coolbrith, Bret Harte, and Charles Warren Stoddard, he seemed a friendly sort, and he crusaded for high standards in literature. Among his own books, he produced at least one outstanding collection of short stories,* Tales of Soldiers and Civilians *(1891). As he grew older, his attitude darkened; he called San Francisco "the paradise of ignorance, anarchy and general yellowness." In 1913, his personal life a shambles, he walked into the Mexican Revolution and was never heard from again.*

. . . .

THE BUBBLE REPUTATION

HOW ANOTHER MAN'S WAS SOUGHT AND PRICKED

It was a stormy night in the autumn of 1930. The hour was about eleven. San Francisco lay in darkness, for the laborers at the gas works had struck and destroyed the company's property because a newspaper to which a cousin of the manager was a subscriber had censured the course of a potato merchant related by marriage to a member of the Knights of Leisure. Electric lights had not at that period been reinvented. The sky was filled with great masses of black cloud which, driven rapidly across the star-fields by winds unfelt on the earth and momentarily altering their fantastic forms, seemed instinct with a life and activity of their own and endowed with awful powers of evil, to the exercise of which they might at any time set their malignant will.

An observer standing, at this time, at the corner of Paradise avenue and

Great White Throne walk in Sorrell Hill cemetery would have seen a human figure moving among the graves toward the Superintendent's residence. Dimly and fitfully visible in the intervals of thinner gloom, this figure had a most uncanny and disquieting aspect. A long black cloak shrouded it from neck to heel. Upon its head was a slouch hat, pulled down across the forehead and almost concealing the face, which was further hidden by a half-mask, only the beard being occasionally visible as the head was lifted partly above the collar of the cloak. The man wore upon his feet jack-boots whose wide, funnel-shaped legs had settled down in many a fold and crease about his ankles, as could be seen whenever accident parted the bottom of the cloak. His arms were concealed, but sometimes he stretched out the right to steady himself by a headstone as he crept stealthily but blindly over the uneven ground. At such times a close scrutiny of the hand would have disclosed in the palm the hilt of a poniard, the blade of which lay along the wrist, hidden in the sleeve. In short, the man's garb, his movements, the hour—everything proclaimed him a reporter.

But what did he there?

On the morning of that day the editor of the *Daily Malefactor* had touched the button of a bell numbered 216 and in response to the summons Mr. Longbo Spittleworth, reporter, had been shot into the room out of an inclined tube.

"I understand," said the editor, "that you are 216—am I right?"

"That," said the reporter, catching his breath and adjusting his clothing, both somewhat disordered by the celerity of his flight through the tube,— "that is my number."

"Information has reached us," continued the editor, "that the Superintendent of the Sorrel Hill cemetery—one Inhumio, whose very name suggests inhumanity—is guilty of the grossest outrages in the administration of the great trust confided to his hands by the sovereign people."

"The cemetery is private property," faintly suggested 216.

"It is alleged," continued the great man, disdaining to notice the interruption, "that in violation of popular rights he refuses to permit his accounts to be inspected by representatives of the press."

"Under the law, you know, he is responsible to the directors of the cemetery company," the reporter ventured to interject.

"They say," pursued the editor, heedless, "that the inmates are in many cases badly lodged and insufficiently clad, and that in consequence they are usually cold. It is asserted that they are never fed—except to the worms.

Statements have been made to the effect that males and females are permitted to occupy the same quarters, to the incalculable detriment of public morality. Many clandestine villainies are alleged of this fiend in human shape, and it is desirable that his underground methods be unearthed in the *Malefactor*. If he resists we will drag his family skeleton from the privacy of his domestic closet. There is money in it for the paper, fame for you— are you ambitious, 216?"

"I am—bitious."

"Go, then," cried the editor, rising and waving his hand imperiously— "go and 'seek the bubble reputation.'"

"The bubble shall be sought," the young man replied, and leaping into a man-hole in the floor, disappeared. A moment later the editor, who after dismissing his subordinate, had stood motionless, as if lost in thought, sprang suddenly to the man-hole and shouted down it: "Hello, 216?"

"Aye, aye, sir," came up a faint and far reply.

"About that 'bubble reputation'—you understand, I suppose, that the reputation which you are to seek is that of the other man."

In the execution of his duty, in the hope of his employer's approval, in the costume of his profession, Mr. Longbo Spittleworth, otherwise known as 216, has already occupied a place in the mind's eye of the intelligent reader. Alas for poor Mr. Inhumio!

A few days after these events that fearless, independent and enterprising guardian and guide of the public, the San Francisco *Daily Malefactor*, contained a whole-page article whose headlines are here presented with some necessary typographical mitigation:

"Hell Upon Earth! Corruption Rampant in the Management of the Sorrel Hill Cemetery. The Sacred City of the Dead in the Leprous Clutches of a Demon in Human Form. Fiendish Atrocities Committed in 'God's Acre.' The Holy Dead Thrown around Loose. Fragments of Mothers. Segregation of a Beautiful Young Lady Who in Life Was the Light of a Happy Household. A Superintendent Who Is an Ex-Convict. How He Murdered His Neighbor to Start the Cemetery. He Buries His Own Dead Elsewhere. Extraordinary Insolence to a Representative of the Public Press. Little Eliza's Last Words: 'Mamma, Feed Me to the Pigs.' A Moonshiner Who Runs an Illicit Bone-Button Factory in One Corner of the Grounds. Buried Head Downward. Revolting Mausoleistic Orgies. Dancing on the Dead. Devilish Mutilation—a Pile of Late Lamented Noses and Sainted Ears. No Separation of the Sexes; Petition's for Chaperons Unheeded. 'Veal' as Supplied to the Superintendent's Employees. A Miscreant's Record from His Birth. Disgusting Subserviency of Our Contemporaries and Strong Indications of Collusion. Nameless Abnormalities. 'Doubled Up Like a Nut-Cracker.' 'Wasn't Planted White.' Horribly Significant Reduction in the Price of Lard. The Question of the Hour: Whom Do You Fry Your Doughnuts In?"

The Rise of the Regions

Contemporary illusions concerning the Golden State often proclaim the media image of coastal Southern California to be this entire realm's reality. California is far too complex, far too rich, far too mysterious to easily grasp or simply explain, and so is its literature. No one actually resides in the mythical Golden State; everyone lives and dies in particular places. Regions within the state emerge from life and writing here, and because they are particular, they are more revealing.

Four geo-literary zones and one exclusively imaginary realm have developed, each reflecting distinct history and literary outputs: *Greater Bay Area*, extending from Big Sur north toward Oregon, with San Francisco its core. *Southland* is dominated today by the Los Angeles–San Diego freeway culture; it was until the late nineteenth century as wild a west as existed anywhere. *Heartland* consists of the state's rural regions, principally the Great Central Valley, although John Steinbeck has single-handedly made the Salinas Valley a significant contributor. *Wilderness California* is another catchall that includes the state's great stretches of mountains, deserts, forests, and wild coastline—still little-settled if widely used. *Fantasy California*, the state as state of mind, may be most important of all: here imagination, expectation, and disappointment dominate realities of weather, society, and landscape.

The concept of regions should, of course, be seen as an acknowledgment of the state's diversity rather than an ironclad dictum. As novelist James D. Houston explains, "California is really a large mosaic of regions, each with its singular identity and microclimate." It is also important to note that many authors write from and about more than one of the state's regions: Gary Snyder's output reflects Wilderness California as well as the Greater Bay Area. More than a few works seem to rise from the boundaries between regions; in fact, much writing from Fantasy California does just that because the realm is not a physical place but a series of highly subjective reflections from areas real and unreal. For instance, Joan Didion's *Play It As It Lays* reflects both Southland and the terrain of Fantasy.

Greater Bay Area

. . . .

The gold rush and attendant opportunities attracted to the San Francisco region during the late 1840s and the 1850s such estimable if largely forgotten authors—with their signal noms de plume—as Old Box (Alonzo Delano), John Phoenix (George Horatio Derby), Dame Shirley (Louisa Smith Clapp), and Yellow Bird (John Rollin Ridge). In this rough-hewn imitation of an eastern seaport, the rest of the country dramatically and suddenly penetrated California. The 1860s saw the development of a national literary reputation by writers operating in the Bay Area, which boasted the Golden Gate Trinity (Bret Harte, Ina Coolbrith, and Charles Warren Stoddard, the three editors of *The Overland Monthly*), plus their partner Samuel Clemens—a high point in western American letters. Later Ambrose Bierce joined them, as did such worthies as Joaquín Miller, Henry George, Basyard Taylor, and young Josiah Royce. What was most important, perhaps, was that writers of the time reflected a distinctness still associated with the region: "they had defined themselves as a people liberated from the Puritan past," explains Kevin Starr, "glorying in an exuberant lust for life."

Throughout the remainder of the century, this section remained a cultural magnet, attracting diverse artists. By the 1870s, the larger north coast remained frontier, but the Bay Area became a frontier province, complete with its own rather self-conscience avante garde. So-called Bohemian movements have continued flourishing in the Bay Area. Late in the last century, for example, creative people began gathering at Carmel. Some, like Miller, were links to the frontier past; most, however, bespoke a new generation's dynamism: Jack London, Lincoln Steffens, George Sterling, Nora May French, Stoddard, Austin, and a host of lesser-known writers. At one of their frolics, they jointly composed a mock-epic poem entitled "Abalone Song" that begins:

> Oh! some folks boast of quail on toast,
> Because they think it's tony;
> But I'm content to owe my rent,
> And live on abalone . . .

By the early twentieth century when Joaquín Miller, Xavier Martinez, Yone Noguchi, even the venerable Ina Coolbrith, et al., had generated yet another Bohemian enclave in Piedmont, this had become one of America's most productive, most controversial literary regions. The Bay Area's Bohemians—up to and including Jack Kerouac and the beats, Ken Kesey and his merry pranksters, and Richard Brautigan and the hippies—have been everything from lunatics to geniuses (sometimes both). Of course, the region still attracts writers from all over the world.

Jack London

Jack London (1876–1916), a native of Oakland, was a gifted, prolific, but some-times poorly edited writer, who brought great energy and originality to his work. Unsystematically educated, his writing reflects interests in socialism, atavism, astral projection, even Anglo-Saxon destiny, among a great many other things—a mirror of his life and times. When discussing the state in which he was born, the one-time "boy socialist of Oakland" could wax eloquent: "I realize that much of California's romance is passing away, and I want to see to it that, at least, I shall preserve as much of that romance as is possible for me." He certainly preserved some. London's prose was first published in The Overland Monthly, *a fact that symbolically linked him with the Bay Area's first literary "Golden Age."*

. . . .

A RAID ON THE OYSTER PIRATES

Of the fish patrolmen under whom we served at various times, Charley Le Grant and I were agreed, I think, that Neil Partington was the best. He was neither dishonest nor cowardly; and while he demanded strict obedience when we were under his orders, at the same time our relations were those of easy comradeship, and he permitted us a freedom to which we were ordinarily unaccustomed, as the present story will show.

Neil's family lived in Oakland, which is on the Lower Bay, not more than six miles across the water from San Francisco. One day, while scout-ing among the Chinese shrimp-catchers of Point Pedro, he received word that his wife was very ill; and within the hour the Reindeer was bowling along for Oakland, with a stiff northwest breeze astern. We ran up the Oak-land Estuary and came to anchor, and in the days that followed, while Neil was ashore, we tightened up the Reindeer's rigging, overhauled the ballast, scraped down, and put the sloop into thorough shape.

This done, time hung heavy on our hands. Neil's wife was dangerously ill, and the outlook was a week's lie-over, awaiting the crisis. Charley and I roamed the docks, wondering what we should do, and so came upon the oyster fleet lying at the Oakland City Wharf. In the main they were trim, natty boats, made for speed and bad weather, and we sat down on the stringer-piece of the dock to study them.

"A good catch, I guess," Charley said, pointing to the heaps of oysters, assorted in three sizes, which lay upon their decks.

Peddlers were backing their wagons to the edge of the wharf, and from the bargaining and chaffering that went on, I managed to learn the selling price of the oysters.

"That boat must have at least two hundred dollars' worth aboard," I calculated. "I wonder how long it took to get the load?"

"Three or four days," Charley answered. "Not bad wages for two men— twenty-five dollars a day apiece."

The boat we were discussing, the Ghost, lay directly beneath us. Two men composed its crew. One was a squat, broad-shouldered fellow with remarkably long and gorilla-like arms, while the other was tall and well proportioned, with clear blue eyes and a mat of straight black hair. So unusual and striking was this combination of hair and eyes that Charley and I remained somewhat longer than we intended.

And it was well that we did. A stout, elderly man, with the dress and carriage of a successful merchant, came up and stood beside us, looking down upon the deck of the Ghost. He appeared angry, and the longer he looked the angrier he grew.

"Those are my oysters," he said at last. "I know they are my oysters. You raided my beds last night and robbed me of them."

The tall man and the short man on the Ghost looked up.

"Hello, Taft," the short man said, with insolent familiarity. (Among the bayfarers he had gained the nickname of "The Centipede" on account of his long arms.) "Hello, Taft," he repeated, with the same touch of insolence. "Wot'r you growlin' about now?"

"Those are my oysters—that's what I said. You've stolen them from my beds."

"Yer mighty wise, ain't ye?" was the Centipede's sneering reply. "S'pose you can tell your oysters wherever you see 'em?"

"Now, in my experience," broke in the tall man, "oysters is oysters wherever you find 'em, an' they're pretty much alike all the Bay over, and the world over, too, for that matter. We're not wantin' to quarrel with you,

Mr. Taft, but we jes' wish you wouldn't insinuate that them oysters is yours an' that we're thieves an' robbers till you can prove the goods."

"I know they're mine; I'd stake my life on it!" Mr. Taft snorted.

"Prove it," challenged the tall man, who we afterward learned was known as "The Porpoise" because of his wonderful swimming abilities.

Mr. Taft shrugged his shoulders helplessly. Of course he could not prove the oysters to be his, no matter how certain he might be.

"I'd give a thousand dollars to have you men behind the bars!" he cried. "I'll give fifty dollars a head for your arrest and conviction, all of you!"

A roar of laughter went up from the different boats, for the rest of the pirates had been listening to the discussion.

"There's more money in oysters," the Porpoise remarked dryly.

Mr. Taft turned impatiently on his heel and walked away. From out of the corner of his eye, Charley noted the way he went. Several minutes later, when he had disappeared around a corner, Charley rose lazily to his feet. I followed him, and we sauntered off in the opposite direction to that taken by Mr. Taft.

"Come on! Lively!" Charley whispered, when we passed from the view of the oyster fleet.

Our course was changed at once, and we dodged around corners and raced up and down side-streets till Mr. Taft's generous form loomed up ahead of us.

"I'm going to interview him about that reward," Charley explained, as we rapidly overhauled the oyster-bed owner. "Neil will be delayed here for a week, and you and I might as well be doing something in the meantime. What do you say?"

"Of course, of course," Mr. Taft said, when Charley had introduced himself and explained his errand. "Those thieves are robbing me of thousands of dollars every year, and I shall be glad to break them up at any price— yes, sir, at any price. As I said, I'll give fifty dollars a head, and call it cheap at that. They've robbed my beds, torn down my signs, terrorized my watchmen, and last year killed one of them. Couldn't prove it. All done in the blackness of night. All I had was a dead watchman and no evidence. The detectives could do nothing. Nobody has been able to do anything with those men. We have never succeeded in arresting one of them. So I say, Mr.— What did you say your name was?"

"Le Grant," Charley answered.

"So I say, Mr. Le Grant, I am deeply obliged to you for the assistance you offer. And I shall be glad, most glad, sir, to cooperate with you in every way. My watchmen and boats are at your disposal. Come and see me at the San Francisco offices any time, or telephone at my expense. And don't be afraid of spending money. I'll foot your expenses, whatever they are, so long as they are within reason. The situation is growing desperate, and something must be done to determine whether I or that band of ruffians own those oyster beds."

"Now we'll see Neil," Charley said, when he had seen Mr. Taft upon his train to San Francisco.

Not only did Neil Partington interpose no obstacle to our adventure, but he proved to be of the greatest assistance. Charley and I knew nothing of the oyster industry, while his head was an encyclopedia of facts concerning it. Also, within an hour or so, he was able to bring to us a Greek boy of seventeen or eighteen who knew thoroughly well the ins and outs of oyster piracy.

At this point I may as well explain that we of the fish patrol were free lances in a way. While Neil Partington, who was a patrolman proper, received a regular salary, Charley and I, being merely deputies, received only what we earned—that is to say, a certain percentage of the fines imposed on convicted violators of the fish laws. Also, any rewards that chanced our way were ours. We offered to share with Partington whatever we should get from Mr. Taft, but the patrolman would not hear of it. He was only too happy, he said, to do a good turn for us, who had done so many for him.

We held a long council of war, and mapped out the following line of action. Our faces were unfamiliar on the Lower Bay, but as the Reindeer was well known as a fish-patrol sloop, the Greek boy, whose name was Nicholas, and I were to sail some innocent-looking craft down to Asparagus Island and join the oyster pirates' fleet. Here, according to Nicholas's description of the beds and the manner of raiding, it was possible for us to catch the pirates in the act of stealing oysters, and at the same time to get them in our power. Charley was to be on the shore, with Mr. Taft's watchmen and a posse of constables, to help us at the right time.

"I know just the boat," Neil said, at the conclusion of the discussion, "a crazy old sloop that's lying over at Tiburon. You and Nicholas can go over by the ferry, charter it for a song, and sail direct for the beds."

"Good luck be with you, boys," he said at parting, two days later. "Remember, they are dangerous men, so be careful."

Nicholas and I succeeded in chartering the sloop very cheaply; and between laughs, while getting up sail, we agreed that she was even crazier and older than she had been described. She was a big, flat-bottomed, square-sterned craft, sloop-rigged, with a sprung mast, slack rigging, dilapidated sails, and rotten running-gear, clumsy to handle and uncertain in bringing about, and she smelled vilely of coal tar, with which strange stuff she had been smeared from stem to stern and from cabin-roof to centreboard. And to cap it all, Coal Tar Maggie was printed in great white letters the whole length of either side.

It was an uneventful though laughable run from Tiburon to Asparagus Island, where we arrived in the afternoon of the following day. The oyster pirates, a fleet of a dozen sloops, were lying at anchor on what was known as the "Deserted Beds." The Coal Tar Maggie came sloshing into their midst with a light breeze astern, and they crowded on deck to see us. Nicholas and I had caught the spirit of the crazy craft, and we handled her in most lubberly fashion.

"Wot is it?" someone called.

"Name it 'n' ye kin have it!" called another.

"I swan naow, ef it ain't the old Ark itself!" mimicked the Centipede from the deck of the Ghost.

"Hey! Ahoy there, clipper ship!" another wag shouted. "Wot's yer port?"

We took no notice of the joking, but acted, after the manner of green-horns, as though the Coal Tar Maggie required our undivided attention. I rounded her well to windward of the Ghost, and Nicholas ran for'ard to drop the anchor. To all appearances it was a bungle, the way the chain tangled and kept the anchor from reaching the bottom. And to all appearances Nicholas and I were terribly excited as we strove to clear it. At any rate, we quite deceived the pirates, who took huge delight in our predicament.

But the chain remained tangled, and amid all kinds of mocking advice we drifted down upon and fouled the Ghost, whose bowsprit poked square through our mainsail and ripped a hole in it as big as a barn door. The Centipede and the Porpoise doubled up on the cabin in paroxysms of laughter, and left us to get clear as best we could. This, with much unseamanlike performance, we succeeded in doing, and likewise in clearing the anchor-chain, of which we let out about three hundred feet. With only ten feet of water under us, this would permit the Coal Tar Maggie to swing in a circle six hundred feet in diameter, in which circle she would be able to foul at least half the fleet.

The oyster pirates lay snugly together at short hawsers, the weather being fine, and they protested loudly at our ignorance in putting out such an un-warranted length of anchor-chain. And not only did they protest, for they made us heave it in again, all but thirty feet.

Having sufficiently impressed them with our general lubberliness, Nicholas and I went below to congratulate ourselves and to cook supper. Hardly had we finished the meal and washed the dishes, when a skiff ground against the Coal Tar Maggie's side, and heavy feet trampled on deck. Then the Centipede's brutal face appeared in the companionway, and he descended into the cabin, followed by the Porpoise. Before they could seat themselves on a bunk, another skiff came alongside, and another, and another, till the whole fleet was represented by the gathering in the cabin.

"Where'd you swipe the old tub?" asked a squat and hairy man, with cruel eyes and Mexican features.

"Didn't swipe it," Nicholas answered, meeting them on their own ground and encouraging the idea that we had stolen the Coal Tar Maggie. "And if we did, what of it?"

"Well, I don't admire your taste, that's all," sneered he of the Mexican features. "I'd rot on the beach first before I'd take a tub that couldn't get out of its own way."

"How were we to know till we tried her?" Nicholas asked, so innocently as to cause a laugh. "And how do you get the oysters?" he hurried on. "We want a load of them; that's what we came for, a load of oysters."

"What d'ye want 'em for?" demanded the Porpoise.

"Oh, to give away to our friends, of course," Nicholas retorted. "That's what you do with yours, I suppose."

This started another laugh, and as our visitors grew more genial we could see that they had not the slightest suspicion of our identity or purpose.

"Didn't I see you on the dock in Oakland the other day?" the Centipede asked suddenly of me.

"Yep," I answered boldly, taking the bull by the horns. "I was watching you fellows and figuring out whether we'd go oystering or not. It's a pretty good business, I calculate, and so we're going in for it. That is," I hastened to add, "if you fellows don't mind."

"I'll tell you one thing, which ain't two things," he replied, "and that is you'll have to hump yerself an' get a better boat. We won't stand to be disgraced by any such box as this. Understand?"

"Sure," I said. "Soon as we sell some oysters we'll outfit in style."

"And if you show yerself square an' the right sort," he went on, "why, you kin run with us. But if you don't" (here his voice became stern and menacing), "why, it'll be the sickest day of yer life. Understand?"

"Sure," I said.

After that and more warning and advice of similar nature, the conversation became general, and we learned that the beds were to be raided that very night. As they got into their boats, after an hour's stay, we were invited to join them in the raid with the assurance of "the more the merrier."

"Did you notice that short, Mexican-looking chap?" Nicholas asked, when they had departed to their various sloops. "He's Barchi, of the Sporting Life Gang, and the fellow that came with him is Skilling. They're both out now on five thousand dollars' bail."

I had heard of the Sporting Life Gang before, a crowd of hoodlums and criminals that terrorized the lower quarters of Oakland, and two-thirds of which were usually to be found in state's prison for crimes that ranged from perjury and ballot-box stuffing to murder.

"They are not regular oyster pirates," Nicholas continued. "They've just come down for the lark and to make a few dollars. But we'll have to watch out for them."

We sat in the cockpit and discussed the details of our plan till eleven o'clock had passed, when we heard the rattle of an oar in a boat from the direction of the *Ghost*. We hauled up our own skiff, tossed in a few sacks, and rowed over. There we found all the skiffs assembling, it being the intention to raid the beds in a body.

To my surprise, I found barely a foot of water where we had dropped anchor in ten feet. It was the big June run-out of the full moon, and as the ebb had yet an hour and a half to run, I knew that our anchorage would be dry ground before slack water.

Mr. Taft's beds were three miles away, and for a long time we rowed silently in the wake of the other boats, once in a while grounding and our oar blades constantly striking bottom. At last we came upon soft mud covered with not more than two inches of water—not enough to float the boats. But the pirates at once were over the side, and by pushing and pulling on the flat-bottomed skiffs, we moved steadily along.

The full moon was partly obscured by high-flying clouds, but the pirates went their way with the familiarity born of long practice. After half a mile of the mud, we came upon a deep channel, up which we rowed, with dead oyster shoals looming high and dry on either side. At last we reached the picking grounds. Two men, on one of the shoals, hailed us and warned us off. But the Centipede, the Porpoise, Barchi, and Skilling took the lead, and followed by the rest of us, at least thirty men in half as many boats, rowed right up to the watchmen.

"You'd better slide outa this here," Barchi said threateningly, "or we'll fill you so full of holes you wouldn't float in molasses."

The watchmen wisely retreated before so overwhelming a force, and rowed their boat along the channel toward where the shore should be. Besides, it was in the plan for them to retreat.

We hauled the noses of the boats up on the shore side of a big shoal, and all hands, with sacks, spread out and began picking. Every now and again the clouds thinned before the face of the moon, and we could see the big oysters quite distinctly. In almost no time sacks were filled and carried back to the boats, where fresh ones were obtained. Nicholas and I returned often and anxiously to the boats with our little loads, but always found some one of the pirates coming or going.

"Never mind," he said; "no hurry. As they pick farther and farther away, it will take too long to carry to the boats. Then they'll stand the full sacks on end and pick them up when the tide comes in and the skiffs will float to them."

Fully half an hour went by, and the tide had begun to flood, when this came to pass. Leaving the pirates at their work, we stole back to the boats. One by one, and noiselessly, we shoved them off and made them fast in an awkward flotilla. Just as we were shoving off the last skiff, our own, one of the men came upon us. It was Barchi. His quick eye took in the situation at a glance, and he sprang for us; but we went clear with a mighty shove, and he was left floundering in the water over his head. As soon as he got back to the shoal he raised his voice and gave the alarm.

We rowed with all our strength, but it was slow going with so many boats in tow. A pistol cracked from the shoal, a second, and a third; then a regular fusillade began. The bullets spat and spat all about us; but thick clouds had covered the moon, and in the dim darkness it was no more than random firing. It was only by chance that we could be hit.

"Wish we had a little steam launch," I panted.

"I'd just as soon the moon stayed hidden," Nicholas panted back.

It was slow work, but every stroke carried us farther away from the shoal and nearer the shore, till at last the shooting died down, and when the moon did come out we were too far away to be in danger. Not long afterward we answered a shoreward hail, and two Whitehall boats, each pulled by three pairs of oars, darted up to us. Charley's welcome face bent over to us, and he gripped us by the hands while he cried, "Oh, you joys! You joys! Both of you!"

When the flotilla had been landed, Nicholas and I and a watchman rowed out in one of the Whitehalls, with Charley in the sternsheets. Two other Whitehalls followed us, and as the moon now shone brightly, we easily made out the oyster pirates on their lonely shoal. As we drew closer, they fired a rattling volley from their revolvers, and we promptly retreated beyond range.

"Lot of time," Charley said. "The flood is setting in fast, and by the time it's up to their necks there won't be any fight left in them."

So we lay on our oars and waited for the tide to do its work. This was the predicament of the pirates: because of the big run-out, the tide was now rushing back like a mill-race, and it was impossible for the strongest swimmer in the world to make against it the three miles to the sloops. Between the pirates and the shore were we, precluding escape in that direction. On the other hand, the water was rising rapidly over the shoals, and it was only a question of a few hours when it would be over their heads.

It was beautifully calm, and in the brilliant white moonlight we watched them through our night glasses and told Charley of the voyage of the *Coal Tar Maggie*. One o'clock came, and two o'clock, and the pirates were clustering on the highest shoal, waist-deep in water.

"Now this illustrates the value of imagination," Charley was saying. "Taft has been trying for years to get them, but he went at it with bull strength and failed. Now we used our heads . . ."

Just then I heard a scarcely audible gurgle of water, and holding up my hand for silence, I turned and pointed to a ripple slowly widening out in a growing circle. It was not more than fifty feet from us. We kept perfectly quiet and waited. After a minute the water broke six feet away, and a black head and white shoulder showed in the moonlight. With a snort of surprise and of suddenly expelled breath, the head and shoulder went down.

We pulled ahead several strokes and drifted with the current. Four pairs of eyes searched the surface of the water, but never another ripple showed, and never another glimpse did we catch of the black head and white shoulder.

"It's the Porpoise," Nicholas said. "It would take broad daylight for us to catch him."

At a quarter to three the pirates gave their first sign of weakening. We heard cries for help, in the unmistakable voice of the Centipede, and this time, on rowing closer, we were not fired upon. The Centipede was in a truly perilous plight. Only the heads and shoulders of his fellow-marauders showed above the water as they braced themselves against the current, while his feet were off the bottom and they were supporting him.

"Now, lads," Charley said briskly, "we have got you, and you can't get away. If you cut up rough, we'll have to leave you alone and the water will finish you. But if you're good, we'll take you aboard, one man at a time, and you'll all be saved. What do you say?"

"Ay," they chorused hoarsely between their chattering teeth.

"Then one man at a time, and the short men first."

The Centipede was the first to be pulled aboard, and he came willingly, though he objected when the constable put the handcuffs on him. Barchi was next hauled in, quite meek and resigned from his soaking. When we had ten in our boat we drew back, and the second Whitehall was loaded. The third Whitehall received nine prisoners only—a catch of twenty-nine in all.

"You didn't get the Porpoise," the Centipede said exultantly, as though his escape materially diminished our success.

Charley laughed. "But we saw him just the same, a-snorting for shore like a puffing pig."

It was a mild and shivering band of pirates that we marched up the beach to the oyster house. In answer to Charley's knock, the door was flung open, and a pleasant wave of warm air rushed out upon us.

"You can dry your clothes here, lads, and get some hot coffee," Charley announced, as they filed in.

And there, sitting ruefully by the fire, with a steaming mug in his hand, was the Porpoise. With one accord Nicholas and I looked at Charley. He laughed gleefully.

"That comes of imagination," he said. "When you see a thing, you've got to see it all around, or what's the good of seeing it at all? I saw the beach, so I left a couple of constables behind to keep an eye on it. That's all."

Frank Norris

*Frank Norris (1870–1902), born in Chicago, came to San Francisco with his family as a boy of fourteen. He would die in 1902, only thirty-two years old, and leave two books in particular—*McTeague, A Story of San Francisco *(1899) and* The Octopus, A Story of California *(1901)—that mark him as the state's first major novelist. Set in the area of modern-day Hanford, the scene that follows is from* The Octopus. *It developed because settlers who had worked and improved land leased from the monopolistic railroad—the "Octopus" of the novel's title—rose against that powerful institution and its allies. Settlers had been led to believe they could purchase their tracts, but the railroad priced the parcels exorbitantly, precisely because they had been improved. These ironic events are based upon the actual occurrences that led to the notorious Mussel Slough Massacre of May 10, 1880, on which "Shootout" is directly modeled.*

. . . .

SHOOTOUT

Around the bend of the road in front of them came a cloud of dust. From it emerged a horse's head.

"Hello, hello, there's something."

"Remember, we are not to fire first."

"Perhaps that's Hooven; I can't see. Is it? There only seems to be one horse."

"Too much dust for one horse."

Annixter, who had taken his field glasses from Harran, adjusted them to his eyes.

"That's not them," he announced presently, "nor Hooven, either. That's a cart." Then, after another moment, he added, "The butcher's cart from Guadalajara."

The tension was relaxed. The men drew long breaths, settling back in their places.

"Do we let him go on, Governor?"

"The bridge is down. He can't go by and we must not let him go back. We shall have to detain him and question him. I wonder the marshal let him pass."

The cart approached at a lively trot.

"Anybody else in that cart, Mr. Annixter?" asked Magnus. "Look carefully. It may be a ruse. It is strange the marshal should have let him pass."

The leaguers roused themselves again. Osterman laid his hand on the revolver.

"No," called Annixter in another instant, "no, there's only one man in it."

The cart came up, and Cutter and Phelps, clambering from the ditch, stopped it as it arrived in front of the party.

"Hey—what—what?" exclaimed the young butcher, pulling up. "Is that bridge broke?"

But at the idea of being held, the boy protested at top voice, badly frightened, bewildered, not knowing what was to happen next.

"No, no. I got my meat to deliver. Say, you let me go. Say, I ain't got nothing to do with you."

He tugged at the reins, trying to turn the cart about. Cutter, with his jackknife, parted the reins just back of the bit.

"You'll stay where you are, m'son, for awhile. We're not going to hurt you. But you are not going back to town till we say so. Did you pass anybody on the road out of town?"

In reply to the leaguers' questions, the young butcher at last told them he had passed a two-horse buggy and a lot of men on horseback just beyond the railroad tracks. They were headed for Los Muertos.

"That's them all right," muttered Annixter. "They're coming by this road, sure."

The butcher's horse and cart were led to one side of the road, and the horse tied to the fence with one of the severed lines. The butcher himself was passed over to Presley, who locked him in Hooven's barn.

"Well, what the devil," demanded Osterman, "has become of Bismarck?"

In fact, the butcher had seen nothing of Hooven. The minutes were passing, and still he failed to appear.

"What's he up to, anyways?"

"Bet you what you like, they caught him. Just like that crazy Dutchman to get excited and go too near. You can always depend on Hooven to lose his head."

Five minutes passed, then ten. The road toward Guadalajara lay empty, baking and white under the sun.

"Well, the marshal and S. Behrman don't seem to be in any hurry, either."

"Shall I go forward and reconnoiter, Governor?" asked Harran.

But Dabney, who stood next to Annixter, touched him on the shoulder, and without speaking pointed down the road. Annixter looked, then suddenly cried out:

"Here comes Hooven."

The German galloped into sight around the turn of the road, his rifle laid across his saddle. He came on rapidly, pulled up, and dismounted at the ditch.

"Dey're commen," he cried, trembling with excitement. "I watch um long dime bei der side oaf der roadt in der busches. Dey shtop bei der gate odor side der relroadt trecks and talk long dime mit one n'udder. Den dey gome on. Dey're gowun sure dozum monkey doodle pizznes. Me, I see Gritschun put der kertridges in his guhn. I tink dey gowun to gome *my* blace first. Dey gowun to try to put me off, tek my home, bei Gott."

"All right, get down in here and keep quiet, Hooven. Don't fire unless—"

"Here they are."

A half-dozen voices uttered the cry at once.

There could be no mistake this time. A buggy, drawn by two horses, came into view around the curve of the road. Three riders accompanied it, and behind these, seen at intervals in a cloud of dust, were two—three—five—six others.

This, then, was S. Behrman with the United States marshal and his posse. The event that had been so long in preparation, the event which it had been said would never come to pass, the last trial of strength, the last fight between the trust and the people, the direct, brutal grapple of armed men, and law defied, the government ignored—behold, here it was close at hand.

Osterman cocked his revolver, and in the profound silence that had fallen upon the scene, the click was plainly audible from end to end of the line.

"Remember our agreement, gentlemen," cried Magnus in a warning voice. "Mr. Osterman, I must ask you to let down the hammer of your weapon."

No one answered. In absolute quiet, standing motionless in their places, the leaguers watched the approach of the marshal.

Five minutes passed. The riders came on steadily. They drew nearer. The grind of the buggy wheels in the grit and dust of the road and the prolonged clatter of horses' feet began to make themselves heard. The leaguers could distinguish the faces of their enemies.

In the buggy were S. Behrman and Cyrus Ruggles, the latter driving. A tall man in a frock coat and slouched hat—the marshal, beyond question— rode at the left of the buggy; Delaney, carrying a Winchester, at the right. Christian, the real estate broker, S. Behrman's cousin, also with a rifle, could be made out just behind the marshal. Back of these, riding well up, was a group of horsemen, indistinguishable in the dust raised by the buggy's wheels.

Steadily the distance between the leaguers and the posse diminished.

"Don't let them get too close, Governor," whispered Harran.

When S. Behrman's buggy was about one hundred yards from the irrigating ditch, Magnus sprang out upon the road, leaving his revolvers behind him. He beckoned Garnett and Gethings to follow, and the three ranchers, who with the exception of Broderson were the oldest men present, advanced, without arms, to meet the marshal.

Magnus cried aloud:

"Halt where you are."

From their places in the ditch, Annixter, Osterman, Dabney, Harran, Hooven, Broderson, Cutter, and Phelps, their hands laid upon their revolvers, watched silently, alert, keen, ready for anything.

At the Governor's words, they saw Ruggles pull sharply on the reins. The buggy came to a standstill, the riders doing likewise. Magnus approached the marshal, still followed by Garnett and Gethings, and began to speak. His voice was audible to the men in the ditch, but his words could not be made out. They heard the marshal reply quietly enough, and the two shook hands. Delaney came around from the side of the buggy, his horse standing before the team across the road. He leaned from the saddle, listening to what was being said, but made no remark. From time to time, S. Behrman and Ruggles, from their seats in the buggy, interposed a sentence or two into the conversation, but at first, so far as the leaguers could discern, neither Magnus nor the marshal paid them any attention. They saw, however, that the latter repeatedly shook his head, and once they heard him exclaim in a loud voice:

"I only know my duty, Mr. Derrick."

Then Gethings turned about, and seeing Delaney close at hand, addressed an unheard remark to him. The cowpuncher replied curtly, and the words seemed to anger Gethings. He made a gesture, pointing back to the ditch, showing the entrenched leaguers to the posse. Delaney appeared to communicate the news that the leaguers were on hand and prepared to resist to the other members of the party. They all looked toward the ditch and plainly saw the ranchers there, standing to their arms.

But, meanwhile, Ruggles had addressed himself more directly to Magnus, and between the two an angry discussion was going forward. Once, even, Harran heard his father exclaim:

"The statement is a lie, and no one knows it better than yourself."

"Here," growled Annixter to Dabney, who stood next to him in the ditch, "those fellows are getting too close. Look at them edging up. Don't Magnus see that?"

The other members of the marshal's force had come forward from their places behind the buggy and were spread out across the road. Some of them were gathered about Magnus, Garnett, and Gethings; and some were talking together, looking and pointing toward the ditch. Whether acting upon signal or not, the leaguers in the ditch could not tell, but it was certain that one or two of the posse had moved considerably forward. Besides this, Delaney had now placed his horse between Magnus and the ditch, and two others riding up from the rear had followed his example. The posse surrounded the three ranchers, and by now everybody was talking at once.

"Look here," Harran called to Annixter, "this won't do. I don't like the looks of this thing. They all seem to be edging up, and before we know it they may take the Governor and the other men prisoners."

"They ought to come back," declared Annixter.

"Somebody ought to tell them that those fellows are creeping up."

By now the angry argument between the Governor and Ruggles had become more heated than ever. Their voices were raised; now and then they made furious gestures.

"They ought to come back," cried Osterman. "We couldn't shoot now if anything should happen, for fear of hitting them."

"Well, it sounds as though something were going to happen pretty soon."

They could hear Gethings and Delaney wrangling furiously; another deputy joined in.

"I'm going to call the Governor back," exclaimed Annixter, suddenly clambering out of the ditch.

"No, no," cried Osterman, "keep in the ditch. They can't drive us out if we keep here."

Hooven and Harran, who had instinctively followed Annixter, hesitated at Osterman's words, and the three halted irresolutely on the road before the ditch, their weapons in their hands.

"Governor," shouted Harran, "come on back. You can't do anything."

Still the wrangle continued, and one of the deputies, advancing a little from out the group, cried out:

"Keep back there! Keep back there, you!"

"Go to hell, will you?" shouted Harran on the instant. "You're on my land."

"Oh, come back here, Harran," called Osterman. "That ain't going to do any good."

"There—listen," suddenly exclaimed Harran. "The Governor is calling us. Come on; I'm going."

Osterman got out of the ditch and came forward, catching Harran by the arm and pulling him back.

"He didn't call. Don't get excited. You'll ruin everything. Get back into the ditch again."

But Cutter, Phelps, and the old man Dabney, misunderstanding what was happening, and seeing Osterman leave the ditch, had followed his example. All the leaguers were now out of the ditch and a little way down the road, Hooven, Osterman, Annixter, and Harran in front, Dabney, Phelps, and Cutter coming up from behind.

"Keep back, you," cried the deputy again.

In the group around S. Behrman's buggy, Gethings and Delaney were yet quarreling, and the angry debate between Magnus, Garnett, and the marshal still continued.

Till this moment the real estate broker, Christian, had taken no part in the argument, but had kept himself in the rear of the buggy. Now, however, he pushed forward. There was but little room for him to pass, and as he rode by the buggy, his horse scraped his flank against the hub of the wheel. The animal recoiled sharply, and striking against Garnett, threw him to the ground. Delaney's horse stood between the buggy and the leaguers gathered on the road in front of the ditch; the incident, indistinctly seen by them, was misinterpreted.

Garnett had not yet risen when Hooven raised a great shout:

"*Hoch, der Kaiser! Hoch, der vaterland!*"

With the words, he dropped to one knee, and sighting his rifle carefully, fired into the group of men around the buggy.

Instantly the revolvers and rifles seemed to go off of themselves. Both sides, deputies and leaguers, opened fire simultaneously. At first, it was nothing but a confused roar of explosions; then the roar lapsed to an irregular, quick succession of reports, shot leaping after shot; then a moment's silence, and last of all, regular as clock ticks, three shots at exact intervals. Then stillness.

Delaney, shot through the stomach, slid down from his horse, and on his hands and knees crawled from the road into the standing wheat. Christian fell backward from the saddle toward the buggy, and hung suspended in that position, his head and shoulders on the wheel, one stiff leg still across his saddle. Hooven, in attempting to rise from his kneeling position, received a rifle ball squarely in the throat, and rolled forward upon his face. Old Broderson, crying out, "Oh, they've shot me, boys," staggered sideways, his head bent, his hands rigid at his sides, and fell into the ditch. Osterman, blood running back from his mouth and nose, turned about and walked back. Presley helped him across the irrigating ditch and Osterman laid himself down, his head on his folded arms. Harran Derrick dropped where he stood, turning over on his face, and lay motionless, groaning terribly, a pool of blood forming under his stomach. The old man Dabney, silent as ever, received his death, speechless. He fell to his knees, got up again, fell once more, and died without a word. Annixter, instantly killed, fell his length to the ground, and lay without movement, just as he had fallen, one arm across his face.

Ina Coolbrith

Ina Donna Coolbrith (1842–1928) was a niece of Joseph Smith, founder of the Mormon church. Christened Josephine Smith, she later changed her name to Ina Donna Coolbrith (her mother's maiden name) and kept her past a secret even from close friends. A woman of beauty and wit, she was, along with Bret Harte and Charles Warren Stoddard, one of San Francisco's original "Golden Gate Trinity" in the 1860s and an editor of The Overland Monthly. *Eventually designated poet laureate of California, she was also a librarian in Oakland, where she profoundly influenced a young Jack London. She was involved in various literary Bohemian movements and for many years conducted a salon for artists in her East Bay home. Coolbrith's career extended well into this century, so it spanned the entire formative period of this state's English-language literary history.*

THE CALIFORNIA POPPY

Thy satin vesture richer is than looms
Of Orient weave for raiment of her kings.
Not dyes of old Tyre, not precious things
Regathered from the long forgotten tombs
Of buried empires, not the iris plumes
That wave upon the tropic's myriad wings,
Not all proud Sheba's queenly offerings,
Could match the golden marvel of thy blooms.
For thou art nurtured from the treasure veins
Of this fair land; thy golden rootlets sup
Her sands of gold—of gold thy petals spun.
Her golden glory, thou! on hills and plains
Lifting, exultant, every kingly cup,
Brimmed with the golden vintage of the sun.

Joaquín Miller

Joaquín Miller (1841?–1913), who at the urging of Ina Coolbrith appropriated his first name from the legendary Joaquín Murrieta, was one of the genuine characters of early California literature. His given name was Cincinnatus Hiner Miller—no wonder he changed it! He wore unusual clothing, long hair, a beard, and clouded his personal history by stories he told, then changed, then retold. Many view him as this state's prototypical literary Bohemian. He took the salons of London by storm in the 1870s, dressing like a mountain man or miner—boots, sombrero, red flannel shirt— and loosing war whoops that startled the English. Playing his role to the hilt, Miller came to represent California in the eyes of many. Later, he deposited his adopted daughter, Cali-Shasta, at Coolbrith's home, then never returned to collect her. The compassionate, beset Coolbrith cared for the girl until she grew to womanhood and married. Through all his shenanigans, Miller seems to have remained popular—a lovable rogue.

. . . .

DEAD IN THE SIERRAS

His footprints have failed us,
Where berries are red,
And madroños are rankest—
The hunter is dead!

The grizzly may pass
By his half-open door;
May pass and repass
On his path, as of yore.

The panther may crouch
In the leaves on his limb;
May scream and may scream—
It is nothing to him.

Prone, bearded, and breasted
Like columns of stone;
And tall as a pine—
As a pine overthrown!

His camp-fires gone,
What else can be done
Than let him sleep on
Till the light of the sun?

Ay, tombless! What of it?
Marble is dust,
Cold and repellent;
And iron is rust.

Edwin Markham

Edwin Markham (1852–1940), Oregon-born, lived much of his life in California. He became a major figure in 1899 with the publication of "The Man with the Hoe," said at the time to have been the best-known single poem ever written by an American. It was inspired by one of Jean-François Millet's powerful paintings and was considered a masterpiece of proletarian writing. It was also the centerpiece for his major collection, The Man with the Hoe and Other Poems *(1899). Collis P. Huntington, the railroad baron, was so shocked by Markham's "radical" verse that he offered a $750 prize for the best poem refuting it; the money was won by John Vance Cheney, whose award-winning work is now forgotten.*

. . . .

THE MAN WITH THE HOE

Written after seeing Millet's world-famous painting of a brutalized toiler
   in the deep abyss of labor.
God made man in His own image: in the image of God He made him.—*Genesis*

Bowed by the weight of centuries he leans
Upon his hoe and gazes on the ground,
The emptiness of ages in his face,
And on his back the burden of the world.
Who made him dead to rapture and despair,
A thing that grieves not and that never hopes,
Stolid and stunned, a brother to the ox?
Who loosened and let down this brutal jaw?
Whose was the hand that slanted back this brow?
Whose breath blew out the light within this brain?

Is this the Thing the Lord God made and gave
To have dominion over sea and land;
To trace the stars and search the heavens for power;
To feel the passion of Eternity?
Is this the dream He dreamed who shaped the suns
And markt their ways upon the ancient deep?
Down all the caverns of Hell to their last gulf
There is no shape more terrible than this—
More tongued with cries against the world's blind greed—
More filled with signs and portents for the soul—
More packt with danger to the universe.

What gulfs between him and the seraphim!
Slave of the wheel of labor, what to him
Are Plato and the swing of Pleiades?
What the long reaches of the peaks of song,
The rift of dawn, the reddening of the rose?
Thru this dread shape the suffering ages look;
Time's tragedy is in that aching stoop;
Thru this dread shape humanity betrayed,
Plundered, profaned and disinherited,
Cries protest to the Powers that made the world,
A protest that is also prophecy.

O masters, lords and rulers in all lands,
Is this the handiwork you give to God,
This monstrous thing distorted and soul-quencht?
How will you ever straighten up this shape;
Touch it again with immortality;
Give back the upward looking and the light;
Rebuild in it the music and the dream;
Make right the immemorial infamies,
Perfidious wrongs, immedicable woes?

O masters, lords and rulers in all lands,
How will the future reckon with this Man?
How answer his brute question in that hour
When whirlwinds of rebellion shake all shores?

How will it be with kingdoms and with kings—
With those who shaped him to the thing he is—
When this dumb Terror shall rise to judge the world,
After the silence of the centuries?

Toshio Mori

Toshio Mori (1910–80), was born in Oakland during a period of deep anti-Asian prejudice in this state. He was raised in San Leandro, where he aspired first to be a baseball player, then a writer, all the while working in his family's nursery. He accomplished the latter dream, publishing two collections of short stories—Yokohama, California (1949) and The Chauvinist and Other Stories *(1979)—as well as a novel,* The Woman from Hiroshima *(1980). During World War II, he and his family were interred at Topaz Relocation Center in Utah. In 1943, he was the first Japanese-American to have work included in the* Best American Short Story *series. As Jeffrey Paul Chan wrote in* A Literary History of the American West, *"Mori's vision of Japanese-American life before the war is perhaps the only work available that has a unity of vision, that melds the variety of loyalties, experiences and sensibilities." The story that follows is from* Yokohama, California.

· ·

SLANT-EYED AMERICANS

My mother was commenting on the fine California weather. It was Sunday noon, December 7. We were having our lunch, and I had the radio going. "Let's take the afternoon off and go to the city," I said to Mother.

"All right. We shall go," she said dreamily. "Ah, four months ago my boy left Hayward to join the army, and a fine send-off he had. Our good friends—ah, I shall never forget the day of his departure."

"We'll visit some of our friends in Oakland and then take in a movie," I said. "Care to come along, Papa?"

Father shook his head. "No, I'll stay home and take it easy."

"That's his heaven," Mother commented. "To stay home, read the papers over and over, and smoke his Bull Durham."

I laughed. Suddenly the musical program was cut off as a special announcement came over the air: At 7:25 a.m. this morning a squadron

70

of Japanese bombing planes attacked Pearl Harbor. The battle is still in progress.

"What's this? Listen to the announcement," I cried, going to the radio.

Abruptly the announcement stopped and the musicale continued.

"What is it?" Mother asked. "What has happened?"

"The radio reports that the Japanese planes attacked Hawaii this morning," I said incredulously. "It couldn't be true."

"It must be a mistake. Couldn't it have been a part of a play?" asked Mother.

I dialed other stations. Several minutes later one of the stations confirmed the bulletin.

"It must be true," Father said quietly.

I said, "Japan has declared war on the United States and Great Britain."

The room became quiet but for the special bulletin coming in every now and then.

"It cannot be true, yet it must be so," Father said over and over.

"Can it be one of those programs scaring the people about invasion?" Mother asked me.

"No, I'm sure this is a news report," I replied.

Mother's last ray of hope paled and her eyes became dull. "Why did it have to happen? The common people in Japan don't want war, and we don't want war. Here the people are peace-loving. Why cannot the peoples of the earth live together peacefully?"

"Since Japan declared war on the United States it'll mean that you parents of American citizens have become enemy aliens," I said.

"Enemy aliens," my mother whispered.

Night came but sleep did not come. We sat up late in the night hoping against hope that some good news would come, retracting the news of vicious attack and open hostilities.

"This is very bad for the people with Japanese faces," I said.

Father slowly shook his head.

"What shall we do?" asked Mother.

"What can we do?" Father said helplessly.

At the flower market next morning the growers were present but the buyers were scarce. The place looked empty and deserted. "Our business is shot to pieces," one of the boys said.

"Who'll buy flowers now?" another called.

Don Haley, the seedsman, came over looking bewildered. "I suppose you don't need seeds now."

We shook our heads.

"It looks bad," I said. "Will it affect your business?"

"Flower seed sale will drop but the vegetable seeds will move quicker," Don said. "I think I'll have to put more time on the vegetable seeds."

Nobu Hiramatsu who had been thinking of building another greenhouse joined us. He had plans to grow more carnations and expand his business.

"What's going to happen to your plans, Nobu?" asked one of the boys.

"Nothing. I'm going to sit tight and see how the things turn out," he said.

"Flowers and war don't go together," Don said. "You cannot concentrate too much on beauty when destruction is going about you."

"Sure, pretty soon we'll raise vegetables instead of flowers," Grasselli said.

A moment later the market opened and we went back to the tables to sell our flowers. Several buyers came in and purchased a little. The flowers didn't move at all. Just as I was about to leave the place I met Tom Yamashita, the Nisei gardener with a future.

"What are you doing here, Tom? What's the matter with your work?" I asked as I noticed his pale face.

"I was too sick with yesterday's news so I didn't work," he said. "This is the end. I am done for."

"No, you're not. Buck up, Tom," I cried. "You have a good future, don't lose hope."

"Sometimes I feel all right. You are an American, I tell myself. Devote your energy and life to the American way of life. Long before this my mind was made up to become a true American. This morning my Caucasian American friends sympathized with me. I felt good and was grateful. Our opportunity has come to express ourselves and act. We are Americans in thought and action. I felt like leaping to work. Then I got sick again because I got to thinking that Japan was the country that attacked the United States. I wanted to bury myself for shame."

I put my hand on his shoulder. "We all feel the same way, Tom. We're human so we flounder around awhile when an unexpected and big problem confronts us, but now that situation has to be passed by. We can't live in the same stage long. We have to move along, face the reality no matter what's in store for us."

Tom stood silently.

"Let's go to my house and take the afternoon off," I suggested. "We'll face a new world tomorrow morning with boldness and strength. What do you say, Tom?"

"All right," Tom agreed.

At home Mother was anxiously waiting for me. When she saw Tom with me her eyes brightened. Tom Yamashita was a favorite of my mother's.

"Look, a telegram from Kazuo!" she cried to me, holding up an envelope. "Read it and tell me what he says."

I tore it open and read. "He wants us to send $45 for train fare. He has a good chance for a furlough."

Mother fairly leaped in the air with the news. She had not seen my brother for four months. "How wonderful! This can happen only in America."

Suddenly she noticed Tom looking glum, and pushed him in the house. "Cheer up, Tom. This is no time for young folks to despair. Roll up your sleeves and get to work. America needs you."

Tom smiled for the first time and looked at me.

"See, Tom?" I said. "She's quick to recover. Yesterday she was wilted, and she's seventy-three."

"Tom, did you go to your gardens today?" she asked him.

"No."

"Why not?" she asked, and then added quickly. "You young men should work hard all the more, keeping up the normal routine of life. You ought to know, Tom, that if everybody dropped their work everything would go to seed. Who's going to take care of the gardens if you won't?"

Tom kept still.

Mother poured tea and brought the cookies. "Don't worry about your old folks. We have stayed here to belong to the American way of life. Time will tell our true purpose. We remained in America for permanence—not for temporary convenience. We common people need not fear."

"I guess you are right," Tom agreed.

"And America is right. She cannot fail. Her principles will stand the test of time and tyranny. Someday agression will be outlawed by all nations."

Mother left the room to prepare the dinner. Tom got up and began to walk up and down the room. Several times he looked out the window and watched the wind blow over the field.

"Yes, if the gardens are ruined I'll rebuild them," he said. "I'll take charge of every garden in the city. All the gardens of America for that matter. I'll rebuild them as fast as the enemies wreck them. We'll have nature on our side and you cannot crush nature."

I smiled and nodded. "Good for you! Tomorrow we'll get up early in the morning and work, sweat, and create. Let's shake on it."

We solemnly shook hands, and by the grip of his fingers I knew he was ready to lay down his life for America and for his gardens.

"No word from him yet," Mother said worriedly. "He should have arrived yesterday. What's happened to him?"

It was eight in the evening, and we had had no word from my brother for several days.

"He's not coming home tonight. It's too late now," I said. "He should have arrived in Oakland this morning at the latest."

Our work had piled up and we had to work late into the night. There were still some pompons to bunch. Faintly the phone rang in the house.

"The phone!" cried Mother excitedly. "It's Kazuo, sure enough."

In the flurry of several minutes I answered the phone, greeted my brother, and was on my way to San Leandro to drive him home. On the way I tried to think of the many things I wanted to say. From the moment I spotted him waiting on the corner I could not say the thing I wanted to. I took his bag and he got in the car, and for some time we did not say anything. Then I asked him how the weather had been in Texas and how he had been.

"We were waiting for you since yesterday," I said. "Mother is home getting the supper ready. You haven't eaten yet, have you?"

He shook his head. "The train was late getting into Los Angeles. We were eight hours behind time and I should have reached San Francisco this morning around eight."

Reaching home it was the same way. Mother could not say anything. "We have nothing special tonight, wish we had something good."

"Anything would do, Mama," my brother said.

Father sat in the room reading the papers but his eyes were over the sheet and his hands were trembling. Mother scurried about getting his supper ready. I sat across the table from my brother, and in the silence which was action I watched the wave of emotions in the room. My brother was aware of it too. He sat there without a word, but I knew he understood. Not many years ago he was the baby of the family, having never been away from home. Now he was on his own, his quiet confidence actually making him appear larger. Keep up the fire, that was his company's motto. It was evident that he was a soldier. He had gone beyond life and death matter, where the true soldiers of war or peace must travel, and had returned.

For five short days we went about our daily task, picking and bunching the flowers for Christmas, eating heavy meals, and visiting the intimates. It was as if we were waiting for the hour of his departure, the time being so short. Every minute was crowded with privacy, friends, and nursery work. Too soon the time for his train came but the family had little to talk.

"Kazuo, don't worry about home or me," Mother said as we rode into town.

"Take care of yourself," my brother told her.

At the 16th Street Station Mother's close friend was waiting for us. She came to bid my brother good-bye. We had fifteen minutes to wait. My brother bought a copy of *The Coast* to see if his cartoons were in.

"Are you in this month's issue?" I asked.

"I haven't seen it yet," he said, leafing the pages. "Yes, I'm in. Here it is."

"Good!" I said. "Keep trying hard. Someday peace will come, and when you return laughter will reign once again."

My mother showed his cartoon to her friend. The train came in and we got up. It was a long one. We rushed to the Los Angeles-bound coach.

Mother's friend shook hands with my brother. "Give your best to America. Our people's honor depend on you Nisei soldiers."

My brother nodded and then glanced at Mother. For a moment her eyes twinkled and she nodded. He waved good-bye from the platform. Once inside the train we lost him. When the train began to move my mother cried, "Why doesn't he pull up the shades and look out? Others are doing it."

We stood and watched until the last of the train was lost in the night of darkness.

Southland

. . . .

The Southland is a desert-turned-city as a result of water piped from elsewhere. Little touched by the gold rush, it had remained largely Spanish-speaking until 1860; it also had harbored a strong movement to split the state to avoid dominance by the economically and culturally advanced north. "At that time," Lawrence Clark Powell claims, "Los Angeles was the toughest town in the West."

Called "the cow counties" and hardly the literary enclave San Francisco was then, the region nonetheless did produce some interesting frontier writing in the nineteenth century. The pivotal work in Southern California's literary history—and one of the state's most influential books—was Helen Hunt Jackson's 1884 novel *Ramona*. Intended to expose the plight of so-called mission Indians, the book ironically became the major factor in the creation of a romanticized mission past. Jackson's story has an incredible life in popular culture: plays, pageants, movies, books about the book, and even countless people who swear they or their grandparents knew the "real" Ramona. In fact, this appears to be an instance of myth filling a historical vacuum, sucked into reality by promoters and desperate settlers.

Following the late-nineteenth-century land boom, the emergence of Hollywood as a movie capital has led to more than 2,000 novels set there, some of them (*Merton of the Movies* by Harry Leon Wilson, for instance, or *What Makes Sammy Run* by Budd Schulberg) outstanding. As Franklin Walker explains, "nearly all [Hollywood novels] agree that life in the movie colony is artificial, the art meretricious, and the industry the graveyard of talent."

Of perhaps greater significance, fiction of crime and detection became a major forum in Southern California for examining the effects of urban reality. James M. Cain, Raymond Chandler, and Ross Macdonald produced work significant enough to force serious critical attention as well as a new sense of the price exacted by densely populated life on the edge. As Chandler himself explains, his stories are set in "a world gone wrong where the law was something to manipulate for profit and power."

Chandler said something else too. Dashiell Hammett, who also wrote in Hollywood, actually created the "hard-boiled detective" novel as an American form when living in San Francisco. Of him, Chandler observed, "He gave murder back to the kind of people who commit it. If it hadn't been for Hammett we'd be solving English drawing-room mysteries, balancing tea cups on our knees and carrying walking sticks and wearing monocles"— credit given where credit was due.

Helen Hunt Jackson

Helen Hunt Jackson (1831–85), among the most successful American women writers of the nineteenth century, produced Ramona *in 1884. In* A Literary History of Southern California, *Franklin Walker calls it "the literary document most important in its influence on the growth of the Spanish tradition in Southern California." Having earlier written a nonfiction book detailing government injustice toward Indians,* A Century of Dishonor *(1881), she had hoped her novel would dramatize the plight of "mission Indians." Results disappointed her; after reading a prestigious— and quite favorable—review, she said, "Not one word for my Indians! I put my heart and soul in the book for them. It is a dead failure." Nevertheless, as Lawrence Clark Powell observed in* California Classics, *she produced "the best California book of its kind—an historical romance of a vanished way of life." The brief passage that follows offers a sense of why Jackson's version of the Hispanic past was so compelling to nineteenth-century readers.*

. . . .

SHEEP-SHEARING TIME

It was sheep-shearing time in Southern California; but sheep-shearing was late at the Señora Moreno's. The Fates had seemed to combine to put it off. In the first place, Felipe Moreno had been ill. He was the Señora's eldest son, and since his father's death had been at the head of his mother's house. Without him, nothing could be done on the ranch, the Señora thought. It had been always, "Ask Señor Felipe," "Go to Señor Felipe," "Señor Felipe will attend to it," ever since Felipe had had the dawning of a beard on his handsome face.

In truth, it was not Felipe, but the Señora, who really decided all questions from greatest to least, and managed everything on the place, from the sheep-pastures to the artichoke-patch; but nobody except the Señora herself knew this. An exceedingly clever woman for her day and generation was Señora Gonzaga Moreno,—as for that matter, exceedingly clever for any day and generation; but exceptionally clever for the day and generation to which she belonged. Her life, the mere surface of it, if it had been written, would have made a romance, to grow hot and cold over: sixty years of the best of old Spain and the wildest of New Spain, Bay of Biscay, Gulf of Mexico, Pacific Ocean,—the waves of them all had tossed destinies for the Señora. The Holy Catholic Church had had its arms round her from first to last; and that was what had brought her safe through, she would have said, if she had ever said anything about herself, which she never did,—one of her many wisdoms. So quiet, so reserved, so gentle an exterior never was known to veil such an imperious and passionate nature, brimful of storm, always passing through stress; never thwarted, except at peril of those who did it; adored and hated by turns, and each at the hottest. A tremendous force, wherever she appeared, was Señora Moreno; but no stranger would suspect it, to see her gliding about, in her scanty black gown, with her rosary hanging at her side, her soft dark eyes cast down, and an expression of mingled melancholy and devotion on her face. She looked simply like a sad, spiritual-minded old lady, amiable and indolent, like her race, but sweeter and more thoughtful than their wont. Her voice heightened this mistaken impression. She was never heard to speak either loud or fast. There was at times even a curious hesitancy in her speech, which came near being a stammer, or suggested the measured care with which people speak who have been cured of stammering. It made her often appear as if she did not know her own mind: at which people sometimes took heart; when, if they had only known the truth, they would have known that the speech hesitated solely because the Señora knew her mind so exactly that she was finding it hard to make the words convey it as she desired, or in a way to best attain her ends.

About this very sheep-shearing there had been, between her and the head shepherd, Juan Canito, called Juan Can for short, and to distinguish him from Juan Jose, the upper herdsman of the cattle, some discussions which would have been hot and angry ones in any other hands than the Señora's.

Juan Canito wanted the shearing to begin, even though Señor Felipe were ill in bed, and though that lazy shepherd Luigo had not yet got back with the flock that had been driven up the coast for pasture. "There were plenty of sheep on the place to begin with," he said one morning,—"at least a thousand;" and by the time they were done, Luigo would surely be back with the rest; and as for Señor Felipe's being in bed, had not he, Juan Canito, stood at the packing bag, and handled the wool, when Señor Felipe was a boy? Why could he not do it again? The Señora did not realize how time was going; there would be no shearers to be hired presently, since the Señora was determined to have none but Indians. Of course, if she would employ Mexicans, as all the other ranches in the valley did, it would be different; but she was resolved upon having Indians,—"God knows why," he interpolated surlily, under his breath.

"I do not quite understand you, Juan," interrupted Señora Moreno at the precise instant the last syllable of this disrespectful ejaculation had escaped Juan's lips; "speak a little louder. I fear I am growing deaf in my old age."

What gentle, suave, courteous tones! and the calm dark eyes rested on Juan Canito with a look to the fathoming of which he was as unequal as one of his own sheep would have been. He could not have told why he instantly and involuntarily said, "Beg your pardon, Señora."

"Oh, you need not ask my pardon, Juan," the Señora replied with exquisite gentleness; "it is not you who are to blame, if I am deaf. I have fancied for a year I did not hear quite as well as I once did. But about the Indians, Juan; did not Señor Felipe tell you that he had positively engaged the same band of shearers we had last autumn, Alessandro's band from Temecula? They will wait until we are ready for them. Señor Felipe will send a messenger for them. He thinks them the best shearers in the country. He will be well enough in a week or two, he thinks, and the poor sheep must bear their loads a few days longer. Are they looking well, do you think, Juan? Will the crop be a good one? General Moreno used to say that you could reckon up the wool-crop to a pound, while it was on the sheep's backs."

"Yes, Señora," answered the mollified Juan; "the poor beasts look wonderfully well considering the scant feed they have had all winter. We'll not come many pounds short of our last year's crop, if any. Though, to be sure, there is no telling in what case that—Luigo will bring his flock back."

The Señora smiled, in spite of herself, at the pause and gulp with which Juan had filled in the hiatus where he had longed to set a contemptuous epithet before Luigo's name.

This was another of the instances where the Señora's will and Juan Canito's had clashed and he did not dream of it, having set it all down as usual to the score of young Señor Felipe.

Harry Leon Wilson

Harry Leon Wilson (1867–1939) was a small-town boy from Illinois who produced what many consider to be the first great Hollywood novel, Merton of the Movies *(1922). Once the editor of the humor weekly* Puck *(1896–1902), this longtime resident of Carmel was a Bohemian companion of Jack London, Mary Austin, and George Sterling. Nonetheless, it was an extended stay in the Southland, where he haunted movie studios, that produced his most famous California novel, from which the following is excerpted. He also produced another widely read novel with an alliterative title,* Ruggles of Red Gap *(1915).*

. . . .

OUT THERE WHERE MEN ARE MEN

From the dressing room the following morning, arrayed in the Buck Benson outfit, unworn since that eventful day on the Gashwiler lot, Merton accompanied Baird to a new set where he would work that day. Baird was profuse in his admiration of the cowboy embellishments, the maroon chaps, the new boots, the hat, the checked shirt and gay neckerchief.

"I'm mighty glad to see you so sincere in your work," he assured Merton. "A lot of these hams I hire get to kidding on the set and spoil the atmosphere, but don't let it bother you. One earnest leading man, if he'll just stay earnest, will carry the piece. Remember that—you got a serious part."

"I'll certainly remember," Merton earnestly assured him.

"Here we are; this is where we begin the Western stuff," said Baird. Merton recognized the place. It was the High Gear Dance Hall where the Montague girl had worked. The name over the door was now "The Come All Ye," and there was a hitching rack in front to which were tethered half-a-dozen saddled horses.

Inside, the scene was set as he remembered it. Tables for drinking were about the floor, and there was a roulette wheel at one side. A red-shirted bartender, his hair plastered low over his brow, leaned negligently on the bar. Scattered around the room were dance-hall girls in short skirts, and a number of cowboys.

"First, I'll wise you up a little bit," said Baird. "You've come out here to work on a ranche in the great open spaces, and these cowboys all love you and come to town with you every time, and they'll stand by you when the detective from New York gets here. Now—let's see—I guess first we'll get your entrance. You come in the front door at the head of them. You've ridden in from the ranche. We get the horseback stuff later. You all come in yelling and so on, and the boys scatter, some to the bar and some to the wheel, and some sit down to the tables to have their drinks and some dance with the girls. You distribute money to them from a paper sack. Here's the sack." From a waiting property boy he took a paper sack. "Put this in your pocket and take it out whenever you need money.

"It's the same sack, see, that the kid put the stolen money in, and you saved it after returning the money. It's just a kind of an idea of mine," he vaguely added, as Merton looked puzzled at this.

"All right, sir." He took the sack, observing it to contain a rude imitation of bills, and stuffed it into his pocket.

"Then, after the boys scatter around, you go stand at the end of the bar. You don't join in their sports and pastimes, see? You're serious; you have things on your mind. Just sort of look around the place as if you were holding yourself above such things, even if you do like to give the boys a good time. Now we'll try the entrance."

Cameras were put into place, and Merton Gill led through the front door his band of rollicking good fellows. He paused inside to give them bills from the paper sack. They scattered to their dissipations. Their leader austerely posed at one end of the bar and regarded the scene with disapproving eyes. Wine, women, and the dance were not for him. He produced again the disillusioned look that had won Henshaw.

"Fine," said Baird. "Gun it, boys."

The scene was shot, and Baird spoke again: "Hold it, everybody; go on with your music, and you boys keep up the dance until Mother's entrance, then you quit and back off."

Merton was puzzled by this speech, but continued his superior look, breaking it with a very genuine shock of surprise when his old mother tottered in at the front door. She was still the disconsolate creature of the day before, bedraggled, sad-eyed, feeble, very aged, and still she carried her bucket and the bundle of rags with which she had mopped. Baird came forward again.

"Oh, I forgot to tell you. Of course you had your old mother follow you out here to the great open spaces, but the poor old thing has cracked under the strain of her hard life, see what I mean? All her dear ones have been leaving the old nest and going out over the hills one by one—you were the last to go—and now she isn't quite right, see?

"You have a good home on the ranche for her, but she won't stay put. She follows you around, and the only thing that keeps her quiet is mopping, so you humour her; you let her mop. It's the only way. But of course it makes you sad. You look at her now, then go up and hug her the way you did yesterday; you try to get her to give up mopping, but she won't, so you let her go on. Try it."

Merton went forward to embrace his old mother. Here was tragedy indeed, a bit of biting pathos from a humble life. He gave the best that was in him as he enfolded the feeble old woman and strained her to his breast, murmuring to her that she must give it up—give it up.

The old lady wept, but was stubborn. She tore herself from his arms and knelt on the floor. "I just got to mop, I just got to mop," she was repeating in a cracked voice. "If I ain't let to mop I git rough till I'm simply a scandal."

It was an affecting scene, marred only by one explosive bit of coarse laughter from an observing cowboy at the close of the old mother's speech. Merton Gill glanced up in sharp annoyance at this offender. Baird was quick in rebuke.

"The next guy that laughs at this pathos can get off the set," he announced, glaring at the assemblage. There was no further outbreak and the scene was filmed.

Lawrence Clark Powell

Lawrence Clark Powell (1906–   ), born in Washington, D.C., where his father was a citrus expert, was raised in Pasadena. "Larry" Powell is among California's most distinguished and versatile men of letters, and is a successful regional essayist, critic—his books California Classic *(1971) and* Southwest Classics *(1974) are themselves now considered to be classics—as well as novelist. He has in all produced four novels (*The Blue Train *[1977],* The River Between *[1979],* El Morro *[1984], and* Portrait of My Father *[1986]) since retiring as founder and first dean of UCLA's library school over twenty years ago. Larry Powell, always a writer, was never a stereotypical librarian, as Wayne Weigand pointed out in* Library Journal: *"Earthy, salty, brash Westerner, defender of the traditional book, friend of the belletristic authors, defender of intellectual freedom, a world traveler, an excellent speaker, an extrovert." He remains an author who has captured Southern California's enduring link with the American Southwest, as well as its largely forgotten small-town past.*

. . . .

LAND OF BOYHOOD

I'd rather write about the town [Pasadena] than go there. It's now all out of proportion. The trees have grown and the houses haven't. What to my boyhood eyes were stately mansions among small trees are now just houses, dwarfed by great bluegums and tall palms. What was my earthly paradise— the blocks-square, lath-shaded Rust Nursery—long ago was lost to urban development. It was my playground, smelling of damp earth and growing things. Sunlight came through the laths in golden bars. Sometimes the Japanese gardeners would let me help water. My special friend was Sugimoto. My father said he was a wizard with plants.

Today the town is peopled with strangers. The old many-childrened families are gone—the Casses, the Fugits, the McEnirys. Boys I played and fought with are risen high or fallen low, or neither, or dead. The girls I fancied are grandmothers or greater.

Until after the second war, South Pasadena was bounded by hills and orange groves and the tracks of the Pacific Electric. I used to sell the *Evening Herald* at Oneonta Junction (the name was from the birthplace in New York of Henry E. Huntington). They cost a penny a paper. Once a passenger on a Sierra Madre car mistakenly gave me a two-and-a-half dollar gold piece. In size and color it resembled a shiny new copper penny. By the time I realized what he had given me, the Big Red Car bearing the man was gone. I quit for the day, a wealthy independent merchant.

Those tracks along Huntington Drive were torn up after the war, as well as the ones up Fair Oaks Avenue. The world's finest interurban electrical railway system was replaced by the world's greatest gasoline-fired, smog-producing transportation system. The hills where the coyotes cried are now peopled. Where I hunted the high mustard for rabbits are now streets and sidewalks, and houses that look pretty much alike. Over the first range the toyon grew. At Christmas we bunched and sold its berries from door to door as California holly. Beyond, the Arroyo Seco's spring floods were yet unchecked by the dam to be built at Devil's Gate.

Nearby was Dippy Hill, named by us from Dr. Bishop's sanitarium for the mentally ill. We never teased the unfortunates who wandered the grounds, talking to themselves. We were afraid to. Boys are rarely compassionate. It was a love of fighting, rather than compassion, that caused me to defend a French war orphan, adopted by Henri St. Pierre, the secretary of the YMCA. The boy's knee breeches led to his being taunted, and so I championed him in rough and tumble. Leon Dostert grew to fame as General Pershing's personal interpreter in World War II, and as the developer of the instantaneous translation system used at the United Nations. He's dead now.

There was another young foreigner who required occasional defending, a skinny Dutch boy with a big name—Cornelis Evertse Groenewegen. His father was the head gardener at the Raymond Hotel. This gave us the run of the great barn where the horses were kept. Later the father had charge of the planting on the new UCLA campus at Westwood. The huge eucalyptus *viminalis* that today line Westwood Boulevard were raised by him as seedlings in five gallon cans. During my early years at UCLA I used to seek him out in the Botanical Garden and talk of past times. As he aged, the old Dutchman came to look like a masterpiece by Rembrandt.

The wide terrace in front of the Raymond Hotel, looking down on the golf course and the town, made an ideal parking place at night when we had given up hunting rabbits for fairer game. It was a secure world whose crime was mostly ours. Why did Old Lady Black persist in drying walnuts on a table in her backyard, thereby inviting us to help ourselves? Why did Old Man White have his tangerine tree right next to our wall? "I don't mind him taking a few," he complained to my parents, "but can't he climb without breaking the branches?"

Another neighbor had a fondness for drink. We used to spy on him drinking alone in his backyard, shout "Boozy" at him, and then run. Those were the years of Prohibition. The doctor prescribed port wine for my mother when she became anemic. I used to sneak down cellar and smell the heady fragrance of the cork. Glue-sniffing, marijuana and the like were undreamed of then, at least in South Pasadena.

Hildegarde Flanner

Hildegarde Flanner (1899–1987), who was born in Indianapolis, lived most of her life in California. She was a protégé of Olive Percival, the literary maven of Arroyo Seco, and became, as historian Kevin Starr has correctly observed, the poet laureate of Pasadena at a time when that community dominated the Southland's emerging literary life. That group included M.F.K. Fisher, Ward Ritchie, Carlyle Ferren MacIntyre, L. C. Powell and, indirectly at least, Robinson Jeffers. Flanner was, writes Starr, "the Edwardian girl, seriously interested in faith, doubt, mysticism, gardens and flowers." She epitomized the literary spirit of Pasadena.

. . . .

NOON ON ALAMEDA STREET

Sun, when it shines on traffic, has a look
Of loaded radiance that might explode,
Yet keeps its kindle like a meaning known
Only to motors in the city road,

Only to fury lifted of all horns
Mourning to themselves a thing to come,
For we have heard delirium in a claxon,
Seen revelation lit on chromium.

On Alameda Street the earth is turning
Secret among old sluices and their kind:
The voice of men among machines at noon
Comes like a sigh from history to the mind,

For in this noon there is no light like light
(Oh, tell us, dark on asphalt, of the sun),
But brightness spawning upon dirty glass,
But fever smoking at meridian,

But men and women riding in their graves
With hands upon a wheel they cannot keep
Clear in the rapt confusion of the crowd,
Crowd and the fate of motion and of sleep.

THE SNAKE AT SHINGLE SPRINGS

Oh, what a fine snake, a very fine snake,
All a long perfect very long snake
With two ivory stripes upon the black,
No foolishness like spots and dots and rings,
No strident castanettes and such things.
As I see him I think
The best snakes in California
Live at Shingle Springs,
And this one quiet, so tranquil
Across the road, a still snake, snake very still.
He brings a thought of such consummate pause
As Egypt of the tombs willed on the swift ones
Of the desert and the Nile,
Cool and lacking superfluities,
Caught so, immortal for a while.

I stop . . . return . . . and look again.

It grieves me to mention
How gay and intent our weather is in May,
How many things are singing, until it seems
Thorns, weeds and ivies sing, even
The oak gall on the pierced twig sings, sings.

Why does the Lord permit the innocent to suffer?
They get in the way.
Farewell, and all the pity of farewell,
You beautiful dead of Shingle Springs.

Raymond Chandler

Raymond Chandler (1888–1959), Chicago-born, was arguably the finest of all detective writers. In a period of four years, 1939–43, he produced four classic novels: The Big Sleep (1939); Farewell, My Lovely (1940); The High Window (1942); and The Lady in the Lake (1943). Chandler himself was quick to point out that he didn't invent the "hard-boiled" school of detective fiction: "I have never made any secret of my opinion that [Dashiell] Hammett deserves most or all of the credit." But it was as an artist who truly grasped Southern California that Chandler is most remembered. According to Powell, he "stopped the Los Angeles kaleidoscope; he arrested its spinning, so confusing to most writers who have tried to see the city clearly . . . he fixed in prose of poetic intensity the brilliant bits and pieces, until we find in his 'Big Four' a glittering mosaic of greater Los Angeles."

. . . .

I'LL BE WAITING

At one o'clock in the morning, Carl, the night porter, turned down the last of three table lamps in the main lobby of the Windermere Hotel. The blue carpet darkened a shade or two and the walls drew back into remoteness. The chairs filled with shadowy loungers. In the corners were memories like cobwebs.

Tony Reseck yawned. He put his head on one side and listened to the frail, twittery music from the radio room beyond a dim arch at the far side of the lobby. He frowned. That should be his radio room after one A.M. Nobody should be in it. That red-haired girl was spoiling his nights.

The frown passed and a miniature of a smile quirked at the corners of his lips. He sat relaxed, a short, pale, paunchy, middle-aged man with long, delicate fingers clasped on the elk's tooth on his watch chain; the long delicate fingers of a sleight-of-hand artist, fingers with shiny, molded nails and tapering first joints, fingers a little spatulate at the ends. Handsome fingers. Tony Reseck rubbed them gently together and there was peace in his quiet sea-gray eyes.

The frown came back on his face. The music annoyed him. He got up with a curious litheness, all in one piece, without moving his clasped hands from the watch chain. At one moment he was leaning back relaxed, and the next he was standing balanced on his feet, perfectly still, so that the movement of rising seemed to be a thing perfectly perceived, an error of vision. . . .

He walked with small, polished shoes delicately across the blue carpet and under the arch. The music was louder. It contained the hot, acid blare, the frenetic, jittering runs of a jam session. It was too loud. The red-haired girl sat there and stared silently at the fretted part of the big radio cabinet as though she could see the band with its fixed professional grin and the sweat running down its back. She was curled up with her feet under her on a davenport which seemed to contain most of the cushions in the room. She was tucked among them carefully, like a corsage in the florist's tissue paper.

She didn't turn her head. She leaned there, one hand in a small fist on her peach-colored knee. She was wearing lounging pajamas of heavy ribbed silk embroidered with black lotus buds.

"You like Goodman, Miss Cressy?" Tony Reseck asked.

The girl moved her eyes slowly. The light in there was dim, but the violet of her eyes almost hurt. They were large, deep eyes without a trace of thought in them. Her face was classical and without expression.

She said nothing.

Tony smiled and moved his fingers at his sides, one by one, feeling them move. "You like Goodman, Miss Cressy?" he repeated gently.

"Not to cry over," the girl said tonelessly.

Tony rocked back on his heels and looked at her eyes. Large, deep, empty eyes. Or were they? He reached down and muted the radio.

"Don't get me wrong," the girl said. "Goodman makes money, and a lad that makes legitimate money these days is a lad you have to respect. But this jitterbug music gives me the backdrop of a beer flat. I like something with roses in it."

"Maybe you like Mozart," Tony said.

"Go on, kid me," the girl said.

"I wasn't kidding you, Miss Cressy. I think Mozart was the greatest man that ever lived—and Toscanini is his prophet."

"I thought you were the house dick." She put her head back on a pillow and stared at him through her lashes.

"Make me some of that Mozart," she added.

"It's too late," Tony sighed. "You can't get it now."

She gave him another long lucid glance. "Got the eye on me, haven't you, flatfoot?" She laughed a little, almost under her breath. "What did I do wrong?"

Tony smiled his toy smile. "Nothing, Miss Cressy. Nothing at all. But you need some fresh air. You've been five days in this hotel and you haven't been outdoors. And you have a tower room."

She laughed again. "Make me a story about it. I'm bored."

"There was a girl here once had your suite. She stayed in the hotel a whole week, like you. Without going out at all, I mean. She didn't speak to anybody hardly. What do you think she did then?"

The girl eyed him gravely. "She jumped her bill."

He put his long delicate hand out and turned it slowly, fluttering the fingers, with an effect almost like a lazy wave breaking. "Unh-uh. She sent down for her bill and paid it. Then she told the hop to be back in half an hour for her suitcases. Then she went out on her balcony."

The girl leaned forward a little, her eyes still grave, one hand capping her peach-colored knee. "What did you say your name was?"

"Tony Reseck."

"Sounds like a hunky."

"Yeah," Tony said. "Polish."

"Go on, Tony."

"All the tower suites have private balconies, Miss Cressy. The walls of them are too low for fourteen stories above the street. It was a dark night, that night, high clouds." He dropped his hand with a final gesture, a farewell gesture. "Nobody saw her jump. But when she hit, it was like a big gun going off."

"You're making it up, Tony." Her voice was a clean dry whisper of sound.

He smiled his toy smile. His quiet sea-gray eyes seemed almost to be smoothing the long waves of her hair. "Eve Cressy," he said musingly. "A name waiting for lights to be in."

"Waiting for a tall dark guy that's no good, Tony. You wouldn't care why. I was married to him once. I might be married to him again. You can make a lot of mistakes in just one lifetime." The hand on her knee opened slowly until the fingers were strained back as far as they would go. Then they closed quickly and tightly, and even in that dim light the knuckles shone like the little polished bones. "I played him a low trick once. I put him in a bad place—without meaning to. You wouldn't care about that either. It's just that I owe him something."

He leaned over softly and turned the knob on the radio. A waltz formed itself dimly on the warm air. A tinsel waltz, but a waltz. He turned the volume up. The music gushed from the loudspeaker in a swirl of shadowed melody. Since Vienna died, all waltzes are shadowed.

The girl put her head on one side and hummed three or four bars and stopped with a sudden tightening of her mouth.

"Eve Cressy," she said. "It was in lights once. At a bum night club. A dive. They raided it and the lights went out."

He smiled at her almost mockingly. "It was no dive while you were there, Miss Cressy . . . That's the waltz the orchestra always played when the old porter walked up and down in front of the hotel entrance, all swelled up with his medals on his chest. *The Last Laugh*. Emil Jannings. You wouldn't remember that one, Miss Cressy."

" 'Spring, Beautiful Spring,' " she said. "No, I never saw it."

He walked three steps away from her and turned. "I have to go upstairs and palm doorknobs. I hope I didn't bother you. You ought to go to bed now. It's pretty late."

The tinsel waltz stopped and a voice began to talk. The girl spoke through the voice. "You really thought something like that—about the balcony?"

He nodded. "I might have," he said softly. "I don't any more."

"No chance, Tony." Her smile was a dim lost leaf. "Come and talk to me some more. Redheads don't jump, Tony. They hang on—and wither."

He looked at her gravely for a moment and then moved away over the carpet. The porter was standing in the archway that led to the main lobby. Tony hadn't looked that way yet, but he knew somebody was there. He always knew if anybody was close to him. He could hear the grass grow, like the donkey in *The Blue Bird*.

The porter jerked his chin at him urgently. His broad face above the uniform collar looked sweaty and excited. Tony stepped up close to him and they went together through the arch and out to the middle of the dim lobby.

"Trouble?" Tony asked wearily.

"There's a guy outside to see you, Tony. He won't come in. I'm doing a wipe-off on the plate glass of the doors and he comes up beside me, a tall guy. 'Get Tony,' he says, out of the side of his mouth."

Tony said: "Uh-huh," and looked at the porter's pale blue eyes. "Who was it?"

"Al, he said to say he was."

Tony's face became as expressionless as dough. "Okey." He started to move off.

The porter caught his sleeve. "Listen, Tony. You got any enemies?"

Tony laughed politely, his face still like dough.

"Listen, Tony." The porter held his sleeve tightly. "There's a big black car down the block, the other way from the hacks. There's a guy standing beside it with his foot on the running board. This guy that spoke to me, he wears a dark-colored, wrap-around overcoat with a high collar turned up against his ears. His hat's way low. You can't hardly see his face. He says, 'Get Tony,' out of the side of his mouth. You ain't got any enemies, have you, Tony?"

"Only the finance company," Tony said. "Beat it."

He walked slowly and a little stiffly across the blue carpet, up the three shallow steps to the entrance lobby with the three elevators on one side and the desk on the other. Only one elevator was working. Beside the open doors, his arms folded, the night operator stood silent in a neat blue uniform with silver facings. A lean, dark Mexican named Gomez. A new boy, breaking in on the night shift.

The other side was the desk, rose marble, with the night clerk leaning on it delicately. A small neat man with a wispy reddish mustache and cheeks so rosy they looked roughed. He stared at Tony and poked a nail at his mustache.

Tony pointed a stiff index finger at him, folded the other three fingers tight to his palm, and flicked his thumb up and down on the stiff finger. The clerk touched the other side of his mustache and looked bored.

Tony went on past the closed and darkened newsstand and the side entrance to the drugstore, out to the brassbound plate-glass doors. He stopped just inside them and took a deep, hard breath. He squared his shoulders, pushed the doors open and stepped out into the cold damp night air.

The street was dark, silent. The rumble of traffic on Wilshire, two blocks away, had no body, no meaning. To the left were two taxis. Their drivers leaned against a fender, side by side, smoking. Tony walked the other way. The big dark car was a third of a block from the hotel entrance. Its lights were dimmed and it was only when he was almost up to it that he heard the gentle sound of its engine turning over.

A tall figure detached itself from the body of the car and strolled toward him, both hands in the pockets of the dark overcoat with the high collar. From the man's mouth a cigarette tip glowed faintly, a rusty pearl.

They stopped two feet from each other.

The tall man said, "Hi, Tony. Long time no see."

"Hello, Al. How's it going?"

"Can't complain." The tall man started to take his right hand out of his overcoat pocket, then stopped and laughed quietly. "I forgot. Guess you don't want to shake hands."

"That don't mean anything," Tony said. "Shaking hands. Monkeys can shake hands. What's on your mind, Al?"

"Still the funny little fat guy, eh, Tony?"

"I guess." Tony winked his eyes tight. His throat felt tight.

"You like your job back there?"

"It's a job."

Al laughed his quiet laugh again. "You take it slow, Tony. I'll take it fast. So it's a job and you want to hold it. Oke. There's a girl named Eve Cressy flopping in your quiet hotel. Get her out. Fast and right now."

"What's the trouble?"

The tall man looked up and down the street. A man behind in the car coughed lightly. "She's hooked with a wrong number. Nothing against her personal, but she'll lead trouble to you. Get her out, Tony. You got maybe an hour."

"Sure," Tony said aimlessly, without meaning.

Al took his hand out of his pocket and stretched it against Tony's chest. He gave him a light, lazy push. "I wouldn't be telling you just for the hell of it, little fat brother. Get her out of there."

"Okey," Tony said, without any tone in his voice.

The tall man took back his hand and reached for the car door. He opened it and started to slip in like a lean black shadow.

Then he stopped and said something to the men in the car and got out again. He came back to where Tony stood silent, his pale eyes catching a little dim light from the street.

"Listen, Tony. You always kept your nose clean. You're a good brother, Tony."

Tony didn't speak.

Al leaned toward him, a long urgent shadow, the high collar almost touching his ears. "It's trouble business, Tony. The boys won't like it, but I'm telling you just the same. This Cressy was married to a lad named Johnny Ralls. Ralls is out of Quentin two, three days, or a week. He did a three-spot for manslaughter. The girl put him there. He ran down an old man one night when he was drunk, and she was with him. He wouldn't stop. She told him to go in and tell it, or else. He didn't go in. So the Johns come for him."

Tony said, "That's too bad."

"It's kosher, kid. It's my business to know. This Ralls flapped his mouth in stir about how the girl would be waiting for him when he got out, all set to forgive and forget, and he was going straight to her."

Tony said, "What's he to you?" His voice had a dry, stiff crackle, like thick paper.

Al laughed. "The trouble boys want to see him. He ran a table at a spot on the Strip and figured out a scheme. He and another guy took the house for fifty grand. The other lad coughed up, but we still need Johnny's twenty-five. The trouble boys don't get paid to forget."

Tony looked up and down the dark street. One of the taxi drivers flicked a cigarette stub in a long arc over the top of one of the cabs. Tony watched it fall and spark on the pavement. He listened to the quiet sound of the big car's motor.

"I don't want any part of it," he said. "I'll get her out."

Al backed away from him, nodding. "Wise kid. How's mom these days?"

"Okey," Tony said.

"Tell her I was asking for her."

"Asking for her isn't anything," Tony said.

Al turned quickly and got into the car. The car curved lazily in the middle of the block and drifted toward the corner. Its lights went up and sprayed on a wall. It turned a corner and was gone. The lingering smell of its exhaust drifted past Tony's nose. He turned and walked back to the hotel and into it. He went along to the radio room.

The radio still muttered, but the girl was gone from the davenport in front of it. The pressed cushions were hollowed out by her body. Tony reached down and touched them. He thought they were still warm. He turned the radio off and stood there, turning a thumb slowly in front of his body, his hand flat against his stomach. Then he went back through the lobby toward the elevator bank and stood beside a majolica jar of white sand. The clerk fussed behind a pebbled-glass screen at one end of the desk. The air was dead.

The elevator bank was dark. Tony looked at the indicator of the middle car and saw that it was at 14.

"Gone to bed," he said under his breath.

The door of the porter's room beside the elevators opened and the little Mexican night operator came out in street clothes. He looked at Tony with a quiet sidewise look out of eyes the color of dried-out chestnuts.

"Good night, boss."

"Yeah," Tony said absently.

He took a thin dappled cigar out of his vest pocket and smelled it. He examined it slowly, turning it around in his neat fingers. There was a small tear along the side. He frowned at that and put the cigar away.

There was a distant sound and the hand on the indicator began to steal around the bronze dial. Light glittered up in the shaft and the straight line of the car floor dissolved the darkness below. The car stopped and the doors opened, and Carl came out of it.

His eyes caught Tony's with a kind of jump and he walked over to him, his head on one side, a thin shine along his pink upper lip.

"Listen, Tony."

Tony took his arm in a hard swift hand and turned him. He pushed him quickly, yet somehow casually, down the steps to the dim main lobby and steered him into a corner. He let go of the arm. His throat tightened again, for no reason he could think of.

"Well?" he said darkly. "Listen to what?"

The porter reached into a pocket and hauled out a dollar bill. "He gimme this," he said loosely. His glittering eyes looked past Tony's shoulder at nothing. They winked rapidly. "Ice and ginger ale."

"Don't stall," Tony growled.

"Guy in Fourteen-B," the porter said.

"Lemme smell your breath."

The porter leaned toward him obediently.

"Liquor," Tony said harshly.

"He gimme a drink."

Tony looked down at the dollar bill. "Nobody's in Fourteen-B. Not on my list," he said.

"Yeah. There is." The porter licked his lips and his eyes opened and shut several times. "Tall dark guy."

"All right," Tony said crossly. "All right. There's a tall dark guy in Fourteen-B and he gave you a buck and a drink. Then what?"

"Gat under his arm," Carl said, and blinked.

Tony smiled, but his eyes had taken on the lifeless glitter of thick ice. "You take Miss Cressy up to her room?"

Carl shook his head. "Gomez. I saw her go up."

"Get away from me," Tony said between his teeth. "And don't accept any more drinks from the guests."

He didn't move until Carl had gone back into his cubbyhole by the elevators and shut the door. Then he moved silently up the three steps and stood in front of the desk, looking at the veined rose marble, the onyx pen set, the fresh registration card in its leather frame. He lifted a hand and smacked it down hard on the marble. The clerk popped out from behind the glass screen like a chipmunk coming out of its hole.

Tony took a flimsy out of his breast pocket and spread it on the desk. "No Fourteen-B on this," he said in a bitter voice.

The clerk wisped politely at his mustache. "So sorry. You must have been out to supper when he checked in."

"Who?"

"Registered as James Watterson, San Diego." The clerk yawned.

"Ask for anybody?"

The clerk stopped in the middle of the yawn and looked at the top of Tony's head. "Why yes. He asked for a swing band. Why?"

"Smart, fast and funny," Tony said. "If you like 'em that way." He wrote on his flimsy and stuffed it back into his pocket. "I'm going upstairs and palm doorknobs. There's four tower rooms you ain't rented yet. Get up on your toes, son. You're slipping."

"I make out," the clerk drawled, and completed his yawn. "Hurry back, pop. I don't know how I'll get through the time."

"You could shave that pink fuzz off your lip," Tony said, and went across to the elevators.

He opened up a dark one and lit the dome light and shot the car up to fourteen. He darkened it again, stepped out and closed the doors. This lobby was smaller than any other, except the one immediately below it. It had a single blue-paneled door in each of the walls other than the elevator wall. On each door was a gold number and letter with a gold wreath around it. Tony walked over to 14A and put his ear to the panel. He heard nothing. Eve Cressy might be in bed asleep, or in the bathroom, or out on the balcony. Or she might be sitting there in the room, a few feet from the door, looking at the wall. Well, he wouldn't expect to be able to hear her sit and look at the wall. He went over to 14B and put his ear to that panel. This was different. There was a sound in there. A man coughed. It sounded somehow like a solitary cough. There were no voices. Tony pressed the small nacre button beside the door.

Steps came without hurry. A thickened voice spoke through the panel. Tony made no answer, no sound. The thickened voice repeated the question. Lightly, maliciously, Tony pressed the bell again.

Mr. James Watterson, of San Diego, should now open the door and give forth noise. He didn't. A silence fell beyond that door that was like the silence of a glacier. Once more Tony put his ear to the wood. Silence utterly.

He got out a master key on a chain and pushed it delicately into the lock of the door. He turned it, pushed the door inward three inches and withdrew the key. Then he waited.

"All right," the voice said harshly. "Come in and get it."

Tony pushed the door wide and stood there, framed against the light from the lobby. The man was tall, black-haired, angular and white-faced. He held a gun. He held it as though he knew about guns.

"Step right in," he drawled.

Tony went in through the door and pushed it shut with his shoulder. He kept his hands a little out from his sides, the clever fingers curled and slack. He smiled his quiet little smile.

"Mr. Watterson?"

"And after that what?"

"I'm the house detective here."

"It slays me."

The tall, white-faced, somehow handsome and somehow not handsome man backed slowly into the room. It was a large room with a low balcony around two sides of it. French doors opened out on the little private open-air balcony that each of the tower rooms had. There was a grate set for a log fire behind a paneled screen in front of a cheerful davenport. A tall misted glass stood on a hotel tray beside a deep, cozy chair. The man backed toward this and stood in front of it. The large, glistening gun drooped and pointed at the floor.

"It slays me," he said. "I'm in the dump an hour and the house copper gives me the buzz. Okey, sweetheart, look in the closet and bathroom. But she just left."

"You didn't see her yet," Tony said.

The man's bleached face filled with unexpected lines. His thickened voice edged toward a snarl. "Yeah? Who didn't I see yet?"

"A girl named Eve Cressy."

The man swallowed. He put his gun down on the table beside the tray. He let himself down into the chair backwards, stiffly, like a man with a touch of lumbago. Then he leaned forward and put his hands on his kneecaps and smiled brightly between his teeth. "So she got here, huh? I didn't ask about her yet. I'm a careful guy. I didn't ask yet."

"She's been here five days," Tony said. "Waiting for you. She hasn't left the hotel a minute."

The man's mouth worked a little. His smile had a knowing tilt to it. "I got delayed a little up north," he said smoothly. "You know how it is. Visiting old friends. You seem to know a lot about my business, copper."

"That's right, Mr. Ralls."

The man lunged to his feet and his hand snapped at the gun. He stood leaning over, holding it on the table, staring. "Dames talk too much," he said with a muffled sound in his voice as though he held something soft between his teeth and talked through it.

"Not dames, Mr. Ralls."

"Huh?" The gun slithered on the hard wood of the table. "Talk it up, copper. My mind reader just quit."

"Not dames, guys. Guys with guns."

The glacier silence fell between them again. The man straightened his body out slowly. His face was washed clean of expression, but his eyes were haunted. Tony leaned in front of him, a shortish plump man with a quiet, pale, friendly face and eyes as simple as forest water.

"They never run out of gas—those boys," Johnny Ralls said, and licked at his lip. "Early and late, they work. The old firm never sleeps."

"You know who they are?" Tony said softly.

"I could maybe give nine guesses. And twelve of them would be right."

"The trouble boys," Tony said, and smiled a brittle smile.

"Where is she?" Johnny Ralls asked harshly.

"Right next door to you."

The man walked to the wall and left his gun lying on the table. He stood in front of the wall, studying it. He reached up and gripped the grillwork of the balcony railing. When he dropped his hand and turned, his face had lost some of its lines. His eyes had a quieter glint. He moved back to Tony and stood over him.

"I've got a stake," he said. "Eve sent me some dough and I built it up with a touch I made up north. Case dough, what I mean. The trouble boys talk about twenty-five grand." He smiled crookedly. "Five *C's* I can count. I'd have a lot of fun making them believe that, I would."

"What did you do with it?" Tony asked indifferently.

"I never had it, copper. Leave that lay. I'm the only guy in the world that believes it. It was a little deal that I got suckered on."

"I'll believe it," Tony said.

"They don't kill often. But they can be awful tough."

"Mugs," Tony said with a sudden bitter contempt. "Guys with guns. Just mugs."

Johnny Ralls reached for his glass and drained it empty. The ice cubes tinkled softly as he put it down. He picked his gun up, danced it on his palm, then tucked it, nose down, into an inner breast pocket. He stared at the carpet.

"How come you're telling me this, copper?"

"I thought maybe you'd give her a break."

"And if I wouldn't?"

"I kind of think you will," Tony said.

Johnny Ralls nodded quietly. "Can I get out of here?"

"You could take the service elevator to the garage. You could rent a car. I can give you a card to the garage man."

"You're a funny little guy," Johnny Ralls said.

Tony took out a worn ostrich-skin billfold and scribbled on a printed card. Johnny Ralls read it, and stood holding it, tapping it against a thumbnail.

"I could take her with me," he said, his eyes narrow.

"You could take a ride in a basket too," Tony said. "She's been here five days, I told you. She's been spotted. A guy I know called me up and told me to get her out of here. Told me what it was all about. So I'm getting you out instead."

"They'll love that," Johnny Ralls said. "They'll send you violets."

"I'll weep about it on my day off."

Johnny Ralls turned his hand over and stared at the palm. "I could see her, anyway. Before I blow. Next door to here, you said?"

Tony turned on his heel and started for the door. He said over his shoulder, "Don't waste a lot of time, handsome. I might change my mind."

The man said, almost gently: "You might be spotting me right now, for all I know."

Tony didn't turn his head. "That's a chance you have to take."

He went on to the door and passed out of the room. He shut it carefully, silently, looked once at the door of 14A and got into his dark elevator. He rode it down to the linen-room floor and got out to remove the basket that held the service elevator open at that floor. The door slid quietly shut. He held it so that it made no noise. Down the corridor, light came from the open door of the housekeeper's office. Tony got back into his elevator and went on down to the lobby.

The little clerk was out of sight behind his pebbled-glass screen, auditing accounts. Tony went through the main lobby and turned into the radio room. The radio was on again, soft. She was there, curled on the davenport again. The speaker hummed to her, a vague sound so low that what it said was as wordless as the murmur of trees. She turned her head slowly and smiled at him.

"Finished palming doorknobs? I couldn't sleep worth a nickel. So I came down again. Okey?"

He smiled and nodded. He sat down in a green chair and patted the plump brocade arms of it. "Sure, Miss Cressy."

"Waiting is the hardest kind of work, isn't it? I wish you'd talk to that radio. It sounds like a pretzel being bent."

Tony fiddled with it, got nothing he liked, set it back where it had been.

"Beer-parlor drunks are all the customers now."

She smiled at him again.

"I don't bother you being here, Miss Cressy?"

"I like it. You're a sweet little guy, Tony."

He looked stiffly at the floor and a ripple touched his spine. He waited for it to go away. It went slowly. Then he sat back, relaxed again, his neat fingers clasped on his elk's tooth. He listened. Not to the radio—to far-off, uncertain things, menacing things. And perhaps to just the safe whir of wheels going away into a strange night.

"Nobody's all bad," he said out loud.

The girl looked at him lazily. "I've met two or three I was wrong on, then."

He nodded. "Yeah," he admitted judiciously. "I guess there's some that are."

The girl yawned and her deep violet eyes half closed. She nestled back into the cushions. "Sit there for a while, Tony. Maybe I could nap."

"Sure. Not a thing for me to do. Don't know why they pay me."

She slept quickly and with complete stillness, like a child. Tony hardly breathed for ten minutes. He just watched her, his mouth a little open. There was a quiet fascination in his limpid eyes, as if he was looking at an altar.

Then he stood up with infinite care and padded away under the arch to the entrance lobby and the desk. He stood at the desk listening for a little while. He heard a pen rustling out of sight. He went around the corner to the row of house phones in little glass cubbyholes. He lifted one and asked the night operator for the garage.

It rang three or four times and then a boyish voice answered: "Windermere Hotel. Garage speaking."

"This is Tony Reseck. That guy Watterson I gave a card to. He leave?"

"Sure, Tony. Half an hour almost. Is it your charge?"

"Yeah," Tony said. "My party. Thanks. Be seein' you."

He hung up and scratched his neck. He went back to the desk and slapped a hand on it. The clerk wafted himself around the screen with his greeter's smile in place. It dropped when he saw Tony.

"Can't a guy catch up on his work?" he grumbled.

"What's the professional rate on Fourteen-B?"

The clerk stared morosely. "There's no professional rate in the tower."

"Make one. The fellow left already. Was there only an hour."

"Well, well," the clerk said airily. "So the personality didn't click tonight. We get a skip-out."

"Will five bucks satisfy you?"

"Friend of yours?"

"No. Just a drunk with delusions of grandeur and no dough."

"Guess we'll have to let it ride, Tony. How did he get out?"

"I took him down the service elevator. You was asleep. Will five bucks satisfy you?"

"Why?"

The worn ostrich-skin wallet came out and a weedy five slipped across the marble. "All I could shake him for," Tony said loosely.

The clerk took the five and looked puzzled. "You're the boss," he said, and shrugged. The phone shrilled on the desk and he reached for it. He listened and then pushed it toward Tony. "For you."

Tony took the phone and cuddled it close to his chest. He put his mouth close to the transmitter. The voice was strange to him. It had a metallic sound. Its syllables were meticulously anonymous.

"Tony? Tony Reseck?"

"Talking."

"A message from Al. Shoot?"

Tony looked at the clerk. "Be a pal," he said over the mouthpiece. The clerk flicked a narrow smile at him and went away. "Shoot," Tony said into the phone.

"We had a little business with a guy in your place. Picked him up scramming. Al had a hunch you'd run him out. Tailed him and took him to the curb. Not so good. Backfire."

Tony held the phone very tight and his temples chilled with the evaporation of moisture. "Go on," he said. "I guess there's more."

"A little. The guy stopped the big one. Cold. Al—Al said to tell you goodbye."

Tony leaned hard against the desk. His mouth made a sound that was not speech.

"Get it?" The metallic voice sounded impatient, a little bored. "This guy had him a rod. He used it. Al won't be phoning anybody any more."

Tony lurched at the phone, and the base of it shook on the rose marble. His mouth was a hard dry knot.

The voice said: "That's as far as we go, bub. G'night." The phone clicked dryly, like a pebble hitting a wall.

Tony put the phone down in its cradle very carefully, so as not to make any sound. He looked at the clenched palm of his left hand. He took a handkerchief out and rubbed the palm softly and straightened the fingers out with his other hand. Then he wiped his forehead. The clerk came around the screen again and looked at him with glinting eyes.

"I'm off Friday. How about lending me that phone number?"

Tony nodded at the clerk and smiled a minute frail smile. He put his handkerchief away and patted the pocket he had put it in. He turned and walked away from the desk, across the entrance lobby, down the three shallow steps, along the shadowy reaches of the main lobby, and so in through the arch to the radio room once more. He walked softly, like man moving in a room where somebody is very sick. He reached the chair he had sat in before and lowered himself into it inch by inch. The girl slept on, motionless, in that curled-up looseness achieved by some women and all cats. Her breath made no slightest sound against the vague murmur of the radio.

Tony Reseck leaned back in the chair and clasped his hands on his elk's tooth and quietly closed his eyes.

Heartland

. . . .

Although California's vast farming valleys—the Central, the Salinas, the Imperial, the Napa, and others—boasted at best a slim literary history of note prior to the 1930s, they have become in the past sixty years regions of considerable note to readers. Creative writing has been rich and diverse in the state's Heartland and for good reason: the population is rich and diverse.

The Great Central Valley is Heartland's apotheosis, and it is also the world's most productive and diverse agricultural region. As a result, it has attracted an ethnically and socially assorted series of migrants to work in its fields: Chinese, Japanese, Italian, Portuguese, Sikh, German, Filipino, Mexican, Okie, and Black—well over one hundred groups. Heartland boasts people and experiences aplenty.

If it appears that this region has typified the California dream, however, there is a difference for in it virtually the only path to a better life has been hard, physical labor. This is not the Golden State most dreamers have envisioned, so it has tended to attract the tough, the determined, possibly the desperate. Parochialism and xenophobia are certainly not unknown here, but neither are determination and courage. Today Heartland may be spawning more native-born writers of quality than any other section of the state.

Certainly, since the emergence of three natives in the 1930s—William Saroyan, William Everson, and John Steinbeck—it has produced a steady stream of innovative literature that defies this region's bumpkin stereotype. And Arnold Rojas, a vaquero-turned-writer, soon provided a unique series of literary portraits of those tough cowboys who toiled these ranges before, during, and after the Americanization of the region.

As was true of Rojas's vaquero tales, much Heartland writing starts with the soil, the physical reality from which so many people wrest their livings. This is typified by "The Squatters' Camp," a powerful essay describing some of the harsh conditions that led Steinbeck to write *The Grapes of Wrath*—arguably the state's most important novel. You will not find beaches or palm trees in these works, but you will find passion and truth and determination.

William Saroyan

William Saroyan (1908–81), winner of the Pulitzer Prize, an Academy Award, and the New York Drama Critics Circle Award, among many other honors, was born and raised in Fresno. He did not graduate from high school, but he did develop into one of America's most original writers. His short-story collections such as The Daring Young Man on the Flying Trapeze and Other Stories *(1934) and* My Name is Aram *(1940) were literary landmarks; so were dramas like* The Time of Your Life *(1939) and* My Heart's in the Highlands *(1939). He also published novels, essays, memoirs and, of course, an Oscar-winning script for* The Human Comedy. *Sadly, William Saroyan is—for reasons that are not entirely clear—perhaps the most underappreciated of all major California authors. His literary output was uneven, but at his best his prose soared and he offered original, sometimes magical visions of what it means to be human.*

· ·

ONE OF OUR FUTURE POETS, YOU MIGHT SAY

When I was the fourteenth brightest pupil in the class of fifteen third-graders at Emerson School, the Board of Education took a day off one day to think things over.

This was years ago.

I was eight going on nine or at the most nine going on ten, and good-natured.

In those days the average Board of Education didn't make a fuss over the children of a small town and if some of the children seemed to be doltish, the average Board of Education assumed that this was natural and let it go at that.

Certain Presbyterian ministers, however, sometimes looked into a sea of young faces and said: You are the future leaders of America, the future captains of industry, the future statesmen, and, I might say, the future poets. This sort of talk always pleased me because I liked to imagine what sort of future captains of industry pals of mine like Jimmy Volta and Frankie Sousa were going to make.

I knew these boys.

They were great baseball players, but by nature idiots, or, in more scientific terminology, high-grade cretins: healthy, strong, and spirited. I didn't think they would be apt to develop into captains of industry and neither did they. If they were asked what career they intended to shape for themselves, they would honestly say, I don't know. Nothing, I guess.

Ordinarily, however, our Board of Education had no such glorious faith as this in the young hoodlums it was trying to teach to read and write.

Nevertheless, one day our Board of Education took a day off to think things over quietly and after seven hours of steady thinking decided to put every public school pupil through a thorough physical examination to solve, if possible, the mystery of health in the young inhabitants of the slums.

According to documentary proof, published and tabulated, all the inhabitants of my neighborhood should have had badly shaped heads, sunken chests, faulty bone structure, hollow voices, no energy, distemper, and six or seven other minor organic defects.

According to the evidence before each public school teacher, however, these ruffians from the slums had well-shaped heads, sound chests, handsome figures, loud voices, too much energy, and a continuous compulsion to behave mischievously.

Something was wrong somewhere.

Our Board of Education decided to try to find out what.

They *did* find out.

They found out that the published and tabulated documentary proof was wrong.

It was at this time that I first learned with joy and fury that I was a poet. I remember being in the Civic Auditorium of my home town at high noon with six hundred other future statesmen, and I remember hearing my name sung out by old Miss Ogilvie in a clear hysterical soprano.

The time had arrived for me to climb the seventeen steps to the stage, walk to the center of the stage, strip to the waist, inhale, exhale, and be measured all over.

There was a moment of confusion and indecision, followed quickly by a superhuman impulse to behave with style, which I did, to the horror and bewilderment of the whole Board of Education, three elderly doctors, a half-dozen registered nurses, and six hundred future captains of industry.

Instead of climbing the seventeen steps to the stage, I *leaped*.

I remember old Miss Ogilvie turning to Mr. Rickenbacker, Superintendent of Public Schools, and whispering fearfully: This is Garoghlanian— one of our future poets, I might say.

Mr. Rickenbacker took one quick look at me and said: Oh, I see. Who's he sore at?

Society, old Miss Ogilvie said.

Oh, I see, Mr. Rickenbacker said. So am I, but I'll be damned if I can jump like that. Let's say no more about it.

I flung off my shirt and stood stripped to the waist, a good deal of hair bristling on my chest.

You see? Miss Ogilvie said. A writer.

Inhale, Mr. Rickenbacker said.

For how long? I asked.

As long as possible, Mr. Rickenbacker said.

I began to inhale. Four minutes later I was still doing so. Naturally, the examining staff was a little amazed. They called a speedy meeting while I continued to inhale. After two minutes of heated debate the staff decided to ask me to stop inhaling. Miss Ogilvie explained that unless they *asked* me to stop I would be apt to go on inhaling all afternoon.

That will be enough for the present, Mr. Rickenbacker said.

Already? I said. I'm not even started.

Now exhale, he said.

For how long? I said.

My God! Mr. Rickenbacker said.

You'd better tell him, Miss Ogilvie said. Otherwise he'll exhale all afternoon.

Three or four minutes, Mr. Rickenbacker said.

I exhaled four minutes and was then asked to put on my shirt and go away.

How are things? I asked the staff. Am I in pretty good shape?

Let's say no more about it, Mr. Rickenbacker said. Please go away.

The following year our Board of Education decided to give no more physical examinations. The examinations went along all right as far as future captains of industry were concerned, and future statesmen, but when it came to future poets the examinations ran helter-skelter and amuck, and nobody knew what to do or think.

John Steinbeck

John Steinbeck (1902–68), California's only Nobel Prize winner for literature (1962) and arguably the state's most accomplished native-born writer, was a novelist of great and compassionate vision. In a series of books that appeared in the 1930s—To a God Unknown (1933), Tortilla Flat (1935), In Dubious Battle (1936), Of Mice and Men (1937), and The Grapes of Wrath (1939)—he elevated California's literature and forever buried the notion that major writers could not develop here. Steinbeck was also a notably versatile writer, producing plays, short stories, and both long and short nonfiction of high quality. The piece that follows is from The Harvest Gypsies (originally titled Their Blood is Strong [1938]), a series of intense essays that were written while the Salinas native did the research that led to his landmark novel, The Grapes of Wrath.

· ·

THE SQUATTERS' CAMPS

The squatters' camps are located all over California. Let us see what a typical one is like. It is located on the banks of a river, near an irrigation ditch or on a side road where a spring of water is available. From a distance it looks like a city dump, and well it may, for the city dumps are the sources for the material of which it is built. You can see a litter of dirty rags and scrap iron, of houses built of weeds, of flattened cans or of paper. It is only on close approach that it can be seen that these are homes.

Here is a house built by a family who have tried to maintain a neatness. The house is about 10 feet by 10 feet, and it is built completely of corrugated paper. The roof is peaked, the walls are tacked to a wooden frame. The dirt floor is swept clean, and along the irrigation ditch or in the muddy river the wife of the family scrubs clothes without soap and tries to rinse out the mud in muddy water. The spirit of this family is not quite broken, for the children, three of them, still have clothes, and the family possesses three old quilts and a soggy, lumpy mattress. But the money so needed for food cannot be used for soap nor for clothes.

With the first rain the carefully built house will slop down into a brown, pulpy mush; in a few months the clothes will fray off the children's bodies while the lack of nourishing food will subject the whole family to pneumonia when the first cold comes.

Five years ago this family had fifty acres of land and a thousand dollars in the bank. The wife belonged to a sewing circle and the man was a member of the grange. They raised chickens, pigs, pigeons and vegetables and fruit for their own use; and their land produced the tall corn of the middle west. Now they have nothing.

If the husband hits every harvest without delay and works the maximum time, he may make four hundred dollars this year. But if anything happens, if his old car breaks down, if he is late and misses a harvest or two, he will have to feed his whole family on as little as one hundred and fifty.

But there is still pride in this family. Wherever they stop they try to put the children in school. It may be that the children will be in a school for as much as a month before they are moved to another locality.

Here, in the faces of the husband and his wife, you begin to see an expression you will notice on every face; not worry, but absolute terror of the starvation that crowds in against the borders of the camp. This man has tried to make a toilet by digging a hole in the ground near his paper house and surrounding it with an old piece of burlap. But he will only do things like that this year. He is a newcomer and his spirit and decency and his sense of his own dignity have not been quite wiped out. Next year he will be like his next door neighbor.

This is a family of six; a man, his wife and four children. They live in a tent the color of the ground. Rot has set in on the canvas so that the flaps and the sides hang in tatters and are held together with bits of rusty baling wire. There is one bed in the family and that is a big tick lying on the ground inside the tent.

They have one quilt and a piece of canvas for bedding. The sleeping arrangement is clever. Mother and father lie down together and two children lie between them. Then, heading the other way, the other two children lie, the littler ones. If the mother and father sleep with their legs spread wide, there is room for the legs of the children.

There is more filth here. The tent is full of flies clinging to the apple box that is the dinner table, buzzing about the foul clothes of the children, particularly the baby, who has not been bathed nor cleaned for several days. This family has been on the road longer than the builder of the paper house. There is no toilet here, but there is a clump of willows nearby where human feces lie exposed to the flies—the same flies that are in the tent.

Two weeks ago there was another child, a four year old boy. For a few weeks they had noticed that he was kind of lackadaisical, that his eyes had been feverish. They had given him the best place in the bed, between father and mother. But one night he went into convulsions and died, and the next morning the coroner's wagon took him away. It was one step down.

They know pretty well that it was a diet of fresh fruit, beans and little else that caused his death. He had no milk for months. With this death there came a change of mind in his family. The father and mother now feel that paralyzed dullness with which the mind protects itself against too much sorrow and too much pain.

And this father will not be able to make a maximum of four hundred dollars a year any more because he is no longer alert; he isn't quick at piecework, and he is not able to fight clear of the dullness that has settled on him. His spirit is losing caste rapidly.

The dullness shows in the faces of this family, and in addition there is a sullenness that makes them taciturn. Sometimes they still start the older children off to school, but the ragged little things will not go; they hide in ditches or wander off by themselves until it is time to go back to the tent, because they are scorned in the school.

The better-dressed children shout and jeer, the teachers are quite often impatient with these additions to their duties, and the parents of the "nice" children do not want to have disease carriers in the schools.

The father of this family once had a little grocery store and his family lived in back of it so that even the children could wait on the counter. When the drought set in there was no trade for the store any more.

This is the middle class of the squatters' camp. In a few months this family will slip down to the lower class. Dignity is all gone, and spirit has turned to sullen anger before it dies.

The next door neighbor family of man, wife and three children of from three to nine years of age, have built a house by driving willow branches into the ground and wattling weeds, tin, old paper and strips of carpet against them. A few branches are placed over the top to keep out the noonday sun. It would not turn water at all. There is no bed. Somewhere the family has found a big piece of old carpet. It is on the ground. To go to bed the members of the family lie on the ground and fold the carpet up over them.

The three year old child has a gunny sack tied about his middle for clothing. He has the swollen belly caused by malnutrition.

He sits on the ground in the sun in front of the house, and the little black fruit flies buzz in circles and land on his closed eyes and crawl up his nose until he weakly brushes them away.

They try to get at the mucous in the eye-corners. This child seems to have the reactions of a baby much younger. The first year he had a little milk, but he has had none since.

He will die in a very short time. The older children may survive. Four nights ago the mother had a baby in the tent, on the dirty carpet. It was born dead, which was just as well because she could not have fed it at the breast; her own diet will not produce milk.

After it was born and she had seen that it was dead, the mother rolled over and lay still for two days. She is up today, tottering around. The last baby, born less than a year ago, lived a week. This woman's eyes have the glazed, far-away look of a sleep walker's eyes. She does not wash clothes any more. The drive that makes for cleanliness has been drained out of her and she hasn't the energy. The husband was a share-cropper once, but he couldn't make it go. Now he has lost even the desire to talk. He will not look directly at you for that requires will, and will needs strength. He is a bad field worker for the same reason. It takes him a long time to make up his mind, so he is always late in moving and late in arriving in the fields. His top wage, when he can find work now, which isn't often, is a dollar a day.

The children do not even go to the willow clump any more. They squat where they are and kick a little dirt. The father is vaguely aware that there is a culture of hookworm in the mud along the river bank. He knows the children will get it on their bare feet. But he hasn't the will nor the energy to resist. Too many things have happened to him. This is the lower class of the camp.

This is what the man in the tent will be in six months; what the man in the paper house with its peaked roof will be in a year, after his house has washed down and his children have sickened or died, after the loss of dignity and spirit have cut him down to a kind of subhumanity.

Helpful strangers are not well-received in this camp. The local sheriff makes a raid now and then for a wanted man, and if there is labor trouble the vigilantes may burn the poor houses. Social workers, survey workers have taken case histories. They are filed and open for inspection. These families have been questioned over and over about their origins, number of children living and dead. The information is taken down and filed. That is that. It has been done so often and so little has come of it.

And there is another way for them to get attention. Let an epidemic break out, say typhoid or scarlet fever, and the country doctor will come to the camp and hurry the infected cases to the pest house. But malnutrition is not infectious, nor is dysentery, which is almost the rule among the children.

The county hospital has no room for measles, mumps, whooping cough; and yet these are often deadly to hunger-weakened children. And although we hear much about the free clinics for the poor, these people do not know how to get the aid and they do not get it. Also, since most of their dealings with authority are painful to them, they prefer not to take the chance.

This is the squatters' camp. Some are a little better, some much worse. I have described three typical families. In some of the camps there are as many as three hundred families like these. Some are so far from water that it must be bought at five cents a bucket.

And if these men steal, if there is developing among them a suspicion and hatred of well-dressed, satisfied people, the reason is not to be sought in their origin nor in any tendency to weakness in their character.

William Everson

William Everson (1912–), who also published under the name Brother Antoninus, was the first major poet produced by the Great Central Valley. His initial collection of verse, San Joaquin *(1938) remains a regional landmark. The Selma native was exposed to the poetry of Robinson Jeffers while attending Fresno State College in 1930, and was powerfully influenced by the Carmel writer's work. Everson, who was for a time a Dominican monk, is much concerned with the sacred in his verse, though he by no means limits his exploration to conventional religion; instead, he examines what he calls "the gods of the solar system" and "the gods of the solar plexus"—a modern shaman who understands the literary power of regional roots. The poems that follow are from* The Residual Years *(1948).*

. . . .

THE RESIDUAL YEARS

As long as we looked lay the low country.
As long as we looked
Were the ranchos miled in their open acres,
The populous oaks and the weedy weirs.
There were birds in the rushes.

And deep in the grass stood the silent cattle.
And all about us the leveled light.
Roads bent to the bogs;
Fenced from the fields they wound in the marshes.
We saw slim-legged horses.

We saw time in the air.
We saw indeed to the held heart of an older order,
That neither our past nor that of our fathers

116

Knew part in the forming,
An expansive mode remarked through the waste of residual years,
Large in its outline,
Turning up from its depth these traces and wisps
That hung yet on through a cultural close
We had thought too faint to recapture.

MUSCAT PRUNING

All these dormant fields are held beneath the fog.
The scraggy vines, the broken weeds, the cold moist ground
Have known it now for days.
My fingers are half-numbed around the handles of the shears,
But I have other thoughts.
There is a flicker swooping from the grove on scalloped wings,
His harsh cry widening through the fog.
After his call the silence holds the drip-sound of the trees,
Muffling the hushed beat under the mist.
Over the field the noise of other pruners
Moves me to my work.
I have a hundred vines to cut before dark.

WINTER PLOWING

Before my feet the plowshare rolls the earth,
Up and over,
Splitting the loam with a soft tearing sound.
Between the horses I can see the red blur of a far peach orchard,
Half obscured in drifting sheets of morning fog.
A score of blackbirds circles around me on shining wings.
They alight beside me and scramble almost under my feet
In search of upturned grubs.
The fragrance of the earth rises like tule-pond mist,
Shrouding me in impalpable folds of sweet cool smell,
Lulling my senses to the rhythm of the running plow,
The jingle of the harness,
And the thin cries of the gleaming bent-winged birds.

WEEDS

All night long in the high meadow
They shielded the city-light from their eyes
Under towering grass.
Weeds warded them:
Dock hung in his hair,
Mallow marred with its subtle stain
Her rumpled skirt.
Near midnight air chilled,
They drew about them his heavy coat,
(Soldier's gear brought to such usage!)
And hoarded their heat.
Toward three they dozed,
All cramped and cold,
And went down in the dawn,
Limping under the early eyes,
Went their way,
Went out to the world,
To the War,
Bearing mallow, dock,
The odor of weed and the weed stain,
And the harsh print of the earth.

Arnold Rojas

Arnold R. Rojas (1896–1988) ran away from an orphanage in San Luis Obispo in 1902 and fled to the Great Central Valley. "I wanted to become a vaquero and I did," he said. Fifty years later, after decades of herding cattle and caring for horses, "Chief" Rojas began writing—first vignettes for The Bakersfield Californian, *then a series of books—beginning with* California Vaqueros *(1953). Who were the vaqueros? "By vaquero," he explained, "I mean the man who rode the range for a hundred years or more before the United States took possession of Mexico's territory." The stories and books of Rojas were literally without rivals, and they remain the finest record we have of California's Hispanic cowboys. All his published work was collected and reissued under the titles* These Were the Vaqueros *(1974) and* Vaqueros and Buckaroos *(1979).*

. . . .

THE WATCH

Nacho, one of the vaqueros, always wore a vest in the pockets of which he carried pencils and a notebook like a regular bossman. As though this were not enough useless weight to carry, on a trip to Buttonwillow he bought a "dollar watch" to add to his impedimenta. On his return to the wagon Lupe Valenzuela, the cook, gave him a piece of buckskin to use in lieu of a watch chain. He tied one end of the thong to the watch and the other to a buttonhole of the vest and put the watch in one of the pockets. Buckskin is the strongest of leathers so the watch was secure.

A day or two later he was riding a cold-backed gray. The other men, watching the horse travel with a hump in its back, looked at each other and grinned expectantly. The crew rode on and in a short time came to a narrow gully and jumped their horses over it. The gray jumped over too, but when he landed on the other side he kept right on jumping. At the first jump the watch dropped out of the vest pocket and swung in an arc and hit the buckeroo on the nose. The next jump, the watch gave him a black eye and as long as the horse bucked the watch swung. As we have said, buckskin is the strongest of leathers so if the horse had not quit bucking the watch "would have beat me to death" as the vaquero afterward said. He untied the buckskin thong, took the pencils out of the pockets (he had lost the notebook) and with what was left of the watch threw them as far away as he could.

Wilderness California

. . . .

Few seem to understand the dimensions of California's undeveloped land. The Mojave and Colorado deserts border it to the east and south. A remarkable and varied coastline marks the west. The north is Bigfoot country, with both virgin and second-growth forests as dense as any in America. The northeast is a volcanic moonscape. Moreover, this state is spined by mountains: the Cascades, the Sierra Nevada, the Klamaths, the Marbles, the Trinity Alps, the Tehachapis, and the Coast Ranges, among others, make this a bumpy state indeed.

What is most interesting in the distinguished body of writing produced in or about Wilderness California is that in the work of the finest writers the topography of the land is never far from the topography of the soul. Look, for example, at the literary reclamation of the desert. Those barren lands had once been crossed by pioneers too intent on survival to notice the unique landscape surrounding them. By the turn of the century, however, the arid lands could be studied and sometimes romanticized. It was one of those interesting cases where changing circumstances allowed people to reenvision an area.

John C. Van Dyke's *The Desert* (1901) was the first in a series of books that changed the way those ostensible wastelands were viewed. Charles Fletcher Lummis, A. J. Burdick, J. Smeaton Chase, and George Wharton James also contributed important volumes, but arguably the finest of all Californian desert books, the most mystical and eloquent, is Mary Hunter Austin's *The Land of Little Rain* (1903).

This state's mountains and forests boast as distinguished a cadre of authors as do its deserts. The master here, of course, is John Muir. His work ranged from romantic to scientific, from graphic to lyrical. Another of California's great mountaineers, Clarence King, left startling descriptions of many wilderness peaks and valleys in *Mountaineering in the Sierra Nevada* (1872). His fellow member of California's first geological survey party,

William Henry Brewer, produced an equally memorable volume with his *Up and Down California in 1860–64* (1930). When those young scientists wrote, nearly all the state was still wilderness. In this century, naturalist Sally Carrigher created a delightful picture from Sequoia National Park in *One Day at Beetle Rock* (1944), and David Rains Wallace produced a memorable literary journey of the state's far north in *The Klamath Knot* (1983).

Sometimes ignored when considering Wilderness California is its impact on poets and novelists, yet it has inspired some of the state's finest literature. For instance, George R. Stewart wrote about Sierra forests when he produced two of his most memorable novels, *Storm* (1941) and *Fire* (1949), and one of Walter Van Tilburg Clark's strongest and most magical novels, *The Track of the Cat* (1949), is set in eastern Sierra cattle country. None is superior to Robinson Jeffers's remarkable poetry, such as the samples that follow, where the symbolic power of California's wildlife and coastline and hills are given artistic life of a high order indeed.

John Muir

John Muir (1838–1914) is among America's greatest nature writers and most in-veterate mountaineers. Born in Scotland, he immigrated to America in 1849 and settled in California in 1868. He was an adventurer and major conservationist, a founder of the Sierra Club, and intimately involved with the preservation of Yosemite Valley. In books such as My First Summer in the Sierra *(1911),* The Yosemite *(1912), and* The Mountains of California *(1894)—from which the following piece is ex-cerpted—Muir helped teach westerners not to take the wonders of their region for granted. How important was Muir to his adopted state? Answers Lawrence Clark Powell: "If I were to choose a single Californian to occupy the Hall of Fame, it would be this tenacious Scot."*

. . . .

THE RANGE OF LIGHT

Go where you may within the bounds of California, mountains are ever in sight, charming and glorifying every landscape. Yet so simple and massive is the topography of the State in general views, that the main central portion displays only one valley, and two chains of mountains which seem almost perfectly regular in trend and height: the Coast Range on the west side, the Sierra Nevada on the east. These two ranges coming together in curves on the north and south inclose a magnificent basin, with a level floor more than 400 miles long, and from 35 to 60 miles wide. This is the grand Cen-tral Valley of California, the waters of which have only one outlet to the sea through the Golden Gate. But with this general simplicity of features there is great complexity of hidden detail. The Coast Range, rising as a grand green barrier against the ocean, from 2000 to 8000 feet high, is com-posed of innumerable forest-crowned spurs, ridges, and rolling hill-waves which inclose a multitude of smaller valleys; some looking out through long, forest-lined vistas to the sea; others, with but few trees, to the Central Valley; while a thousand others yet smaller are embosomed and concealed in mild, round-browed hills, each with its own climate, soil, and productions.

Making your way through the mazes of the Coast Range to the summit of any of the inner peaks or passes opposite San Francisco, in the clear spring-time, the grandest and most telling of all California landscapes is outspread before you. At your feet lies the great Central Valley glowing golden in the sunshine, extending north and south farther than the eye can reach, one smooth, flowery, lake-like bed of fertile soil. Along its eastern margin rises the mighty Sierra, miles in height, reposing like a smooth, cumulous cloud in the sunny sky, and so gloriously colored, and so luminous, it seems to be not clothed with light, but wholly composed of it, like the wall of some celestial city. Along the top, and extending a good way down, you see a pale, pearl-gray belt of snow; and below it a belt of blue and dark purple, marking the extension of the forests; and along the base of the range a broad belt of rose-purple and yellow, where lie the miner's gold-fields and the foot-hill gardens. All these colored belts blending smoothly make a wall of light ineffably fine, and as beautiful as a rainbow, yet firm as adamant.

When I first enjoyed this superb view, one glowing April day, from the summit of the Pacheco Pass, the Central Valley, but little trampled or plowed as yet, was one furred, rich sheet of golden compositæ, and the luminous wall of the mountains shone in all its glory. Then it seemed to me the Sierra should be called not the Nevada, or Snowy Range, but the Range of Light. And after ten years spent in the heart of it, rejoicing and wondering, bathing in its glorious floods of light, seeing the sunbursts of morning among the icy peaks, the noonday radiance on the trees and rocks and snow, the flush of the alpenglow, and a thousand dashing waterfalls with their marvelous abundance of irised spray, it still seems to me above all others the Range of Light, the most divinely beautiful of all the mountain-chains I have ever seen.

The Sierra is about 500 miles long, 70 miles wide, and from 7000 to nearly 15,000 feet high. In general views no mark of man is visible on it, nor anything to suggest the richness of the life it cherishes, or the depth and grandeur of its sculpture. None of its magnificent forest-crowned ridges rises much above the general level to publish its wealth. No great valley or lake is seen, or river, or group of well-marked features of any kind, standing out in distinct pictures. Even the summit-peaks, so clear and high in the sky, seem comparatively smooth and featureless. Nevertheless, glaciers are still at work in the shadows of the peaks, and thousands of lakes and meadows shine and bloom beneath them, and the whole range is furrowed with cañons to a depth of from 2000 to 5000 feet, in which once flowed majestic glaciers, and in which now flow and sing a band of beautiful rivers.

Though of such stupendous depth, these famous cañons are not raw, gloomy, jagged-walled gorges, savage and inaccessible. With rough passages here and there they still make delightful pathways for the mountaineer, conducting from the fertile lowlands to the highest icy fountains, as a kind of mountain streets full of charming life and light, graded and sculptured by the ancient glaciers, and presenting, throughout all their courses, a rich variety of novel and attractive scenery, the most attractive that has yet been discovered in the mountain-ranges of the world.

In many places, especially in the middle region of the western flank of the range, the main cañons widen into spacious valleys or parks, diversified like artificial landscape-gardens, with charming groves and meadows, and thickets of blooming bushes, while the lofty, retiring walls, infinitely varied in form and sculpture, are fringed with ferns, flowering-plants of many species, oaks, and evergreens, which find anchorage on a thousand narrow steps and benches; while the whole is enlivened and made glorious with rejoicing streams that come dancing and foaming over the sunny brows of the cliffs to join the shining river that flows in tranquil beauty down the middle of each one of them.

The walls of these park valleys of the Yosemite kind are made up of rocks mountains in size, partly separated from each other by narrow gorges and side-cañons; and they are so sheer in front, and so compactly built together on a level floor, that, comprehensively seen, the parks they inclose look like immense halls or temples lighted from above. Every rock seems to glow with life. Some lean back in majestic repose; others, absolutely sheer, or nearly so, for thousands of feet, advance their brows in thoughtful attitudes beyond their companions, giving welcome to storms and calms alike, seemingly conscious yet heedless of everything going on about them, awful in stern majesty, types of permanence, yet associated with beauty of the frailest and most fleeting forms; their feet set in pine-groves and gay emerald meadows, their brows in the sky; bathed in light, bathed in floods of singing water, while snow-clouds, avalanches, and the winds shine and surge and wreathe about them as the years go by, as if into these mountain mansions Nature had taken pains to gather her choicest treasures to draw her lovers into close and confiding communion with her.

Mary Hunter Austin

Mary Hunter Austin (1868–1934), a native of Illinois, migrated with her family in 1888 to the parched southern end of the Great Central Valley south of Bakersfield. There she began the observations and literary experiments that would make her one of her generation's most prominent authors. In 1903, with the publication of the first of what would be thirty-five books, The Land of Little Rain, *she immediately established herself as a major voice for America's deserts. She was later a prominent member of the artistic colony at Carmel and, later still, a central figure among the so-called Bohemians at Santa Fe, New Mexico, where she continued her study of American Indian cultures. Her 1923 book* The American Rhythm *presented her versions of poems and songs from Native American cultures. She also wrote novels, plays, and an interesting autobiography,* Earth Horizon *(1932).*

. . . .

MY NEIGHBOR'S FIELD

It is one of those places God must have meant for a field from all time, lying very level at the foot of the slope that crowds up against Kearsarge, falling slightly toward the town. North and south it is fenced by low old glacial ridges, boulder strewn and untenable. Eastward it butts on orchard closes and the village gardens, brimming over into them by wild brier and creeping grass. The village street, with its double row of unlike houses, breaks off abruptly at the edge of the field in a footpath that goes up the streamside, beyond it, to the source of waters.

The field is not greatly esteemed of the town, not being put to the plough nor affording firewood, but breeding all manner of wild seeds that go down in the irrigating ditches to come up as weeds in the gardens and grass plots. But when I had no more than seen it in the charm of its spring smiling, I knew I should have no peace until I had bought ground and built me a house beside it, with a little wicket to go in and out at all hours, as afterward came about.

Edswick, Roeder, Connor, and Ruffin owned the field before it fell to my neighbor. But before that the Paiutes, mesne lords of the soil, made a campoodie by the rill of Pine Creek; and after, contesting the soil with them, cattle-men, who found its foodful pastures greatly to their advantage; and bands of blethering flocks shepherded by wild, hairy men of little speech, who attested their rights to the feeding ground with their long staves upon each other's skulls. Edswick homesteaded the field about the time the wild tide of mining life was roaring and rioting up Kearsarge, and where the village now stands built a stone hut, with loopholes to make good his claim against cattle-men or Indians. But Edswick died and Roeder became master of the field. Roeder owned cattle on a thousand hills, and made it a recruiting ground for his bellowing herds before beginning the long drive to market across a shifty desert. He kept the field fifteen years, and afterward falling into difficulties, put it out as security against certain sums. Connor, who held the securities, was cleverer than Roeder and not so busy. The money fell due the winter of the Big Snow, when all the trails were forty feet under drifts, and Roeder was away in San Francisco selling his cattle. At the set time Connor took the law by the forelock and was adjudged possession of the field. Eighteen days later Roeder arrived on snowshoes, both feet frozen, and the money in his pack. In the long suit at law ensuing, the field fell to Ruffin, that clever one-armed lawyer with the tongue to wile a bird out of the bush, Connor's counsel, and was sold by him to my neighbor, whom from envying his possession I call Naboth.

Curiously, all this human occupancy of greed and mischief left no mark on the field, but the Indians did, and the unthinking sheep. Round its corners children pick up chipped arrow points of obsidian, scattered through it are kitchen middens and pits of old sweathouses. By the south corner, where the campoodie stood, is a single shrub of "hoopee" (*Lycium andersonii*), maintaining itself hardly among alien shrubs, and near by, three low rakish trees of hackberry, so far from home that no prying of mine has been able to find another in any cañon east or west. But the berries of both were food for the Paiutes, eagerly sought and traded for as far south as Shoshone Land. By the fork of the creek where the shepherds camp is a single clump of mesquite of the variety called "screw bean." The seed must have shaken there from some sheep's coat, for this is not the habitat of mesquite, and except for other single shrubs at sheep camps, none grows freely for a hundred and fifty miles south or east.

Naboth has put a fence about the best of the field, but neither the Indians nor the shepherds can quite forego it. They make camp and build their wattled huts about the borders of it, and no doubt they have some sense of home in its familiar aspect.

As I have said, it is a low-lying field, between the mesa and the town, with no hillocks in it, but a gentle swale where the waste water of the creek goes down to certain farms, and the hackberry-trees, of which the tallest might be three times the height of a man, are the tallest things in it. A mile up from the water gate that turns the creek into supply pipes for the town, begins a row of long-leaved pines, threading the watercourse to the foot of Kearsarge. These are the pines that puzzle the local botanist, not easily determined, and unrelated to other conifers of the Sierra slope; the same pines of which the Indians relate a legend mixed of brotherliness and the retribution of God. Once the pines possessed the field, as the worn stumps of them along the streamside show, and it would seem their secret purpose to regain their old footing. Now and then some seedling escapes the devastating sheep a rod or two down-stream. Since I came to live by the field one of these has tiptoed above the gully of the creek, beckoning the procession from the hills, as if in fact they would make back toward that skyward-pointing finger of granite on the opposite range, from which, according to the legend, when they were bad Indians and it a great chief, they ran away. This year the summer floods brought the round, brown, fruitful cones to my very door, and I look, if I live long enough, to see them come up greenly in my neighbor's field.

It is interesting to watch this retaking of old ground by the wild plants, banished by human use. Since Naboth drew his fence about the field and restricted it to a few wild-eyed steers, halting between the hills and the shambles, many old habitués of the field have come back to their haunts. The willow and brown birch, long ago cut off by the Indians for wattles, have come back to the streamside, slender and virginal in their spring greenness, and leaving long stretches of the brown water open to the sky. In stony places where no grass grows, wild olives sprawl; close-twigged, blue-gray patches in winter, more translucent greenish gold in spring than any aureole. Along with willow and birch and brier, the clematis, that shyest plant of water borders, slips down season by season to within a hundred yards of the village street. Convinced after three years that it would come no nearer, we spent time fruitlessly pulling up roots to plant in the garden. All this while, when no coaxing or care prevailed upon any transplanted slip to grow, one was coming up silently outside the fence near the wicket, coiling so secretly in the rabbit-brush that its presence was never suspected until it flowered delicately along its twining length. The horehound comes through the fence and under it, shouldering the pickets off the railings; the brier rose mines under the horehound; and no care, though I own I am not a close weeder, keeps the small pale moons of the primrose from rising to the night moth under my apple-trees. The first summer in the new place, a clump of cypripediums came up by the irrigating ditch at the bottom of the lawn. But the clematis will not come inside, nor the wild almond.

I have forgotten to find out, though I meant to, whether the wild almond grew in that country where Moses kept the flocks of his father-in-law, but if so one can account for the burning bush. It comes upon one with a flame-burst as of revelation; little hard red buds on leafless twigs, swelling unnoticeably, then one, two, or three strong suns, and from tip to tip one soft fiery glow, whispering with bees as a singing flame. A twig of finger size will be furred to the thickness of one's wrist by pink five-petaled bloom, so close that only the blunt-faced wild bees find their way in it. In this latitude late frosts cuts off the hope of fruit too often for the wild almond to multiply greatly, but the spiny, taprooted shrubs are resistant to most plant evils.

It is not easy always to be attentive to the maturing of wild fruit. Plants are so unobtrusive in their material processes, and always at the significant moment some other bloom has reached its perfect hour. One can never fix the precise moment when the rosy tint the field has from the wild almond passes into the inspiring blue of lupines. One notices here and there a spike of bloom, and a day later the whole field royal and ruffling lightly to the wind. Part of the charm of the lupine is the continual stir of its plumes to airs not suspected otherwhere. Go and stand by any crown of bloom and the tall stalks do but rock a little as for drowsiness, but look off across the field, and on the stillest days there is always a trepidation in the purple patches.

From midsummer until frost the prevailing note of the field is clear gold, passing into the rusty tone of bigelovia going into a decline, a succession of color schemes more admirably managed than the transformation scene at the theatre. Under my window a colony of cleome made a soft web of bloom that drew me every morning for a long still time; and one day I discovered that I was looking into a rare fretwork of fawn and straw colored twigs from which both bloom and leaf had gone, and I could not say if it had been for a matter of weeks or days. The time to plant cucumbers and set out cabbages may be set down in the almanac, but never seed-time nor blossom in Naboth's field.

Certain winged and mailed denizens of the field seem to reach their heyday along with the plants they most affect. In June the leaning towers of the white milkweed are jeweled over with red and gold beetles, climbing dizzily. This is that milkweed from whose stems the Indians flayed fibre to make snares for small game, but what use the beetles put it to except for a displaying ground for their gay coats, I could never discover. The white butterfly crop comes on with the bigelovia bloom, and on warm mornings makes an airy twinkling all across the field. In September young linnets grow out of the rabbit-brush in the night. All the nests discoverable in the neighboring orchards will not account for the numbers of them. Somewhere, by the same secret process by which the field matures a million more seeds than it needs, it is maturing redhooded linnets for their devouring. All the purlieus of bigelovia and artemisia are noisy with them for a month. Suddenly as they come as suddenly go the fly-by-nights, that pitch and toss on dusky barred wings above the field of summer twilights. Never one of these nighthawks will you see after linnet time, though the hurtle of their wings makes a pleasant sound across the dusk in their season.

For two summers a great red-tailed hawk has visited the field every afternoon between three and four o'clock, swooping and soaring with the airs of a gentleman adventurer. What he finds there is chiefly conjectured, so secretive are the little people of Naboth's field. Only when leaves fall and the light is low and slant, one sees the long clean flanks of the jackrabbits, leaping like small deer, and of late afternoons little cotton-tails scamper in the runways. But the most one sees of the burrowers, gophers, and mice is the fresh earthwork of their newly opened doors, or the pitiful small shreds the butcher-bird hangs on spiny shrubs.

It is a still field, this of my neighbor's, though so busy, and admirably compounded for variety and pleasantness,—a little sand, a little loam, a grassy plot, a stony rise or two, a full brown stream, a little touch of humanness, a footpath trodden out by moccasins. Naboth expects to make town lots of it and his fortune in one and the same day; but when I take the trail to talk with old Seyavi at the campoodie, it occurs to me that though the field may serve a good turn in those days it will hardly be happier. No, certainly not happier.

Robinson Jeffers

Robinson Jeffers (1887–1962), son of a theologian and brother of an astronomer—
links with the worlds of mythology and science that would dominate his poetry—
was a world traveler by the time he was sixteen and his family moved to Southern
California. He later graduated from Occidental College and, after various adven-
tures and misadventures, settled with his wife Una at Carmel. His name is now
closely identified with that region just as his poetry has been said to define it. But
his poetry did far more than that: Jeffers employed nature both for its own sake and
to place humans in the great scheme of existence; our species, he asserted, is im-
portant but not central to the cosmos. As a result, some critics called his approach
"inhumanism." Others consider him America's finest twentieth-century poet.

. . . .

VULTURE

I had walked since dawn and lay down to rest on a bare hillside
Above the ocean. I saw through half-shut eyelids a vulture wheeling high
   up in heaven,
And presently it passed again, but lower and nearer, its orbit narrowing, I
   understood then
That I was under inspection. I lay death-still and heard the flight-feathers
Whistle above me and make their circle and come nearer.
I could see the naked red head between the great wings
Bear downward staring. I said, "My dear bird, we are wasting time here.
These old bones will still work; they are not for you." But how beautiful
   he looked, gliding down
On those great sails; how beautiful he looked, veering away in the
   sea-light over the precipice. I tell you solemnly
That I was sorry to have disappointed him. To be eaten by that beak and

become part of him, to share those wings and those eyes—
What a sublime end of one's body, what an enskyment; What a life
after death.

AUTUMN EVENING

Though the little clouds ran southward still, the quiet autumnal
Cool of the late September evening
Seemed promising rain, rain, the change of the year, the angel
Of the sad forest. A heron flew over
With that remote ridiculous cry, "Quawk," the cry
That seems to make silence more silent. A dozen
Flops of the wing, a drooping glide, at the end of the glide
The cry, and a dozen flops of the wing.
I watched him pass on the autumn-colored sky; beyond him
Jupiter shone for evening star.
The sea's voice worked into my mood, I thought "No matter
What happens to men . . . the world's well made though."

HURT HAWKS

I

The broken pillar of the wing jags from the clotted shoulder,
The wing trails like a banner in defeat,
No more to use the sky forever but live with famine
And pain a few days: cat nor coyote
Will shorten the week of waiting for death, there is game without talons.
He stands under the oak-bush and waits
The lame feet of salvation; at night he remembers freedom
And flies in a dream, the dawns ruin it.
He is strong and pain is worse to the strong, incapacity is worse.
The curs of the day come and torment him
At distance, no one but death the redeemer will humble that head,
The intrepid readiness, the terrible eyes.
The wild God of the world is sometimes merciful to those
That ask mercy, not often to the arrogant.
You do not know him, you communal people, or you have forgotten him;
Intemperate and savage, the hawk remembers him;
Beautiful and wild, the hawks, and men that are dying, remember him.

II

I'd sooner, except the penalties, kill a man than a hawk; but the great
  redtail
Had nothing left but unable misery
From the bone too shattered for mending, the wing that trailed under his
  talons when he moved.
We had fed him six weeks, I gave him freedom,
He wandered over the foreland hill and returned in the evening, asking for
  death,
Not like a beggar, still eyed with the old
Implacable arrogance. I gave him the lead gift in the twilight. What fell
  was relaxed,
Owl-downy, soft feminine feathers; but what
Soared: the fierce rush: the night-herons by the flooded river cried fear at
  its rising
Before it was quite unsheathed from reality.

136

Fantasy California

. . . .

Spanish settlement of California is believed to have begun in the 1530s when a few brave souls ventured onto its southern reaches. Nothing those adventurers experienced, however, lived up to the image of California that had already been created by Garci Ordoñez de Montalvo in a popular Spanish novel, *Las sergas de Esplandian* (1510). His California was an island "very near the Terrestrial Paradise and inhabited by black women without a single man among them and living in the manner of Amazons."

Welcome to Fantasy California, a land where imagination and expectation outstripped reality, or where reality could simply be ignored. Not even Venice Beach or Telegraph Avenue has lived up to the expectations of de Montalvo's black Amazons riding griffins garbed in gold, so exaggeration has often battled with disappointment here.

For many, this imaginary realm seems to be the *only* California, the place where America abuts the future. This is the land of suntans and bleached blondes, of wacky cults and New-Age scams, of nobel laureates and television game shows. It is the land of *more*. Sang Deanna Durbin and Robert Paige in a 1945 movie:

> The climate is better
> The ocean is wetter
> The mountains are higher
> The deserts are drier
> The hills have more splendor
> The girls have more gender
> Ca-li-for-ni-ay!

Fantasy California has, in any case, produced an intriguing body of literature in all of the physical regions. To this richly imaginative area can be assigned books as diverse as Evelyn Waugh's *The Loved One* (set in the Southland, 1948), Ernest Callenbach's *Ecotopia* (Wilderness California, 1975), Robert Roper's *Royo County* (Heartland, 1974), and Cyra McFadden's *The Serial* (Greater Bay Area, 1977).

The apotheosis of Fantasy California's literature, however, is Nathaniel West's *The Day of the Locust* (1939), which is excerpted below. A hint of West's disillusionment with California may be gleaned from a letter he wrote in 1933 shortly after he had become a Hollywood screenwriter:

> This place is Asbury Park, New Jersey. . . . in other words, phooey on Cal. Another thing, this stuff about easy work is all wrong. My hours are from ten in the morning to six at night with a full day on Saturdays. There's no fooling here.

West actually wrote about a world gone mad as reflected in his version of one small section of the state. As a result, he produced a novel that typifies this imaginary realm, a dark mirror limning the gap between expectation and reality.

Garci Ordóñez de Montalvo

Garci Rodriguez Ordóñez de Montalvo (14??–15??), a Spanish novelist, published a book called Las sergas de Esplandián *(The Adventures of Esplandián) that created in advance of any actual experience a vision of California. While the author remains a somewhat shadowy figure—the name is rendered several different ways in Spanish texts: Garci-Ordóñez de Montalvo, Garci-Rodriguez de Montalvo, and Garci Rodriguez Ordóñez de Montalvo are the principal variations. In any case, in either 1508 or 1510—again, Spanish scholars don't agree on the date—over thirty years before the Cabrillo expedition viewed this realm's west coast and over twenty-five before Cortez named what is now the tip of lower California, de Montalvo sent his hero on a mythical journey. It remains the initial, the most fanciful, and, as a result, perhaps the ultimate vision of California as state of mind. Of course, de Montalvo never visited the real place.*

. . . .

AN ISLAND CALLED CALIFORNIA

Know ye that on the right hand of the Indies there is an island called California, very near the Terrestrial Paradise and inhabited by black women without a single man among them and living in the manner of Amazons. They are robust of body, strong and passionate in heart, and of great valor. Their island is one of the most rugged in the world with bold rocks and crags. Their arms are all of gold, as is the harness of the wild beasts which, after taming, they ride. In all the island there is no other metal.

They live in well-excavated caves. They have ships in which they go to raid other places, and the men they capture they carry off with them, later to be killed as will be told. At other times, being at peace with their opponents, they consort with them freely and have carnal relations from which it results that many of them become pregnant. If they give birth to a female they keep her, but if to a male they kill him. The reason for this, as is known, is that they are firmly resolved to keep the males at so small a number that without trouble they can control them with all their lands, saving those thought necessary to perpetuate the race.

In this island called California, with the great roughness of the land and the multitude of wild animals, are many griffins the like of which are not found in any other part of the world. In the season when the griffins give birth to their young, these women cover themselves with thick hides and go out to snare the little griffins, taking them to their caves where they raise them. And being quite a match for these griffins, they feed them the men taken as prisoners and the males to which they have given birth. All this is done with such skill that the griffins become thoroughly accustomed to them and do them no harm. Any male who comes to the island is killed and eaten by the griffins. Even if the latter are gorged they do not fail to seize them, fly high in the air with them, and, when tired of carrying them, let them fall to their death.

Over this island of California rules a queen, Calafía, statuesque in proportions, more beautiful than all the rest, in the flower of her womanhood, eager to perform great deeds, valiant and spirited, and ambitious to excel all those who have ruled before her.

Walt Whitman

Walt Whitman (1819–92), a pivotal figure in the history of American literature, "liberated" English-language poetry by infusing it with the vocabulary and rhythm and vigor of vernacular speech. He also understood that the westward migration was a quintessential American activity that involved all citizens, even those who remained in the East. In "Pioneers! O Pioneers!" he wrote:

> *These are of us, they are with us,*
> *All for primal needed work, while the followers there in embryo wait*
> > *behind,*
> *We to-day's procession heading, we the route for travel clearing,*
> > *Pioneers! O Pioneers!*

Of course, California—then a distant, Pacific realm called "the far coast"—was the ultimate destination. It became in the minds of many a correlate of national ambition. Whitman had a vision of California that powerfully articulated the belief in manifest destiny—that America was destined to fill the continent and perhaps more, as the following poem demonstrates.

· ·

FACING WEST FROM CALIFORNIA'S SHORES

Facing west from California's shores,
Inquiring, tireless, seeking what is yet unfound,
I, a child, very old, over waves, towards the house of maternity, the land of
    migrations, look afar,
Look off the shores of my Western sea, the circle almost circled;
For starting westward from Hindustan, from the vales of Kashmere,
From Asia, from the north, from the God, the sage, and the hero,
From the south, from the flowery peninsulas and the spice islands,

Long having wander'd since, round the earth having wander'd,
Now I face home again, very pleas'd and joyous,
(But where is what I started for so long ago?
And why is it yet unfound?)

Nathaniel West

Nathaniel West (1903–40), an original writer who was born as Nathan Weinstein in New York, came to Hollywood in 1933 to work as a screenwriter. That same year he published one of his best-known novels, Miss Lonelyhearts. *West was not impressed by what he found in Southern California—life for him was not easy pickings but nearly all work, and unrewarding work at that, so his next novel veered toward the dark side of the California dream. The apocalyptic vision West finally revealed in* The Day of the Locust *was a surreal and grotesque version that seems to have more to do with the image that Hollywood then promoted than with the middle-American, middle-class reality that surrounded him in Southern California. What follows is a chapter from* The Day of the Locust.

. . . .

ADORE

Tod got a lift back to his office in a studio car. He had to ride on the running board because the seats were occupied by two Walloon grenadiers and four Swabian foot. One of the infantrymen had a broken leg, the other extras were only scratched and bruised. They were quite happy about their wounds. They were certain to receive several extra days' pay, and the man with the broken leg thought he might get as much as five hundred dollars.

When Tod arrived at his office, he found Faye waiting to see him. She hadn't been in the battle. At the last moment, the director had decided not to use any vivandières.

To his surprise, she greeted him with warm friendliness. Nevertheless, he tried to apologize for his behavior in the funeral parlor. He had hardly started before she interrupted him. She wasn't angry, but grateful for his lecture on venereal disease. It had brought her to her senses.

She had still another surprise for him. She was living in Homer Simpson's house. The arrangement was a business one. Homer had agreed to board and dress her until she became a star. They were keeping a record of every cent he spent and as soon as she clicked in pictures, she would pay him back with six per cent interest. To make it absolutely legal, they were going to have a lawyer draw up a contract.

She pressed Tod for an opinion and he said it was a splendid idea. She thanked him and invited him to dinner for the next night.

After she had gone, he wondered what living with her would do to Homer. He thought it might straighten him out. He fooled himself into believing this with an image, as though a man were a piece of iron to be heated and then straightened with hammer blows. He should have known better, for if anyone ever lacked malleability Homer did.

He continued to make this mistake when he had dinner with them. Faye seemed very happy, talking about charge accounts and stupid sales clerks. Homer had a flower in his buttonhole, wore carpet slippers and beamed at her continually.

After they had eaten, while Homer was in the kitchen washing dishes, Tod got her to tell him what they did with themselves all day. She said that they lived quietly and that she was glad because she was tired of excitement. All she wanted was a career. Homer did the housework and she was getting a real rest. Daddy's long sickness had tired her out completely. Homer liked to do housework and anyway he wouldn't let her go into the kitchen because of her hands.

"Protecting his investment," Tod said.

"Yes," she replied seriously, "they have to be beautiful."

They had breakfast around ten, she went on, Homer brought it to her in bed. He took a housekeeping magazine and fixed the tray like the pictures in it. While she bathed and dressed, he cleaned the house. Then they went downtown to the stores and she bought all sorts of things, mostly clothes. They didn't eat lunch on account of her figure, but usually had dinner out and went to the movies.

"Then, ice cream sodas," Homer finished for her, as he came out of the kitchen.

Faye laughed and excused herself. They were going to a picture and she wanted to change her dress. When she had left, Homer suggested that they get some air in the patio. He made Tod take the deck chair while he sat on an upturned orange crate.

If he had been careful and had acted decently, Tod couldn't help thinking, she might be living with him. He was at least better looking than Homer.

But then there was her other prerequisite. Homer had an income and lived in a house, while he earned thirty dollars a week and lived in a furnished room.

The happy grin on Homer's face made him feel ashamed of himself. He was being unfair. Homer was a humble, grateful man who would never laugh at her, who was incapable of laughing at anything. Because of this great quality, she could live with him on what she considered a much higher plane.

"What's the matter?" Homer asked softly, laying one of his heavy hands on Tod's knee.

"Nothing. Why?"

Tod moved so that the hand slipped off.

"You were making faces."

"I was thinking of something."

"Oh," Homer said sympathetically.

Tod couldn't resist asking an ugly question.

"When are you two getting married?"

Homer looked hurt.

"Didn't Faye tell about us?"

"Yes, sort of."

"It's a business arrangement."

"Yes?"

To make Tod believe it, he poured out a long, disjointed argument, the one he must have used on himself. He even went further than the business part and claimed that they were doing it for poor Harry's sake. Faye had nothing left in the world except her career and she must succeed for her daddy's sake. The reason she wasn't a star was because she didn't have the right clothes. He had money and believed in her talent, so it was only natural for them to enter into a business arrangement. Did Tod know a good lawyer?

It was a rhetorical question, but would become a real one, painfully insistent, if Tod smiled. He frowned. That was wrong, too.

"We must see a lawyer this week and have papers drawn up."

His eagerness was pathetic. Tod wanted to help him, but didn't know what to say. He was still fumbling for an answer when they heard a woman shouting from the hill behind the garage.

"Adore! Adore!"

She had a high soprano voice, very clear and pure.

"What a funny name," Tod said, glad to change the subject.

"Maybe it's a foreigner," Homer said.

The woman came into the yard from around the corner of the garage. She was eager and plump and very American.

"Have you seen my little boy?" she asked, making a gesture of helplessness. "Adore's such a wanderer."

Homer surprised Tod by standing up and smiling at the woman. Faye had certainly helped his timidity.

"Is your son lost?" Homer said.

"Oh, no—just hiding to tease me."

She held out her hand.

"We're neighbors. I'm Maybelle Loomis."

"Glad to know you, ma'am. I'm Homer Simpson and this is Mr. Hackett." Tod also shook hands with her.

"Have you been living here long?" she asked.

"No. I've just come from the East," Homer said.

"Oh, have you? I've been here ever since Mr. Loomis passed on six years ago. I'm an old settler."

"You like it then?" Tod asked.

"Like California?" she laughed at the idea that anyone might not like it. "Why, it's paradise on earth!"

"Yes," Homer agreed gravely.

"And anyway," she went on, "I have to live here on account of Adore."

"Is he sick?"

"Oh, no. On account of his career. His agent calls him the biggest little attraction in Hollywood."

She spoke so vehemently that Homer flinched.

"He's in the movies?" Tod asked.

"I'll say," she snapped.

Homer tried to placate her.

"That's very nice."

"If it weren't for favoritism," she said bitterly, "he'd be a star. It ain't talent. It's pull. What's Shirley Temple got that he ain't got?"

"Why, I don't know," Homer mumbled.

She ignored this and let out a fearful bellow.

"Adore! Adore!"

Tod had seen her kind around the studio. She was one of that army of women who drag their children from casting office to casting office and sit for hours, weeks, months, waiting for a chance to show what Junior can do.

Some of them are very poor, but no matter how poor, they always manage to scrape together enough money, often by making great sacrifices, to send their children to one of the innumerable talent schools.

"Adore!" she yelled once more, then laughed and became a friendly housewife again, a chubby little person with dimples in her fat cheeks and fat elbows.

"Have you any children, Mr. Simpson?" she asked.

"No," he replied blushing.

"You're lucky—they're a nuisance."

She laughed to show that she didn't really mean it and called her child again.

"Adore . . . Oh, Adore . . ."

Her next question surprised them both.

"Who do you follow?"

"What?" said Tod.

"I mean—in the Search for Health, along the Road of Life?"

They both gaped at her.

"I'm a raw-foodist, myself," she said. "Dr. Pierce is our leader. You must have seen his ads—'Know-All Pierce-All.'"

"Oh, yes," Tod said, "you're vegetarians."

She laughed at his ignorance.

"Far from it. We're much stricter. Vegetarians eat cooked vegetables. We eat only raw ones. Death comes from eating dead things."

Neither Tod nor Homer found anything to say.

"Adore," she began again, "Adore . . ."

This time there was an answer from around the corner of the garage.

"Here I am, mama."

A minute later, a little boy appeared dragging behind him a small sailboat on wheels. He was about eight years old, with a pale, peaked face on a large, troubled forehead. He had great staring eyes. His eyebrows had been plucked and shaped carefully. Except for his Buster Brown collar, he was dressed like a man, in long trousers, vest and jacket.

He tried to kiss his mother, but she fended him off and pulled at his clothes, straightening and arranging them with savage little tugs.

"Adore," she said sternly, "I want you to meet Mr. Simpson, our neighbor."

Turning like a soldier at the command of a drill sergeant, he walked up to Homer and grasped his hand.

"A pleasure, sir," he said, bowing stiffly with his heels together.

"That's the way they do it in Europe," Mrs. Loomis beamed. "Isn't he cute?"

"What a pretty sailboat!" Homer said, trying to be friendly.

Both mother and son ignored his comment. She pointed to Tod, and the child repeated his bow and heel-click.

"Well, we've got to go," she said.

Tod watched the child, who was standing a little to one side of his mother and making faces at Homer. He rolled his eyes back in his head so that only the whites showed and twisted his lips in a snarl.

Mrs. Loomis noticed Tod's glance and turned sharply. When she saw what Adore was doing, she yanked him by the arm, jerking him clear off the ground.

"Adore!" she yelled.

To Tod she said apologetically, "He thinks he's the Frankenstein monster."

She picked the boy up, hugging and kissing him ardently. Then she set him down again and fixed his rumpled clothing.

"Won't Adore sing something for us?" Tod asked.

"No," the little boy said sharply.

"Adore," his mother scolded, "sing at once."

"That's all right, if he doesn't feel like it," Homer said.

But Mrs. Loomis was determined to have him sing. She could never permit him to refuse an audience.

"Sing, Adore," she repeated with quiet menace. "Sing 'Mama Doan Wan' No Peas'."

His shoulders twitched as though they already felt the strap. He tilted his straw sailor over one eye, buttoned up his jacket and did a little strut, then began:

> "Mama doan wan' no peas,
> An' rice, an' cocoanut oil,
> Just a bottle of brandy handy all the day.
> Mama doan wan' no peas,
> Mama doan wan' no cocoanut oil."

His singing voice was deep and rough and he used the broken groan of the blues singer quite expertly. He moved his body only a little, against rather than in time with the music. The gestures he made with his hands were extremely suggestive.

"Mama doan wan' no gin,
Because gin do make her sin,
Mama doan wan' no glass of gin,
Because it's boun' to make her sin,
An' keep her hot and bothered all the day."

He seemed to know what the words meant, or at least his body and his voice seemed to know. When he came to the final chorus, his buttocks writhed and his voice carried a top-heavy load of sexual pain.

Tod and Homer applauded. Adore grabbing the string of his sailboat and circled the yard. He was imitating a tugboat. He tooted several times, then ran off.

"He's just a baby," Mrs. Loomis said proudly, "but he's got loads of talent."

Tod and Homer agreed.

She saw that he was gone again and left hurriedly. They could hear her calling in the brush back of the garage.

"Adore! Adore . . ."

"That's a funny woman," Tod said.

Homer sighed.

"I guess it's hard to get a start in pictures. But Faye is awfully pretty."

Tod agreed. She appeared a moment later in a new flower print dress and picture hat and it was his turn to sigh. She was much more than pretty. She posed, quivering and balanced, on the doorstep and looked down at the two men in the patio. She was smiling, a subtle half-smile uncontaminated by thought. She looked just born, everything moist and fresh, volatile and perfumed. Tod suddenly became very conscious of his dull, insensitive feet bound in dead skin and of his hands, sticky and thick, holding a heavy, rough felt hat.

He tried to get out of going to the pictures with them, but couldn't. Sitting next to her in the dark proved the ordeal he expected it to be. Her self-sufficiency made him squirm and the desire to break its smooth surface with a blow, or at least a sudden obscene gesture, became irresistible.

He began to wonder if he himself didn't suffer from the ingrained, morbid apathy he liked to draw in others. Maybe he could only be galvanized into sensibility and that was why he was chasing Faye.

He left hurriedly, without saying good-bye. He had decided to stop running after her. It was an easy decision to make, but a hard one to carry out.

In order to manage it, he fell back on one of the oldest tricks in the very full bag of the intellectual. After all, he told himself, he had drawn her enough times. He shut the portfolio that held the drawings he had made of her, tied it with a string, and put it away in his trunk.

It was a childish trick, hardly worthy of a primitive witch doctor, yet it worked. He was able to avoid her for several months. During this time, he took his pad and pencils on a continuous hunt for other models. He spent his nights at the different Hollywood churches, drawing the worshipers. He visited the "Church of Christ, Physical" where holiness was attained through the constant use of chestweights and spring grips; the "Church Invisible" where fortunes were told and the dead made to find lost objects; the "Tabernacle of the Third Coming" where a woman in male clothing preached the "Crusade Against Salt"; and the "Temple Moderne" under whose glass and chromium roof "Brain-Breathing, the Secret of the Aztecs" was taught.

As he watched these people writhe on the hard seats of their churches, he thought of how well Alessandro Magnasco would dramatize the contrast between their drained-out feeble bodies and their wild, disordered minds. He would not satirize them as Hogarth or Daumier might, not would he pity them. He would paint their fury with respect, appreciating its awful, anarchic power and aware that they had it in them to destroy civilization.

One Friday night in the "Tabernacle of the Third Coming," a man near Tod stood up to speak. Although his name most likely was Thompson or Johnson and his home town Sioux City, he had the same counter-sunk eyes, like the heads of burnished spikes, that a monk by Magnasco might have. He was probably just in from one of the colonies in the desert near Soboba Hot Springs where he had been conning over his soul on a diet of raw fruit and nuts. He was very angry. The message he had brought to the city was one that an illiterate anchorite might have given decadent Rome. It was a crazy jumble of dietary rules, economics and Biblical threats. He claimed to have seen the Tiger of Wrath stalking the walls of the citadel and the Jackal of Lust skulking in the shrubbery, and he connected these omens with "thirty dollars every Thursday" and meat eating.

Tod didn't laugh at the man's rhetoric. He knew it was unimportant. What mattered were his messianic rage and the emotional response of his hearers. They sprang to their feet, shaking their fists and shouting. On the altar someone began to beat a bass drum and soon the entire congregation was singing "Onward Christian Soldiers."

Interlude: The San Francisco Renaissance

. . . .

In John Steinbeck's *The Grapes of Wrath*, the beleaguered Joad family finally emerges from mountains to be greeted by a vista of the Great Central Valley:

> They drove through Tehachapi in the morning glow, and the sun came up behind them, and then—suddenly they saw the great valley below them. Al jammed on the brake and stopped in the middle of the road, and, "Jesus Christ! Look!" he said. The vineyards, the orchards, the great flat valley, green and beautiful, the trees set in rows, and the farm houses.
>
> And Pa said, "God almighty!" The distant cities, the little towns in the orchard land, and the morning sun, golden on the valley.

That the golden glow of the California dream would soon dissolve in sweat and desperation for the Joads, that it would take a world war to allow them and other dust bowl migrants to achieve what they sought, in no way diminished the power of the dream itself. Their yearning and eventual triumph—the triumph of the human spirit—illustrate that California is neither paradise nor hades, but is in fact a purgatory through which we pass.

A little over a decade later, one more sojourner, Jack Kerouac, would write:

> It seemed like a matter of minutes when we began rolling the foothills before Oakland and suddenly reached a height and saw stretched out ahead of us the fabulous white city of San Francisco on her eleven mystic hills with the blue Pacific and its advancing wall of potato-patch fog, beyond, and smoke and goldenness in the late afternoon of time.

Another time, another golden dream, another candidate for purgatory.

When Kerouac arrived, forces of change and liberation that had been brewing since the social turmoil of the Great Depression and its harsh remedy, World War II, had veered thinking Americans—and thinking Californians—from their previous sanguine paths. In an age of conformity, some discontented folks would symbolically identify with Kerouac, the transplanted New Englander, and a cadre of creative, rebellious men and women in the mid-1950s gathering in San Francisco's North Beach as well as New York's Greenwich Village. Younger "Beats" like Michael McClure, Neal Cassady, Philip Whalen, Allen Ginsberg, Lawrence Ferlinghetti, Gary Snyder, Robert Duncan, Diane Di Prima, Gregory Corso, and Bob Kaufman joined established figures such as Henry Miller and Kenneth Rexroth in a reevaluation and rejection of conventional society.

The latter was especially important, and Gary Snyder remembers, "Kenneth is such a catalytic figure for all of us—his presence in San Francisco, his house, literally, was the place that we met." Snyder goes on to explain,

> Anarchism as a credible and viable position was one of Rexroth's greatest contributions for us intellectually. Also, linking that to Kenneth's sense of biology and nature, his belief in poetry as song, which he states clearly in the introduction to *The Signature of All Things* . . . his interest in American Indian song, his interest in Chinese and Japanese poetry, which I started studying before I met Kenneth. But it was beautifully reinforcing to meet Kenneth and get the sense that here was an American poet of an older generation who saw value in that.

They were called the Beat Generation and, later, "beatniks." John Clellon Holmes recalls Kerouac telling him, "Like we were a generation of furtives. You know, with an inner knowledge . . . a kind of 'beatness'. . . . So I guess you might say we're a beat generation." Ironically, the notion of a "Beat Generation" became largely public, the product of media infatuation, especially with the movement's nonconformist aspects: popular magazines ranging from *Life* to *Saturday Review* to *Esquire* examined it, television and radio programs celebrated or excoriated it, comedians parodied its affectations. The names of Kerouac, Snyder, Ginsberg, and Ferlinghetti became well known not only to the younger people they would profoundly influence, but also to those—often older—they would outrage.

Most in both groups never read literature written by Beats, but did read about them and found themselves intrigued by "beatitude"—that word, with its haughty religious allusion to the Biblical "beatitudes," capturing the most pretentious aspect of this loosely organized movement. In fact, for seventeen issues, a literary magazine called *Beatitude* was published in North Beach. At its best it captured the playful tone and temper of a time and place where fake philosophy and poseurs were far more common than saints. As Kaufman wrote in "Selections on a Small Parade,"

> When I see the little Buddhist scouts
> Marching with their Zen mothers
> To tea ceremonies at the rock garden,
> I shake my head. . . . It falls off.

Even those actually immersed in "beatitude" could not always be certain where performing began and ended. Illusion and reality often merged in their lives after they became public figures.

If the core group sounds like an all-male club, it was; in many ways the entire decade—"Beat" and "non-Beat"—was dominated by men, although women such as Carolyn Cassady, Joanna McClure, and Eileen Kauffman would eventually emerge as important influences. Diane Di Prima reflects, "I can't say a lot of really great women writers were ignored in my time, but I can say a lot of potentially great women writers ended up dead or crazy." Time has softened the image of those days, but they could be hard indeed for street people, especially those bent on expressing their independence via drugs and sex and jazz.

No style typifies these writers, but Kerouac's rambling novel *On the Road*—supposedly written in three frantic weeks on a single roll of paper, and not necessarily his or the movement's best work—became the group's most celebrated statement. The novel's nonconformist, threatening theme was stated explicitly: "Young kids in this country, instead of yearning to be jet pilots should have turned their attention to Rimbaud and Shakespeare and struggled to draw their breath in pain to tell a brother's story."

Ginsberg's *Howl*, with its talismanic opening lines—

> I saw the best minds of my generation destroyed by
>   madness, starving, hysterical, naked
> dragging themselves through the negro streets at dawn . . .

—and Ferlinghetti's *A Coney Island of the Mind* were also widely identified with the Beats. Kerouac's later *Dharma Bums*, *Big Sur*, and *Mexico City Blues*, possibly more important as literature than *On the Road*, added the exotic element of Buddhism and the quest for truth—Amiri Baraka (who was there) explains, "I think with the Beat thing it was a question of people trying to be honest and forthright"—a variation that would be more fully and persistently developed in the poetry of Gary Snyder:

> stay together
> learn the flowers
> go light.

Snyder, an accomplished and enduring poet, remains the strongest link between those heady days and contemporary American writing.

Of the "big four"—Kerouac, Ginsberg, Ferlinghetti, and Snyder—only the latter two are truly California authors. Snyder lives and writes in the Sierra Nevada near Grass Valley, and Ferlinghetti's City Lights Books, both store and publishing house, is a San Francisco institution.

Many others passed through, some on a pilgrimage from Greenwich Village to North Beach and back. More than a few, such as poet and dramatist Kenneth Patchen, not only revealed the influence of music, but began performing their work to the accompaniment of jazz or bongo drums in Bay Area night spots. In fact, the nonlinear, spontaneous, anarchic forms of jazz—especially "bop" or the cool tones of West Coast styles—became major models for many writers of the time.

Disillusioned by the commercial and superficial society in which they found themselves, burdened by hangers-on, these people attempted in both their writing and their lives to achieve countercultural styles. They abjured taboos: no words were too strong, no subjects forbidden—unless they were the words and subjects favored by the middle class (a term they often used with considerable scorn).

Many of these writers composed their work with a certain sense of desperation in a time dominated by nuclear threat, the Cold War, and McCarthyism. Employing alcohol, "speed," marijuana, and other drugs, some sought easy routes to enlightenment or bliss, making them precursors of the far more general but less artistically productive "hippie" period that would follow. Slim on consistent ideology despite their affection for impressive abstractions ("truth," "karma," "freedom," "satori," etc.) these writers tended to offer critiques without remedies, or remedies without examples, but they did so with great energy and originality. Snyder, with his merging of Native American ecological insights and Zen Buddhism, was a major exception.

In the fall of 1955, a poetry reading at Six Gallery brought together

Kerouac, Snyder, Ginsberg, McClure, Ferlinghetti, and Whalen, among others—some reading, some attending. It was a symbolic event of great portent in this state's literary history. Why San Francisco? Dennis McNally calls the city "a conscious sanctuary for personal freedom," and Snyder says simply, "San Francisco taught me what a city could be, and saved me having to go to Europe." In other words, the city itself, with its ethnic and racial diversity, its history of radicalism, its avant-garde traditions, was an important player in this short, intense drama. As a result, points out novelist Herbert Gold, Bohemians eventually were "bivouacked in a North Beach concentration so dense that one strategic bomb could have wiped out most of the nation's resources of unrhymed verse."

At the end of the fifties, Kerouac wrote in *Mexico City Blues*,

> It's all indeed in Love;
> Love not of Loved Object
> Cause no object exists,
> Love of objectlessness,
> When nothing exists . . .

He and others often took "love" literally, so no matter how quasireligious their words, hedonism was as central to their vision as was Buddhism; in fact, personal excesses would plow a considerable furrow through the artists and their many hangers-on. In the next decade, there would be hippies, a not altogether lovely "Summer of Love," a "Human Be-In," acid rock, and a drug epidemic. There would also be Ken Kesey and Richard Brautigan and Lenore Kandel, Barbara Dane and Joan Baez and the Jefferson Airplane—unofficial extensions of the earlier creative cluster. The question of who begat what remains unanswered.

Nevertheless, by breaking with existing paradigms, Beat poets and writers opened paths of possibility for everyone who has followed them, and the state's literature has altered and burgeoned as a result. As Michael McClure would later write, "We danced on borrowed feet."

But how they danced!

Allen Ginsberg

Allen Ginsberg (1926–   ) is a New Jersey-born poet whose Howl and Other Poems *(1956), and the obscenity trial that followed its publication, in many ways remains the single most memorable development of the period. His passionate poetry—which leans toward east-Asian mysticism and radical left-wing politics, combined with his sprawling,* Whitmanesque *style—has led many critics to call his work prototypical of Beat expression.*

. . . .

A SUPERMARKET IN CALIFORNIA

What thoughts I have of you tonight, Walt Whitman, for I walked down the sidestreets under the trees with a headache self-conscious looking at the full moon.
In my hungry fatigue, and shopping for images, I went into the neon fruit supermarket, dreaming of your enumerations!
What peaches and what penumbras! Whole families shopping at night! Aisles full of husbands! Wives in the avocados, babies in the tomatoes!—and you, Garcia Lorca, what were you doing down by the watermelons?

I saw you, Walt Whitman, childless, lonely old grubber, poking among the meats in the refrigerator and eyeing the grocery boys.
I heard you asking questions of each: Who killed the pork chops? What price bananas? Are you my Angel?
I wandered in and out of the brilliant stacks of cans following you, and followed in my imagination by the store detective.
We strode down the open corridors together in our solitary fancy tasting artichokes, possessing every frozen delicacy, and never passing the cashier.

Where are we going, Walt Whitman? The doors close in an hour. Which way does your beard point tonight?
(I touch your book and dream of our odyssey in the supermarket and feel absurd.)
Will we walk all night through solitary streets? The trees add shade to shade, lights out in the houses, we'll both be lonely.
Will we stroll dreaming of the lost America of love past blue automobiles in driveways, home to our silent cottage?
Ah, dear father, graybeard, lonely old courage-teacher, what America did you have when Charon quit poling his ferry and you got out on a smoking bank and stood watching the boat disappear on the black waters of Lethe?

Jack Kerouac

Jack Kerouac (1922–69) remains perhaps the writer most identified with the "beat-niks," as columnist Herb Caen labeled them. In a series of novels beginning with On the Road *(1957), this ex-football player from Massachusetts captured a generation's restlessness and quest for alternative visions of truth. As novelist James D. Houston says in* A Literary History of the American West *(1987), "Kerouac's books pointed the way for a generation of American writers as well as for a generation or two of American seekers." Many critics consider* The Dharma Bums *(1958)— the autobiographical novel with thinly veiled characters (Japhy Ryder/Gary Snyder, Alvah Goldbook/Allen Ginsberg, etc.) from which the following excerpt is taken— to be the one that best captures the spirit of the Bay Area during that singular time.*

. . . .

DHARMA BUMS

The little Saint Teresa bum was the first genuine Dharma Bum I'd met, and the second was the number one Dharma Bum of them all and in fact it was he, Japhy Ryder, who coined the phrase. Japhy Ryder was a kid from eastern Oregon brought up in a log cabin deep in the woods with his father and mother and sister, from the beginning a woods boy, an ax-man, farmer, interested in animals and Indian lore so that when he finally got to college by hook or crook he was already well equipped for his early studies in anthropology and later in Indian myth and in the actual texts of Indian mythology. Finally he learned Chinese and Japanese and became an Oriental scholar and discovered the greatest Dharma Bums of them all, the Zen Lunatics of China and Japan. At the same time, being a Northwest boy with idealistic tendencies, he got interested in oldfashioned I.W.W. an-archism and learned to play the guitar and sing old worker songs to go with his Indian songs and general folksong interests. I first saw him walk-ing down the street in San Francisco the following week (after hitchhiking the rest of the way from Santa Barbara in one long zipping ride given me, as though anybody'll believe this, by a beautiful darling young blonde in a snow-white strapless bathing suit and barefooted with a gold bracelet on her ankle, driving a next-year's cinnamon-red Lincoln Mercury, who wanted benzedrine so she could drive all the way to the City and when I said I had some in my duffel bag yelled "Crazy!")—I saw Japhy loping along in that curious long stride of the mountainclimber, with a small knapsack on his back filled with books and toothbrushes and whatnot which was his small "goin-to-the-city" knapsack as apart from his big full rucksack complete with sleeping bag, poncho, and cookpots. He wore a little goatee, strangely Oriental-looking with his somewhat slanted green eyes, but he didn't look like a Bohemian at all, and was far from being a Bohemian (a hanger-onner around the arts). He was wiry, suntanned, vigorous, open, all howdies and glad talk and even yelling hello to bums on the street and when asked a question answered right off the bat from the top or bottom of his mind I don't know which and always in a sprightly sparkling way.

"Where did you meet Ray Smith?" they asked him when we walked into The Place, the favorite bar of the hepcats around the Beach.

"Oh I always meet my Bodhisattvas in the street!" he yelled, and ordered beers.

It was a great night, a historic night in more ways than one. He and some other poets (he also wrote poetry and translated Chinese and Japanese poetry into English) were scheduled to give a poetry reading at the Gallery Six in town. They were all meeting in the bar and getting high. But as they stood and sat around I saw that he was the only one who didn't look like a poet, though poet he was indeed. The other poets were either horn-rimmed intellectual hepcats with wild black hair like Alvah Goldbook, or delicate pale handsome poets like Ike O'Shay (in a suit), or out-of-this-world genteel-looking Renaissance Italians like Francis DaPavia (who looks like a young priest), or bow-tied wild-haired old anarchist fuds like Rheinhold Cacoethes, or big fat bespectacled quiet booboos like Warren Coughlin. And all the other hopeful poets were standing around, in various costumes, worn-at-the-sleeves corduroy jackets, scuffly shoes, books sticking out of their pockets. But Japhy was in rough workingman's clothes he'd bought secondhand in Goodwill stores to serve him on mountain climbs and hikes and for sitting in the open at night, for campfires, for hitchhiking up and down the Coast. In fact in his little knapsack he also had a funny green alpine cap that he wore when he got to the foot of a mountain, usually with a yodel, before starting to tromp up a few thousand feet. He wore mountain-climbing boots, expensive ones, his pride and joy, Italian make, in which he clomped around over the sawdust floor of the bar like an oldtime lumberjack. Japhy wasn't big, just about five foot seven, but strong and wiry and fast and muscular. His face was a mask of woeful bone, but his eyes twinkled like the eyes of old giggling sages of China, over that little goatee, to offset the rough look of his handsome face. His teeth were a little brown, from early backwoods neglect, but you never noticed that and he opened his mouth wide to guffaw at jokes. Sometimes he'd quiet down and just stare sadly at the floor, like a man whittling. He was merry at times. He showed great sympathetic interest in me and in the story about the little Saint Teresa bum and the stories I told him about my own experiences hopping freights or hitchhiking or hiking in woods. He claimed at once that I was a great "Bodhisattva," meaning "great wise being" or "great wise angel," and that I was ornamenting this world with my sincerity. We had the same favorite Buddhist saint, too: Avalokitesvara, or, in Japanese, Kwannon the Eleven-Headed. He knew all the details of Tibetan, Chinese, Mahayana, Hinayana, Japanese and even Burmese Buddhism but I warned him at once I didn't give a goddamn about the mythology and all the names and national flavors of Buddhism, but was just interested in the first of Sakyamuni's four noble truths, *All life is suffering*. And to an extent interested in the third, *The suppression of suffering can be achieved*, which I didn't quite believe was possible then. (I hadn't yet digested the Lankavatara Scripture which eventually shows you that there's nothing in the world but the mind itself, and therefore all's possible including the suppression of suffering.) Japhy's buddy was the aforementioned booboo big old goodhearted Warren Coughlin a hundred and eighty pounds of poet meat, who was advertised by Japhy (privately in my ear) as being more than meets the eye.

"Who is he?"

"He's my big best friend from up in Oregon, we've known each other a long time. At first you think he's slow and stupid but actually he's a shining diamond. You'll see. Don't let him cut you to ribbons. He'll make the top of your head fly away, boy, with a choice chance word."

"Why?"

"He's a great mysterious Bodhisattva I think maybe a reincarnation of Asagna the great Mahayana scholar of the old centuries."

"And who am I?"

"I dunno, maybe you're Goat."

"Goat?"

"Maybe you're Mudface."

"Who's Mudface?"

"Mudface is the mud in your goatface. What would you say if someone was asked the question 'Does a dog have the Buddha nature?' and said 'Woof!' "

"I'd say that was a lot of silly Zen Buddhism." This took Japhy back a bit. "Lissen Japhy," I said, "I'm not a Zen Buddhist, I'm a serious Buddhist, I'm an oldfashioned dreamy Hinayana coward of later Mahayanism," and so forth into the night, my contention being that Zen Buddhism didn't concentrate on kindness so much as on confusing the intellect to make it perceive the illusion of all sources of things. "It's *mean*," I complained. "All those Zen Masters throwing young kids in the mud because they can't answer their silly word questions."

"That's because they want them to realize mud is better than words, boy." But I can't recreate the exact (will try) brilliance of all Japhy's answers and come-backs and come-ons with which he had me on pins and needles all the time and did eventually stick something in my crystal head that made me change my plans in life.

Lawrence Ferlinghetti

Lawrence Ferlinghetti (1919–), a notable poet, also published Ginsberg's Howl *under the aegis of City Light books. Originally from New York, his City Lights Bookshop in San Francisco remains the symbolic heart of the beat movement, and his* A Coney Island of the Mind *(1958) is among the movement's landmark publications. The titles of two of his other collections of poetry are themselves revealing of the beat world:* Picture of the Gone World *(1955) and* Starting from San Francisco *(1961).*

. . . .

DOG

The dog trots freely in the street
and sees reality
and the things he sees
are bigger than himself
and the things he sees
are his reality
Drunks in doorways
Moons on trees
The dog trots freely thru the street
and the things he sees
are smaller than himself
Fish on newsprint
Ants in holes
Chickens in Chinatown windows
their heads a block away
The dog trots freely in the street
and the things he smells
smell something like himself
The dog trots freely in the street

past puddles and babies
cats and cigars
poolrooms and policemen
He doesn't hate cops
He merely has no use for them
and he goes past them
and past the dead cows hung up whole
in front of the San Francisco Meat Market
He would rather eat a tender cow
than a tough policeman
though either might do
And he goes past the Romeo Ravioli Factory
and past Coit's Tower
and past Congressman Doyle
He's afraid of Coit's Tower
but he's not afraid of Congressman Doyle
although what he hears is very discouraging
very depressing
very absurd
to a sad young dog like himself
to a serious dog like himself
But he has his own free world to live in
His own fleas to eat
He will not be muzzled
Congressman Doyle is just another
fire hydrant
to him
The dog trots freely in the street
and has his own dog's life to live
and to think about
and to reflect upon
touching and tasting and testing everything
investigating everything
without benefit of perjury
a real realist
with a real tale to tell
and a real tail to tell it with
a real live

                barking
                            democratic dog
engaged in real
                            free enterprise
with something to say
                            about ontology
something to say
                    about reality
                            and how to see it
                                    and how to hear it
with his head cocked sideways
                    at streetcorners
as if he is just about to have
                    his picture taken
                            for Victor Records
                    listening for
                            His Master's Voice
            and looking
                    like a living questionmark
                                    into the
                            great gramophone
                            of puzzling existence
with its wondrous hollow horn
            which always seems
            just about to spout forth
                            some Victorious answer
                            to everything

Kenneth Rexroth

Kenneth Rexroth (1905–82), an Indiana native, was a longtime fixture in San Francisco's literary scene and "the least-read major poet of our time," according to critic William Lockwood. Rexroth posed two questions for aspiring poets: "Who speaks? Who listens?" In "Prophets on the Burning Shore," critic Dennis McNally cited Rexroth as a central element in San Francisco's Renaissance: "The city had Kenneth Rexroth, rejected from Communist Party membership in the 30s for being too individualistic, an elder brother who dispensed radical political talk along with poetry news and opinions on his program on public radio station KPFA in Berkeley, itself a unique element in the Bay Area's cultural life." Rexroth was all those things and a gifted translator as well.

. . . .

SPRING RAIN

The smoke of our campfire lowers
And coagulates under
The redwoods, like low-lying
Clouds. Fine mist fills the air. Drops
Rattle down from all the leaves.
As the evening comes on
The treetops vanish in fog.
Two saw-whet owls utter their
Metallic sobbing cries high
Overhead. As it gets dark
The mist turns to rain. We are
All alone in the forest.
No one is near us for miles.
In the firelight mice scurry
Hunting crumbs. Tree toads cry like

Tiny owls. Deer snort in the
Underbrush. Their eyes are green
In the firelight like balls of
Foxfire. This morning I read
Mei Yao Chen's poems, all afternoon
We walked along the stream through
Woods and meadows full of June
Flowers. We chased frogs in the
Pools and played with newts and young
Grass snakes. I picked a wild rose
For your hair. You brought
New flowers for me to name.
Now it is night and our fire
Is a red throat open in
The profound blackness, full of
The throb and hiss of the rain.

Robert Duncan

Robert Duncan (1919–88), born in Oakland and a graduate of Bakersfield High
School, was one of the few beats who actually grew up in California. Duncan was
a member of the so-called Black Mountain poets' group that also included Charles
Olson, Ed Dorn, and Robert Creeley, among others. Critic William Lockwood
(in "Present Trends in Western Poetry") says that Duncan's poetry "can be simply
focussed and rich in its capacity for transforming the outer world in accordance
with the inner radiance he discovers in his own soul." He remained a major figure
in the Bay Area's poetry scene for most of the next four decades, a teacher in the
poetics program at New College who influenced countless younger writers.

. . . .

MY MOTHER WOULD BE A FALCONRESS

My mother would be a falconress,
And I, her gay falcon treading her wrist,
would fly to bring back
from the blue of the sky to her, bleeding, a prize,
where I dream in my little hood with many bells
jangling when I'd turn my head.

My mother would be a falconress,
and she sends me as far as her will goes.
She lets me ride to the end of her curb
where I fall back in anguish.
I dread that she will cast me away,
for I fall, I mis-take, I fail in her mission.

She would bring down the little birds.
And I would bring down the little birds.
When will she let me bring down the little birds,
pierced from their flight with their necks broken,
their heads like flowers limp from the stem?

I tread my mother's wrist and would draw blood.
Behind the little hood my eyes are hooded.
I have gone back into my hooded silence,
talking to myself and dropping off to sleep.

For she has muffled my dreams in the hood she has made me,
sewn round with bells, jangling when I move.
She rides with her little falcon upon her wrist.
She uses a barb that brings me to cower.
She sends me abroad to try my wings
and I come back to her. I would bring down
the little birds to her
I may not tear into, I must bring back perfectly.

I tear at her wrist with my beak to draw blood,
and her eye holds me, anguisht, terrifying.
She draws a limit to my flight.
Never beyond my sight, she says.
She trains me to fetch and to limit myself in fetching.
She rewards me with meat for my dinner.
But I must never eat what she sends me to bring her.

Yet it would have been beautiful, if she would have carried me,
always, in a little hood with the bells ringing,
at her wrist, and her riding
to the great falcon hunt, and me
flying up to the curb of my heart from her heart
to bring down the skylark from the blue to her feet,
straining, and then released for the flight.

My mother would be a falconress,
and I her gerfalcon, raised at her will,
from her wrist sent flying, as if I were her own
pride, as if her pride
knew no limits, as if her mind
sought in me flight beyond the horizon.

Ah, but high, high in the air I flew.
And far, far beyond the curb of her will,
were the blue hills where the falcons nest.
And then I saw west to the dying sun—
it seemed my human soul went down in flames.

I tore at her wrist, at the hold she had for me,
until the blood ran hot and I heard her cry out,
far, far beyond the curb of her will

to horizons of stars beyond the ringing hills of the world where the
     falcons nest
I saw, and I tore at her wrist with my savage beak.
I flew, as if sight flew from the anguish in her eye beyond her sight,
sent from my striking loose, from the cruel strike at her wrist,
striking out from the blood to be free of her.

My mother would be a falconress,
and even now, years after this,
when the wounds I left her had surely heald,
and the woman is dead,
her fierce eyes closed, and if her heart
were broken, it is stilld

I would be a falcon and go free.
I tread her wrist and wear the hood,
talking to myself, and would draw blood.

Bob Kaufman

Bob Kaufman (1931?–86) was the thirteenth of fourteen children whose father was Jewish and whose mother was black. At thirteen he became a cabin boy on a freighter and remained with the merchant marine for twenty years. In the 1950s he met Kerouac, Ginsberg, and Corso in Los Angeles and eventually joined them in San Francisco, where he became a favorite at poetry readings. Kaufman was also a founder of Beatitude, *the North Beach poetry magazine. His poetry has found a wide audience in Britain where he has been regarded as a major figure, and his poem "West Coast Sounds—1956" is a quick picture of all the prominent beats. "I Have Folded My Sorrows," from* Solitudes Crowded with Loneliness *(1959), is considered by many critics to be his finest single poem.*

. . . .

I HAVE FOLDED MY SORROWS

I have folded my sorrows into the mantle of summer night,
Assigning each brief storm its allotted space in time,
Quietly pursuing catastrophic histories buried in my eyes.
And yes, the world is not some unplayed Cosmic Game,
And the sun is still ninety-three million miles from me,
And in the imaginary forest, the shingled hippo becomes the gay unicorn.
No, my traffic is not with addled keepers of yesterday's disasters,
Seekers of manifest disembowelment on shafts of yesterday's pains.
Blues come dressed like introspective echoes of a journey.
And yes, I have searched the rooms of the moon on cold summer nights.
And yes, I have refought those unfinished encounters. Still, they remain
    unfinished.
And yes, I have at times wished myself something different.

The tragedies are sung nightly at the funerals of the poet;
The revisited soul is wrapped in the aura of familiarity.

A Contemporary Sampler

California remains America's favorite destination. As a result, it houses an amazing variety of writers, both native-born and transplants: for every local visionary like Maxine Hong Kingston or Richard Rodriguez or Ella Leffland there is a sharp migrant perspective from the likes of Sara Vogan or Morton Marcus or Herbert Gold. There are in fact so many authors of all kinds that no single volume, including this one, is apt to provide more than a sample of the state's contemporary letters.

Older regional and subregional distinctions endure—the beach and harsh street life remain prominent in writing from Southern California, just as rural realities still inform much literature from the Great Central Valley— but there is also a steady, perhaps inexorable homogenization at work as population grows, as electronic media invades, as popular culture becomes performed reality. Increasingly, cities in that same Great Central Valley grow indistinguishable from those in Southern California: from within, Van Nuys and Bakersfield are nearly indistinguishable, and both are still filling with migrants.

Despite the continued stream of accomplished authors relocating to the Golden State from elsewhere, the single most impressive literary development in post-World War II California has been the remarkable burgeoning of home-grown authors. Look, for instance, at what has happened in Fresno.

That agricultural hub is the scene of a poetic fluorescence. The work of the group now proudly called "The Fresno Poets" increasingly graces the most prestigious collections of American verse. Writers such as Gary Soto, Sherley Anne Williams, Leonard Adame, Greg Pape, Roberta Spear, Herbert Scott, Dixie Salazar, Jon Veinberg, David St. John, Luis Omar Salinas, DeWayne Rail, Robert Vasquez, Larry Levis, Ernesto Trejo, C. W. Moulton—the list could be much, much longer—were nurtured in the Central Valley town.

Asked how they account for this creative explosion, the poets themselves point toward Philip Levine.

Thirty years ago Levine was hired by Fresno State College, a school that boasted no particular literary reputation and no creative writing program at all. Although he acknowledges that Fresno's literary emergence "had something to do with my being here and doing a decent job," Levine credits the special quality of his pupils, "people who have a little dirt in their teeth." And there was another indispensable ingredient: the place itself. The material for literature had long been steeping in the San Joaquin Valley when Levine arrived—human complexity, passion, yearning, and anger. Only William Saroyan and William Everson had previously created memorable literature from local experiences, although John Steinbeck's Joads were better known. Among the Fresno Poets, some Joads are speaking for themselves. Oklahoma-born DeWayne Rail creates this scene in "Pickers":

> Scattered out like a handful of seeds across
>> The field, backs humped to the wind,
>> Faces like clumps of dirt in the white rows,
>> Their hands keep eating cotton.
>> The long sacks fill and puff up tight,
>> Like dreams of the money they're going to make
>> Or of what they'll have for supper.
>> They stagger with the weight to the wagon and scales,
>> Dragging their tracks out in the dust,
>> Faces bent close to the ground,
>> Their hands ragged from the cotton bolls.

As a matter of fact, many local writers have come from poor-to-marginal families and they *expect* life to be hard, whether picking cotton or writing verse. They face life frontally, yet their language is by no means inelegant. Robert Vasquez creates this picture of a boy who found dead baby birds in "Willing Witness:"

> Had I found them still in their blue shells
> like Easter candies, I would have watched them,
> one by one, hit the cement below
> like heavy balls of spit.
> I was nine years old.

Vasquez is, in a sense, a second-generation Fresno Poet, since he studied first with Rail at Fresno City College, then with Levine at Fresno State—a new tradition already perpetuating itself.

> Land flat as hoecake
> Summers hot enough
> to fry one crops fanned
>
> out in fields as
> eyes can see . . .

Another poet who studied with Levine, Sherley Anne Williams, wrote those lines in "The Iconography of Childhood," and she describes her home area as well as anyone who has served an apprenticeship on Valley soil. Fresno, once rated the worst city in America by Rand-McNally and now the nation's fastest-growing community, is producing poetry to rival its fabled raisins thanks to Philip Levine and some local kids who dreamed they could be poets.

That the hub of America's most productive agricultural county is now the country's fastest-growing city illustrates that, despite all of contemporary California's open space, this state is increasingly an urban realm. As a result, high-quality writers with urban views proliferate. Leonard Gardner, for example, in his classic *Fat City*—novel and movie—used Stockton to create a naturalistic cityscape that engulfed characters with the inexorability of quicksand. Amy Tan, in *The Joy Luck Club*, explored the lives of immigrant mothers and American daughters in San Francisco. In Southern California, Luis Valdez revealed a passionate, labyrinthine world of World War II pachucos in his innovative drama—later a movie—*Zoot Suit*. No work has been more harshly urban than the waterfront-bar, skid-row poetry of Charles Bukowski or the tough, often angry Afro-American ghetto explored in the plays of Ed Bullins.

Poets may be this rich state's principal crop: Robert Hass, Dennis Schmitz, Leonard Nathan, Glenna Luchessi, Robert Marine Warden, James Ragan, Nancy Edwards, Gary Thompson, Laurel Ann Bogen, George Keithley, Charles Webb, Jane Hirschfield, Jess Tagami, Jack Grapes, Nellie Wong, Bill Hotchkiss—so many, so diverse. They cluster not only in the urban areas—although they certainly cluster there—but also in enclaves such as the Russian River region in bucolic Sonoma County: David Bromige,

Sharon Dubaou, Marianne Ware, Don Emblen, Elizabeth Herron, et al. It's ironic that the Russian River also now hosts the annual, controversial gatherings of the artistically neutered Bohemian Club.

One reason poets thrive is that literary magazines do too, literally hundreds of them. Some are well known—Marvin Malone's *Wormwood Review*, Frederick A. Raborg's *Amelia*, Howard Junker's *Zyzzyva*, for example—while others were begun this morning and will be gone next month. Says Len Fulton, who has published *The International Directory of Little Magazines and Small Presses* since 1965, "it's easier to 'sum up' a literature fifty years *after* its own time because most of it gets lost." Fulton, operating out of the northern California town of Paradise, has seen to it that much less is lost. Small presses certainly thrive in this state too—again, literally hundreds—some of which have endured and become major forces: Capra Press in Santa Barbara, Heyday Books in Berkeley, Black Sparrow Press in Santa Rosa.

The misnamed Bohemian Club may be a high rollers' association today, but it once housed Bohemian artists, and Northern California has a long history of congeniality toward genuine Bohemian artists and writers. A cluster of lesser-known but very active countercultural authors may be found south at Venice Beach. Finally it is the variety of contemporary California writing that most astounds: more and more places producing more and more diverse literature; more working-class voices; more nonwhites; more traditionalists; more nontraditionalists; more crazies.

Memorable dramas are, for instance, being written by such authors as Ed Bullins, Luis Valdez, Suzanne Lummis, Philip Gotanda, William Babula, and Michael Lynch. Motion-picture scripts represent a major form of literary expression here: Gardner, Bukowski, Valdez, James D. Houston, and Leonard Michaels, among other prominent authors, have written screenplays. Lewis Lapham, Joan Didion, David Rains Wallace, Richard Rodriguez, and Lawrence Clark Powell have contributed incisive essays. William Oandasen, Paula Gunn Allen, Darrell Wilson, Duane Big Eagle, Jack Forbes, and Mary TallMountain are producing poetry and prose that defies conventional classification because it is derived from Native American traditions. The sense of place emerges as a force in the work of Valerie Miner, Christopher Buckley, Joyce Carol Thomas, William Rintoul, David Rains Wallace, and Richard Dokey. Asian-American authors as diverse as David Mas Masumoto, Frank Chin, Oscar Peñaranda, Genny Lim, Gus Lee, Mitsuye Yamada, Al Robles, Garrett Hongo, and Lawson Fusao Inada continue enriching California's letters. The selections that follow, then, represent only a sample of this state's contemporary literary flowering.

Variety, variety, variety. There are so many writers and so many kinds of writing that lists alone might fill a book. The picture that emerges is of a state churning culturally as it explores and defines itself. Asserts William Irwin Thompson,

> California is not so much a state of the Union as it is an *imagination* that seceded from our reality a long time ago. In leading the world in transition from industrial to post-industrial society, California's culture became the first from coal to oil, from steel to plastic, from hardware to software, from materialism to mysticism, from reality to fantasy. California became the first to discover that it was fantasy that led to reality, not the other way around.

Fantasy certainly remains a factor, but reality dominates, and the geo-literary regions—Southland, Heartland, Bay Area, and Wilderness—remain authentic and vital. This diverse collection of places and people gathered under a single name has no core—unless it is that cusp between hope and desperation which brings so many migrants to the state, and the centrality of hard work here. That tough edge of reality finally emerges when it overwhelms the dream of scooping up gold nuggets and picking free fruit, and newcomers understand that *work* is what California offers. Wrote author Nathaniel West after he was recruited by Hollywood: "I'm expected to turn out pages and pages a day. There's no fooling here." Many a grape picker or oil worker has said variations of the same thing—it's hard work: "There's no fooling here."

In contemporary California, the nation's most geographically diverse, ethnically dynamic, and fantasy-burdened state, there is plenty to write about. And the best of this state's writers, like farm boy Art Cuelho in his poem "The Harvest of Wheatville Longing," never forget the real California that produced them:

> I am planted here:
> my first kiss came
> from this land;
> lips of a sagebrush disk
> opened this adobe ground.
> My last longing harvest
> will be found here.

Gary Snyder

Gary Snyder (1931–   ), a major beat-movement link to the present, was impor-
tant in introducing Zen Buddhism to other writers of the 1950s. Snyder has moved
toward a mystical yet practical ecological vision as his poetry has matured, as is
illustrated by "Marin-An." The other two poems are from Riprap *(1959), a series*
he wrote while working on a trail crew in the Yosemite backcountry. "In a curious
mind of renunciation and long day's hard work with shovel, pick, dynamite, and
boulder," he explained, "my language relaxed into itself. . . . and I found myself
writing some poems that surprised me." A native of the Pacific Northwest, Snyder
has been associated with California for four decades. He now lives on San Juan
Ridge in the Sierra Nevada in a cabin he built himself.

. . . .

MARIN-AN

sun breaks over the eucalyptus
grove below the wet pasture,
water's about hot,
I sit in the open window
& roll a smoke.

distant dogs bark, a pair of
cawing crows; the twang
of a pygmy nuthatch high in a pine—
from behind the cypress windrow
the mare moves up, grazing.

a soft continuous roar
comes out of the far valley
of the six-lane highway—thousands
and thousands of cars
driving men to work.

ABOVE PATE VALLEY

We finished clearing the last
Section of trail by noon,
High on the ridge-side
Two thousand feet above the creek
Reached the pass, went on
Beyond the white pine groves,
Granite shoulders, to a small
Green meadow watered by the snow,
Edged with Aspen—sun
Straight high and blazing
But the air was cool.
Ate a cold fried trout in the
Trembling shadows. I spied
A glitter, and found a flake
Black volcanic glass—obsidian—
By a flower. Hands and knees
Pushing the Bear grass, thousands
Of arrowhead leavings over a
Hundred yards. Not one good
Head, just razor flakes
On a hill snowed all but summer,
A land of fat summer deer,
They came to camp. On their
Own trails. I followed my own
Trail here. Picked up the cold-drill,
Pick, singlejack, and sack
Of dynamite.
Ten thousand years.

HAY FOR THE HORSES

He had driven half the night
From far down San Joaquin
Through Mariposa, up the
Dangerous mountain roads,
And pulled in at eight a.m.
With his big truckload of hay behind the barn.
With winch and ropes and hooks
We stacked the bales up clean
To splintery redwood rafters
High in the dark, flecks of alfalfa
Whirling through shingle-cracks of light,
Itch of haydust in the sweaty shirt and shoes.
At lunchtime under Black oak
Out in the hot corral,
—The old mare nosing lunchpails,
Grasshoppers crackling in the weeds—
"I'm sixty-eight" he said,
"I first bucked hay when I was seventeen.
I thought, that day I started,
I sure would hate to do this all my life.
And dammit, that's just what
I've gone and done."

Joan Didion

Joan Didion (1934–), a native of Sacramento, published her first novel, Run River, *in 1963.* Play It As It Lays, *another lauded novel, was released in 1970. Her visions of California are razor sharp and unique, and her prose, as exemplified below, is crystalline.* California: An Interpretive History *by Walton Bean and James J. Rawls asserts, "The most important figure among the new California, and the one who most profoundly invoked the California mythos was . . . Joan Didion." She may or may not be that important—some critics, for instance, consider her perspective to be elitist—but the excellence of Didion's magazine pieces have led to high praise ("Her work galvanized me," reports Richard Rodriguez) and to a series of nonfiction collections, including* Slouching Toward Bethlehem *(1968), from which this essay is reprinted.*

. . . .

NOTES FROM A NATIVE DAUGHTER

It is very easy to sit at a bar in, say, La Scala in Beverly Hills, or Ernie's in San Francisco, and to share in the pervasive delusion that California is only five hours from New York by air. The truth is that La Scala and Ernie's are only five hours from New York by air. California is somewhere else.

Many people in the East (or "back East," as they say in California, although not in La Scala or Ernie's) do not believe this. They have been to Los Angeles or to San Francisco, have driven through a giant redwood and have seen the Pacific glazed by the afternoon sun off Big Sur, and they naturally tend to believe that they have in fact been to California. They have not been, and they probably never will be, for it is a longer and in many ways a more difficult trip than they might want to undertake, one of those trips on which the destination flickers chimerically on the horizon, ever receding, ever diminishing. I happen to know about that trip because I come from

California, come from a family, or a congeries of families, that has always been in the Sacramento Valley.

You might protest that no family has been in the Sacramento Valley for anything approaching "always." But it is characteristic of Californians to speak grandly of the past as if it had simultaneously begun, *tabula rasa*, and reached a happy ending on the day the wagons started west. *Eureka*—"I Have Found It"—as the state motto has it. Such a view of history casts a certain melancholia over those who participate in it; my own childhood was suffused with the conviction that we had long outlived our finest hour. In fact that is what I want to tell you about: what it is like to come from a place like Sacramento. If I could make you understand that, I could make you understand California and perhaps something else besides, for Sacramento *is* California, and California is a place in which a boom mentality and a sense of Chekhovian loss meet in uneasy suspension; in which the mind is troubled by some buried but ineradicable suspicion that things had better work here, because here, beneath that immense bleached sky, is where we run out of continent.

In 1847 Sacramento was no more than an adobe enclosure, Sutter's Fort, standing alone on the prairie; cut off from San Francisco and the sea by the Coast Range and from the rest of the continent by the Sierra Nevada, the Sacramento Valley was then a true sea of grass, grass so high a man riding into it could tie it across his saddle. A year later gold was discovered in the Sierra foothills, and abruptly Sacramento was a town, a town any movie-goer could map tonight in his dreams—a dusty collage of assay offices and wagonmakers and saloons. Call that Phase Two. Then the settlers came— the farmers, the people who for two hundred years had been moving west on the frontier, the peculiar flawed strain who had cleared Virginia, Kentucky, Missouri; they made Sacramento a farm town. Because the land was rich, Sacramento became eventually a rich farm town, which meant houses in town, Cadillac dealers, a country club. In that gentle sleep Sacramento dreamed until perhaps 1950, when something happened. What happened was that Sacramento woke to the fact that the outside world was moving in, fast and hard. At the moment of its waking Sacramento lost, for better or for worse, its character, and that is part of what I want to tell you about.

But the change is not what I remember first. First I remember running a boxer dog of my brother's over the same flat fields that our great-great-grandfather had found virgin and had planted; I remember swimming (albeit nervously, for I was a nervous child, afraid of sinkholes and afraid of snakes, and perhaps that was the beginning of my error) the same rivers we had swum for a century: the Sacramento, so rich with silt that we could barely see our hands a few inches beneath the surface; the American, running clean and fast with melted Sierra snow until July, when it would slow down, and rattlesnakes would sun themselves on its newly exposed rocks. The Sacramento, the American, sometimes the Cosumnes, occasionally the Feather. Incautious children died every day in those rivers; we read about it in the paper, how they had miscalculated a current or stepped into a hole down where the American runs into the Sacramento, how the Berry Brothers had been called in from Yolo County to drag the river but how the bodies remained unrecovered. "They were from away," my grandmother would extrapolate from the newspaper stories. "Their parents had no *business* letting them in the river. They were visitors from Omaha." It was not a bad lesson, although a less than reliable one; children we knew died in the rivers too.

When summer ended—when the State Fair closed and the heat broke, when the last green hop vines had been torn down along the H Street road and the tule fog began rising off the low ground at night—we would go back to memorizing the Products of Our Latin American Neighbors and to visting the great-aunts on Sunday, dozens of great-aunts, year after year of Sundays. When I think now of those winters I think of yellow elm leaves wadded in the gutters outside the Trinity Episcopal Pro-Cathedral on M Street. There are actually people in Sacramento now who call M Street Capitol Avenue, and Trinity has one of those featureless new buildings, but perhaps children still learn the same things there on Sunday mornings:

Q. In what way does the Holy Land resemble the Sacramento Valley?
A. In the type and diversity of its agricultural products.

And I think of the rivers rising, of listening to the radio to hear at what height they would crest and wondering if and when and where the levees would go. We did not have as many dams in those years. The bypasses would be full, and men would sandbag all night. Sometimes a levee would go in the night, somewhere upriver; in the morning the rumor would spread that the Army Engineers had dynamited it to relieve the pressure on the city.

After the rains came spring, for ten days or so; the drenched fields would dissolve into a brilliant ephemeral green (it would be yellow and dry as fire in two or three weeks) and the real-estate business would pick up. It was the time of year when people's grandmothers went to Carmel; it was the time of year when girls who could not even get into Stephens or Arizona or Oregon, let alone Stanford or Berkeley, would be sent to Honolulu, on the *Lurline*. I have no recollection of anyone going to New York, with the exception of a cousin who visited there (I cannot imagine why) and reported that the shoe salesmen at Lord & Taylor were "intolerably rude." What happened in New York and Washington and abroad seemed to impinge not at all upon the Sacramento mind. I remember being taken to call upon a very old woman, a rancher's widow, who was reminiscing (the favored conversational mode in Sacramento) about the son of some contemporaries of hers. "That Johnston boy never did amount to much," she said. Desultorily, my mother protested: Alva Johnston, she said, had won the Pulitzer Prize, when he was working for *The New York Times*. Our hostess looked at us impassively. "He never amounted to anything in Sacramento," she said.

Hers was the true Sacramento voice, and, although I did not realize it then, one not long to be heard, for the war was over and the boom was on and the voice of the aerospace engineer would be heard in the land. VETS NO DOWN! EXECUTIVE LIVING ON LOW FHA!

Later, when I was living in New York, I would make the trip back to Sacramento four and five times a year (the more comfortable the flight, the more obscurely miserable I would be, for it weighs heavily upon my kind that we could perhaps not make it by wagon), trying to prove that I had not meant to leave at all, because in at least one respect California—the California we are talking about—resembles Eden: it is assumed that those who absent themselves from its blessings have been banished, exiled by some perversity of heart. Did not the Donner-Reed Party, after all, eat its own dead to reach Sacramento?

I have said that the trip back is difficult, and it is—difficult in a way that magnifies the ordinary ambiguities of sentimental journeys. Going back to California is not like going back to Vermont, or Chicago; Vermont and Chicago are relative constants, against which one measures one's own change. All that is constant about the California of my childhood is the rate at which it disappears. An instance: on Saint Patrick's Day of 1948 I was taken to see the legislature "in action," a dismal experience; a handful of florid assemblymen, wearing green hats, were reading Pat-and-Mike jokes into the record. I still think of the legislators that way—wearing green hats, or sitting around on the veranda of the Senator Hotel fanning themselves and being entertained by Artie Samish's emissaries. (Samish was the lobbyist who said, "Earl Warren may be the governor of the state, but I'm the gov-

ernor of the legislature.") In fact there is no longer a veranda at the Senator
Hotel—it was turned into an airline ticket office, if you want to embroider
the point—and in any case the legislature has largely deserted the Senator
for the flashy motels north of town, where the tiki torches flame and the
steam rises off the heated swimming pools in the cold Valley night.

It is hard to *find* California now, unsettling to wonder how much of it was
merely imagined or improvised; melancholy to realize how much of anyone's memory is no true memory at all but only the traces of someone else's
memory, stories handed down on the family network. I have an indelibly
vivid "memory," for example, of how Prohibition affected the hop growers
around Sacramento: the sister of a grower my family knew brought home a
mink coat from San Francisco, and was told to take it back, and sat on the
floor of the parlor cradling that coat and crying. Although I was not born
until a year after Repeal, that scene is more "real" to me than many I have
played myself.

I remember one trip home, when I sat alone on a night jet from New
York and read over and over some lines from a W. S. Merwin poem I had
come across in a magazine, a poem about a man who had been a long time
in another country and knew that he must go home:

> . . . But it should be
> Soon. Already I defend hotly
> Certain of our indefensible faults,
> Resent being reminded; already in my mind
> Our language becomes freighted with a richness
> No common tongue could offer, while the mountains
> Are like nowhere on earth, and the wide rivers.

You see the point. I want to tell you the truth, and already I have told you
about the wide rivers.

It should be clear by now that the truth about the place is elusive, and
must be tracked with caution. You might go to Sacramento tomorrow and
someone (although no one I know) might take you out to Aerojet-General,
which has, in the Sacramento phrase, "something to do with rockets." Fifteen thousand people work for Aerojet, almost all of them imported; a
Sacramento lawyer's wife told me, as evidence of how Sacramento was
opening up, that she believed she had met one of them, at an open house
two Decembers ago. ("Couldn't have been nicer, actually," she added en-

thusiastically. "I think he and his wife bought the house next *door* to Mary and Al, something like that, which of course was how *they* met him.") So you might go to Aerojet and stand in the big vendor's lobby where a couple of thousand components salesmen try every week to sell their wares and you might look up at the electrical wallboard that lists Aerojet personnel, their projects and their location at any given time, and you might wonder if I have been in Sacramento lately. MINUTEMAN, POLARIS, TITAN, the lights flash, and all the coffee tables are littered with airline schedules, very now, very much in touch.

But I could take you a few miles from there into towns where the banks still bear names like The Bank of Alex Brown, into towns where the one hotel still has an octagonal-tile floor in the dining room and dusty potted palms and big ceiling fans; into towns where everything—the seed business, the Harvester franchise, the hotel, the department store and the main street—carries a single name, the name of the man who built the town. A few Sundays ago I was in a town like that, a town smaller than that, really, no hotel, no Harvester franchise, the bank burned out, a river town. It was the golden anniversary of some of my relatives and it was 110° and the guests of honor sat on straight-backed chairs in front of a sheaf of gladioluses in the Rebekah Hall. I mentioned visiting Aerojet-General to a cousin I saw there, who listened to me with interested disbelief. Which is the true California? That is what we all wonder.

Let us try out a few irrefutable statements, on subjects not open to interpretation. Although Sacramento is in many ways the least typical of the Valley towns, it *is* a Valley town, and must be viewed in that context. When you say "the Valley" in Los Angeles, most people assume that you mean the San Fernando Valley (some people in fact assume that you mean Warner Brothers), but make no mistake: we are talking not about the valley of the sound stages and the ranchettes but about the real Valley, the Central Valley, the fifty thousand square miles drained by the Sacramento and the San Joaquin Rivers and further irrigated by a complex network of sloughs, cutoffs, ditches, and the Delta-Mendota and Friant-Kern Canals.

A hundred miles north of Los Angeles, at the moment when you drop from the Tehachapi Mountains into the outskirts of Bakersfield, you leave Southern California and enter the Valley. "You look up the highway and it is straight for miles, coming at you, with the black line down the center coming at you and at you . . . and the heat dazzles up from the white slab so that only the black line is clear, coming at you with the whine of the tires, and if you don't quit staring at that line and don't take a few deep breaths and slap yourself hard on the back of the neck you'll hypnotize yourself."

Robert Penn Warren wrote that about another road, but he might have been writing about the Valley road, U.S. 99, three hundred miles from Bakersfield to Sacramento, a highway so straight that when one flies on the most direct pattern from Los Angeles to Sacramento one never loses sight of U.S. 99. The landscape it runs through never, to the untrained eye, varies. The Valley eye can discern the point where miles of cotton seedlings fade into miles of tomato seedlings, or where the great corporation ranches— Kern County Land, what is left of DiGiorgio—give way to private operations (somewhere on the horizon, if the place is private, one sees a house and a stand of scrub oaks), but such distinctions are in the long view irrelevant. All day long, all that moves is the sun, and the big Rainbird sprinklers.

Every so often along 99 between Bakersfield and Sacramento there is a town: Delano, Tulare, Fresno, Madera, Merced, Modesto, Stockton. Some of these towns are pretty big now, but they are all the same at heart, one- and two- and three-story buildings artlessly arranged, so that what appears to be the good dress shop stands beside a W. T. Grant store, so that the big Bank of America faces a Mexican movie house. *Dos Peliculas, Bingo Bingo Bingo.* Beyond the downtown (pronounced *down*town, with the Okie accent that now pervades Valley speech patterns) lie blocks of old frame houses—paint peeling, sidewalks cracking, their occasional leaded amber windows overlooking a Foster's Freeze or a five-minute car wash or a State Farm Insurance office; beyond those spread the shopping centers and the miles of tract houses, pastel with redwood siding, the unmistakable signs of cheap building already blossoming on those houses which have survived the first rain. To a stranger driving 99 in an air-conditioned car (he would be on business, I suppose, any stranger driving 99, for 99 would never get a tourist to Big Sur or San Simeon, never get him to the California he came to see), these towns must seem so flat, so impoverished, as to drain the imagination. They hint at evenings spent hanging around gas stations, and suicide pacts sealed in drive-ins.

But remember:

Q. In what way does the Holy Land resemble the Sacramento Valley?
A. In the type and diversity of its agricultural products.

U.S. 99 in fact passes through the richest and most intensely cultivated agricultural region in the world, a giant outdoor hothouse with a billion-dollar crop. It is when you remember the Valley's wealth that the mono-chromatic flatness of its towns takes on a curious meaning, suggests a habit of mind some would consider perverse. There is something in the Valley mind that reflects a real indifference to the stranger in his air-conditioned car, a failure to perceive even his presence, let alone his thoughts or wants. An implacable insularity is the seal of these towns. I once met a woman in Dallas, a most charming and attractive woman accustomed to the hos-pitality and social hypersensitivity of Texas, who told me that during the four war years her husband had been stationed in Modesto, she had never once been invited inside anyone's house. No one in Sacramento would find this story remarkable ("She probably had no *relatives* there," said someone to whom I told it), for the Valley towns understand one another, share a peculiar spirit. They think alike and they look alike. *I* can tell Modesto from Merced, but I have visited there, gone to dances there; besides, there is over the main street of Modesto an arched sign which reads:

WATER—WEALTH

CONTENTMENT—HEALTH

There is no such sign in Merced.

I said that Sacramento was the least typical of the Valley towns, and it is—but only because it is bigger and more diverse, only because it has had the rivers and the legislature; its true character remains the Valley charac-ter, its virtues the Valley virtues, its sadness the Valley sadness. It is just as hot in the summertime, so hot that the air shimmers and the grass bleaches white and the blinds stay drawn all day, so hot that August comes on not like a month but like an affliction; it is just as flat, so flat that a ranch of my family's with a slight rise on it, perhaps a foot, was known for the hundred-some years which preceded this year as "the hill ranch." (It is known this year as a subdivision in the making, but that is another part of the story.) Above all, in spite of its infusions from outside, Sacramento retains the Valley insularity.

To sense that insularity a visitor need do no more than pick up a copy of either of the two newspapers, the morning *Union* or the afternoon *Bee*. The *Union* happens to be Republican and impoverished and the *Bee* Democratic and powerful ("THE VALLEY OF THE BEES!" as the McClatchys, who own the Fresno, Modesto and Sacramento *Bees*, used to headline their advertisement in the trade press. "ISOLATED FROM ALL OTHER MEDIA INFLUENCE!"), but they read a good deal alike, and the tone of their chief editorial concerns is strange and wonderful and instructive. The *Union*, in a county heavily and reliably Democratic, frets mainly about the possibility of a local takeover by the John Birch Society; the *Bee*, faithful to the letter of its founder's will, carries on overwrought crusades against phantoms it still calls "the power trusts." Shades of Hiram Johnson, whom the *Bee* helped elect governor in 1910. Shades of Robert La Follette, to whom the *Bee* delivered the Valley in 1924. There is something about the Sacramento papers that does not quite connect with the way Sacramento lives now, something pronouncedly beside the point. The aerospace engineers, one learns, read the San Francisco *Chronicle*.

The Sacramento papers, however, simply mirror the Sacramento peculiarity, the Valley fate, which is to be paralyzed by a past no longer relevant. Sacramento is a town which grew up on farming and discovered to its shock that land has more profitable uses. (The chamber of commerce will give you crop figures, but pay them no mind—what matters is the feeling, the knowledge that where the green hops once grew is now Larchmont Riviera, that what used to be the Whitney ranch is now Sunset City, thirty-three thousand houses and a country-club complex.) It is a town in which defense industry and its absentee owners are suddenly the most important facts; a town which has never had more people or more money, but has lost its *raison d'être*. It is a town many of whose most solid citizens sense about themselves a kind of functional obsolescence. The old families still see only one another, but they do not see even one another as much as they once did; they are closing ranks, preparing for the long night, selling their rights-of-way and living on the proceeds. Their children still marry one another, still play bridge and go into the real-estate business together. (There is no other business in Sacramento, no reality other than land—even I, when I was living and working in New York, felt impelled to take a University of California correspondence course in Urban Land Economics.) But late at night when the ice has melted there is always somebody now, some Julian English, whose heart is not quite in it. For out there on the outskirts of town are marshaled the legions of aerospace engineers, who talk their peculiar condescending language and tend their dichondra and plan to stay in the promised land; who are raising a new generation of native Sacramentans and who do not care, really do not care, that they are not asked to join the Sutter Club. It makes one wonder, late at night when the ice is gone; introduces some air into the womb, suggests that the Sutter Club is perhaps not, after all, the Pacific Union or the Bohemian; that Sacramento is not *the* *city*. In just such self-doubts do small towns lose their character.

I want to tell you a Sacramento story. A few miles out of town is a place, six or seven thousand acres, which belonged in the beginning to a rancher with one daughter. That daughter went abroad and married a title, and when she brought the title home to live on the ranch, her father built them a vast house—music rooms, conservatories, a ballroom. They needed a ballroom because they entertained: people from abroad, people from San Francisco, house parties that lasted weeks and involved special trains. They are long dead, of course, but their only son, aging and unmarried, still lives on the place. He does not live in the house, for the house is no longer there. Over the years it burned, room by room, wing by wing. Only the chimneys of the great house are still standing, and its heir lives in their shadow, lives by himself on the charred site, in a house trailer.

That is a story my generation knows; I doubt that the next will know it, the children of the aerospace engineers. Who would tell it to them? Their grandmothers live in Scarsdale, and they have never met a great-aunt. "Old" Sacramento to them will be something colorful, something they read about in *Sunset*. They will probably think that the Redevelopment has always been there, that the Embarcadero, down along the river, with its amusing places to shop and its picturesque fire houses turned into bars, has about it the true flavor of the way it was. There will be no reason for them to know that in homelier days it was called Front Street (the town was not, after all, settled by the Spanish) and was a place of derelicts and missions and itinerant pickers in town for a Saturday-night drunk: VICTORIOUS LIFE MISSION, JESUS SAVES, BEDS 25 ¢ A NIGHT, CROP INFORMATION HERE. They will have lost the real past and gained a manufactured one, and there will be no way for them to know, no way at all, why a house trailer should stand alone on seven thousand acres outside town.

But perhaps it is presumptuous of me to assume that they will be missing something. Perhaps in retrospect this has been a story not about Sacramento at all, but about the things we lose and the promises we break as we grow older; perhaps I have been playing out unawares the Margaret in the poem:

> Margaret, are you grieving
> Over Goldengrove unleaving? . . .
> It is the blight man was born for,
> It is Margaret you mourn for.

Floyd Salas

Floyd Salas (1931–   ), an ex-boxer who graduated from the creative-writing program at San Francisco State College, produced one of the memorable prison novels in American literature, Tattoo the Wicked Cross *(1967). Born in Colorado of a pioneering Hispanic family, the author was raised in California and was the first athlete to win a boxing scholarship at the University of California, Berkeley. A social activist, Salas has published two other novels:* What Now My Love *(1970) and* Lay My Body on the Line *(1978), and edited an anthology of Bay-Area writing,* Close to Home *(1985). He is also a widely published poet and a longtime participant in the Poets-in-the-Schools Program. Salas lives in Berkeley.*

. . . .

TO SERGIE MY SWEET OLD DOG
WHO DIED IN OLD AGE

This is the reality now Sergie
this mound of earth
under the camellia bush
with a bouquet of orange poppies
alive at its foot
the shade that sprinkles it
even in the sunshine
There will always be sprinkles on this gravesite
summer or winter
raining or shining
I sprinkle it now with my tears

One of the poppies is dying though
the brown bud of a withered face
smiles out

through the bent strands
of its petals
peeking up through the bent brim
of an old straw hat
though his blooms all gone
like you did
these last two years

I suck in air to ease the cramp in my gut
Miki my Japanese puppy
nibbles some grass on your grave
A bird trill thrills me
from the big bush over your head
The sun warms me
the long branches of a thin plum tree
burst into beads of green buds
and rows of buttons of white flowers
Poppies
spin like a fleet of flying suns
over the green clover
in the speckled shade
of a knobby pear tree

This is the reality
Sergie

You down in the deep damp hole
the rain seeping into your ears
trickling through the fears
a slow movement
of flesh and bone
back to silt
back to the mud of my backyard
back to these earth clods
spongy with a whole night's rain
This is my pain

This is the reality
Sergie
dogchain
hanging from the doorknob
red cross of its rabies tab
and green heart
of its license

a breeze on me
shadow of leaves
flickering on my page
no you around
on top the ground

No Sergie
to sniff noses with
no sweet
and earthy canine smell

The reality is
there is
no trace of you
here
aside from this small mound of dirt
in the yard
and the warm coral
of my brain
the pain
in my chest

This is the reality
Sergie

WYOMING IS AN INDIAN NAME
Crossing the plateau of Wyoming by van,
March 31, 1983

Hello on your birthday Claire
I speak to the rocks of Wyoming
The Indian call haunts
the snow-speckled hills
Sculptured stratifications of rock
sing of the ages
when this plateau
was an inland sea
I see
the bottom of the ocean
pressed against
the bottom of the snow-leaded sky

It leans on me
heavily
smothering me
like a hot blanket
without you

I take deep breaths
to make sure I live
loneliness
drove the pioneer women of the plains
mad

all day
squeezed between the dry earth
and the sky
for years
can make you cry

Wyoming!
the Indian chants
but his call fades
like a thin spiral of signal smoke
smothered
by miles and miles of flat dirt
that spread out
in a tightening circle
around me
trapping
this shell of a flesh man
in this hull
of a steel car
too far
to touch you
on your birthday
I know what I was doing
thirty-one years ago
on this day Claire
but I didn't know then
a woman was being born
that I'd love now
in this
far future

Maxine Hong Kingston

Maxine Hong Kingston (1940–), a native of Stockton, is conceded to be a major American writer of her generation. She is a stylist whose original, rich view of California has enhanced literary possibilities for writers the world over. The Woman Warrior *(1976), her breakthrough book—from which the following passage is excerpted—was so singular that critics could not classify it: Was it fiction or nonfiction? Was it a biography or a novel? Hong Kingston's portraits of Chinese life do not dwell on generalizations about Chinatown, but instead examine the experiences of individuals that can be extrapolated by readers. She has remained equally original in the two volumes that have followed,* China Men *(1980) and* Tripmaster Monkey: His Fake Book *(1990).*

. . . .

THE AMERICAN FATHER

In 1903 my father was born in San Francisco, where my grandmother had come disguised as a man. Or, Chinese women once magical, she gave birth at a distance, she in China, my grandfather and father in San Francisco. She was good at sending. Or the men of those days had the power to have babies. If my grandparents did no such wonders, my father nevertheless turned up in San Francisco an American citizen.

He was also married at a distance. My mother and a few farm women went out into the chicken yard, and said words over a rooster, a fierce rooster, red of comb and feathers; then she went back inside, married, a wife. She laughs telling this wedding story; he doesn't say one way or the other.

When I asked MaMa why she speaks different from BaBa, she says their parents lived across the river from one another. Maybe his village was America, the river an ocean, his accent American.

My father's magic was also different from my mother's. He pulled the two ends of a chalk stub or a cigarette butt, and between his fingers a new stick of chalk or a fresh cigarette grew long and white. Coins appeared around his knuckles, and number cards turned into face cards. He did not have a patter but was a silent magician. I would learn these tricks when I became a grown-up and never need for cigarettes, money, face cards, or chalk.

He also had the power of going places where nobody else went, and making places belong to him. I could smell his presence. He owned special places the way he owned special things like his copper ashtray from the 1939 World's Fair and his Parker 51. When I explored his closet and desk, I thought, This is a father place; a father belongs here.

One of his places was the dirt cellar. That was under the house where owls bounced against the screens. Rats as big as cats sunned in the garden, fat dust balls among the greens. The rats ran up on the table where the rice or the grapes or the beans were drying and ate with their hands, then took extra in their teeth and leapt off the table like a circus, one rat after another. My mother swung her broom at them, the straw swooping through the air in yellow arcs. That was the house where the bunny lived in a hole in the kitchen. My mother had carried it home from the fields in her apron. Whenever it was hopping noiselessly on the linoleum, and I was there to see it, I felt the honor and blessing of it.

When I asked why the cellar door was kept locked, MaMa said there was a "well" down there. "I don't want you children to fall in the well," she said. Bottomless.

I ran around a corner one day and found the cellar door open. BaBa's white-shirted back moved in the dark. I had been following him, spying on him. I went into the cellar and hid behind some boxes. He lifted the lid that covered the bottomless well. Before he could stop me, I burst out of hiding and saw it—a hole full of shining, bulging, black water, alive, alive, like an eye, deep and alive. BaBa shouted, "Get away." "Let me look. Let me look," I said. "Be careful," he said as I stood on the brink of a well, the end and edge of the ground, the opening to the inside of the world. "What's it called?" I asked to hear him say it. "A well." I wanted to hear him say it again, to tell me again, "Well." My mother had poured rust water from old nails into my ears to improve them.

"What's a well?"

"Water comes out of it," BaBa said. "People draw water out of wells."

"Do they drink it? Where does the water come from?"

"It comes from the earth. I don't think we should drink it without boiling it for at least twenty minutes. Germs."

Poison water.

The well was like a wobble of black jello. I saw silver stars in it. It sparked. It was the black sparkling eye of the planet. The well must lead to the other side of the world. If I fall in, I will come out in China. After a long, long fall, I would appear feet first out of the ground, out of another well, and the Chinese would laugh to see me do that. The way to arrive in China less obtrusively was to dive in head first. The trick would be not to get scared during the long time in the middle of the world. The journey would be worse than the mines.

My father pulled the wooden cover, which was the round lid of a barrel, back over the well. I stepped on the boards, stood in the middle of them, and thought about the bottomless black well beneath my feet, my very feet. What if the cover skidded aside? My father finished with what he was doing; we walked out of the cellar, and he locked the door behind us.

Another father place was the attic of our next house. Once I had seen his foot break through the ceiling. He was in the attic, and suddenly his foot broke through the plaster overhead.

I watched for the day when he left a ladder under the open trap door. I climbed the ladder through the kitchen ceiling. The attic air was hot, too thick, smelling like pigeons, their hot feathers. Rafters and floor beams extended in parallels to a faraway wall, where slats of light slanted from shutters. I did not know we owned such an extravagance of empty space. I raised myself up on my forearms like a prairie dog, then balanced sure-footed on the beams, careful not to step between them and fall through. I climbed down before he returned.

The best of the father places I did not have to win by cunning; he showed me it himself. I had been young enough to hold his hand, which felt splin-tery with calluses "caused by physical labor," according to MaMa. As we walked, he pointed out sights; he named the plants, told time on the clocks, explained a neon sign in the shape of an owl, which shut one eye in daylight. "It will wink at night," he said. He read signs, and I learned the recurring words: *Company, Association, Hui, Tong.* He greeted the old men with a finger to the hat. At the candy-and-tobacco store, Baba bought Lucky Strikes and beef jerky, and the old men gave me plum wafers. The tobac-conist gave me a cigar box and a candy box. The secret place was not on the busiest Chinatown street but the street across from the park. A pedestrian would look into the barrels and cans in front of the store next door, then walk on to the herbalist's with the school supplies and saucers of herbs in the window, examine the dead flies and larvae, and overlook the secret place completely. (The herbs inside the hundred drawers did not have flies.) BaBa stepped between the grocery store and the herb shop into the kind of sheltered doorway where skid-row men pee and sleep and leave liquor bottles. The place seemed out of business; no one would rent it because it was not eyecatching. It might have been a family association office. On the window were dull gold Chinese words and the number the same as our house number. And delightful, delightful, a big old orange cat sat dozing in the window; it had pushed the shut venetian blinds aside, and its fur was flat against the glass. An iron grillwork with many hinges protected the glass. I tapped on it to see whether the cat was asleep or dead; it blinked.

BaBa found the keys on his chain and unlocked the grating, then the door. Inside was an immense room like a bank or a post office. Suddenly no city street, no noise, no people, no sun. Here was horizontal and vertical order, counters and tables in cool gray twilight. It was safe in here. The cat ran across the cement floor. The place smelled like cat piss or eucalyptus berries. Brass and porcelain spittoons squatted in corners. Another cat, a gray one, walked into the open, and I tried following it, but it ran off. I walked under the tables, which had thick legs.

BaBa filled a bucket with sawdust and water. He and I scattered handfuls of the mixture on the floors, and the place smelled like a carnival. With our pushbrooms leaving wet streaks, we swept the sawdust together, which turned gray as it picked up the dirt. BaBa threw his cigarette butts in it. The cat shit got picked up too. He scooped everything into the dustpan he had made out of an oil can.

We put away our brooms, and I followed him to the wall where sheaves of paper hung by their corners, diamond shaped. "Pigeon lottery," he called them. "Pigeon lottery tickets." Yes, in the wind of the paddle fan the soft thick sheaves ruffled like feathers and wings. He gave me some used sheets. Gamblers had circled green and blue words in pink ink. They had bet on those words. You had to be a poet to win, finding lucky ways words go together. My father showed me the winning words from last night's games: "white jade that grows in water," "red jade that grows in earth," or—not so many words in Chinese—"white waterjade," "redearthjade," "firedragon," "waterdragon." He gave me pen and ink, and I linked words of my own:

"rivercloud," "riverfire," the many combinations with *horse, cloud,* and *bird*. The lines and loops connecting the words, which were in squares, a word to a square, made designs too. So this was where my father worked and what he did for a living, keeping track of the gamblers' schemes of words.

We were getting the gambling house ready. Tonight the gamblers would come here from the towns and the fields; they would sail from San Francisco all the way up the river through the Delta to Stockton, which had more gambling than any city on the coast. It would be a party tonight. The gamblers would eat free food and drink free whiskey, and if times were bad, only tea. They'd laugh and exclaim over the poems they made, which were plain and very beautiful: "Shiny water, bright moon." They'd cheer when they won. BaBa let me crank the drum that spun words. It had a little door on top to reach in for the winning words and looked like the cradle that the Forty-niner ancestors had used to sift for gold, and like the drum for the lottery at the Stockton Chinese Community Fourth of July Picnic.

He also let me play with the hole puncher, which was a heavy instrument with a wrought-iron handle that took some strength to raise. I played gambler punching words to win—"cloudswallow," "riverswallow," "river forking," "swallow forking." I also punched perfect round holes in the corners so that I could hang the papers like diamonds and like pigeons. I collected round and crescent confetti in my cigar box.

While I worked on the floor under the tables, BaBa sat behind a counter on his tall stool. With black elastic armbands around his shirtsleeves and an eyeshade on his forehead, he clicked the abacus fast and steadily, stopping to write the numbers down in ledgers. He melted red wax in candle flame and made seals. He checked the pigeon papers, and set out fresh stacks of them. Then we twirled the dials of the safe, wound the grandfather clock, which had a long brass pendulum, meowed at the cats, and locked up. We bought crackly pork on the way home.

According to MaMa, the gambling house belonged to the most powerful Chinese American in Stockton. He paid my father to manage it and to pretend to be the owner. BaBa took the blame for the real owner. When the cop on the beat walked in, Baba gave him a plate of food, a carton of cigarettes, and a bottle of whiskey. Once a month, the police raided with a paddy wagon, and it was also part of my father's job to be arrested. He never got a record, however, because he thought up a new name for himself every time. Sometimes it came to him while the city sped past the barred windows; sometimes just when the white demon at the desk asked him for it, a name came to him, a new name befitting the situation. They never found out his real names or that he had an American name at all. "I got away with aliases," he said, "because the white demons can't tell one Chinese name from another or one face from another." He had the power of naming. He had a hundred dollars ready in an envelope with which he bribed the demon in charge. It may have been a fine, not a bribe, but BaBa saw him pocket the hundred dollars. After that, the police let him walk out the door. He either walked home or back to the empty gambling house to straighten out the books.

Two of the first white people we children met were customers at the gambling house, one small and skinny man, one fat and jolly. They lived in a little house on the edge of the slough across the street from our house. Their arms were covered with orange and yellow hair. The round one's name was Johnson, but what everyone called him was Water Shining, and his partner was White Cloud. They had once won big on those words. Also *Johnson* resembles *Water Shining*, which also has *o*, *s*, and *n* sounds. Like two old China Men, they lived together lonely with no families. They sat in front of stores; they sat on their porch. They fenced a part of the slough for their vegetable patch, which had a wooden sign declaring the names of the vegetables and who they belonged to. They also had a wooden sign over their front door: TRANQUILITY, a wish or blessing or the name of their house. They gave us nickels and quarters; they made dimes come out of noses, ears, and elbows and waved coins in and out between their knuckles. They were white men, but they lived like China Men.

When we came home from school and a wino or hobo was trying the doors and windows, Water Shining came out of his little house. "There's a wino breaking into our house," we told him. It did occur to me that he might be offended at our calling his fellow white man a wino. "It's not just a poor man taking a drink from the hose or picking some fruit and going," I explained.

"What? What? Where? Let's take a look-see," he said, and walked with us to our house, saving our house without a fight.

The old men disappeared one by one before I noticed their going. White Cloud told the gamblers that Water Shining was killed in a farming accident, run over by a tractor. His body had been churned and plowed. White Cloud lived alone until the railroad tracks were leveled, the slough drained, the blackbirds flown, and his house torn down.

My father found a name for me too at the gambling house. "He named you," said MaMa, "after a blonde gambler who always won. He gave you her lucky American name." My blonde namesake must have talked with a cigarette out of the side of her mouth and left red lip prints. She wore a low-cut red or green gambling dress, or she dressed cowgirl in white boots with baton-twirler tassels and spurs; a stetson hung at her back. When she threw down her aces, the leather fringe danced along her arm. And there was applause and buying of presents when she won. "Your father likes blondes," MaMa said. "Look how beautiful," they both exclaimed when a blonde walked by.

But my mother keeps saying those were dismal years. "He worked twelve hours a day, no holidays," she said. "Even on New Year's, no day off. He couldn't come home until two in the morning. He stood on his feet gambling twelve hours straight."

"I saw a tall stool," I said.

"He only got to sit when there were no customers," she said. "He got paid almost nothing. He was a slave; I was a slave." She is angry recalling those days.

After my father's partners stole his New York laundry, the owner of the gambling house, a fellow ex-villager, paid my parents' fares to Stockton, where the brick buildings reminded them of New York. The way my mother repaid him—only the money is repayable—was to be a servant to his, the owner's, family. She ironed for twelve people and bathed ten children. Bitterly, she kept their house. When my father came home from work at two in the morning, she told him how badly the owner's family had treated her, but he told her to stop exaggerating. "He's a generous man," he said.

The owner also had a black servant, whose name was Harry. The rumor was that Harry was a half-man/half-woman, a half-and-half. Two servants could not keep that house clean, where children drew on the wallpaper and dug holes in the plaster. I listened to Harry sing "Sioux City Sue." "Lay down my rag with a hoo hoo hoo," he sang. He squeezed his rag out in the bucket and led the children singing the chorus. Though my father was also as foolishly happy over his job, my mother was not deceived.

When my mother was pregnant, the owner's wife bought her a dozen baby chicks, not a gift; my mother would owe her the money. MaMa would be allowed to raise the chicks in the owner's yard if she also tended his chickens. When the baby was born, she would have chicken to give for birth announcements. Upon his coming home from work one night, the owner's wife lied to him, "The aunt forgot to feed her chickens. Will you do it?" Grumbling about my lazy mother, the owner went out in the rain and slipped in the mud, which was mixed with chicken shit. He hurt his legs and lay there yelling that my mother had almost killed him. "And she makes our whole yard stink with chicken shit," he accused. When the baby was born, the owner's wife picked out the scrawny old roosters and said they were my mother's twelve.

Ironing for the children, who changed clothes several times a day, MaMa had been standing for hours while pregnant when the veins in her legs rippled and burst. After that she had to wear support stockings and to wrap her legs in bandages.

The owner gave BaBa a hundred-and-twenty-dollar bonus when the baby was born. His wife found out and scolded him for "giving charity."

"You deserve that money," MaMa said to BaBa. "He takes all your time. You're never home. The babies could die, and you wouldn't know it."

When their free time coincided, my parents sat with us on apple and orange crates at the tiny table, our knees touching under it. We ate rice and salted fish, which is what peasants in China eat. Everything was nice except what MaMa was saying, "We've turned into slaves. We're the slaves of these villagers who were nothing when they were in China. I've turned into the servant of a woman who can't read. Maybe we should go back to China. I'm tired of being Wah Q," that is, a Sojourner from Wah.

My father said, "No." Angry. He did not like her female intrigues about the chickens and the ironing and the half-man/half-woman.

They saved his pay and the bonuses, and decided to buy a house, the very house they were renting. This was the two-story house around the corner from the owner's house, convenient for my mother to walk to her servant job and my father to the gambling house. We could rent out the bottom floor and make a profit. BaBa had five thousand dollars. Would the owner, who spoke English, negotiate the cash sale? Days and weeks passed, and when he asked the owner what was happening, the owner said, "I decided to buy it myself. I'll let you rent from me. It'll save you money, especially since you're saving to go back to China. You're going back to China anyway." But BaBa had indeed decided to buy a house on the Gold Mountain. And this was before Pearl Harbor and before the Chinese Revolution.

He found another house farther away, not as new or big. He again asked the owner to buy it for him. You would think we could trust him, our fellow villager with the same surname, almost a relative, but the owner bought up this house too—the one with the well in the cellar—and became our landlord again.

My parents secretly looked for another house. They told everyone, "We're saving our money to go back to China when the war is over." But what they really did was to buy the house across from the railroad tracks. It was exactly like the owner's house, the same size, the same floor plan and ginger-bread. BaBa paid six thousand dollars cash for it, not a check but dollar bills, and he signed the papers himself. It was the biggest but most run-down of the houses; it had been a boarding house for old China Men. Rose bushes with thorns grew around it, wooden lace hung broken from the porch eaves, the top step was missing like a moat. The rooms echoed. This was the house with the attic and basement. The owner's wife accused her husband of giving us the money, but she was lying. We made our escape from them. "You don't have to be afraid of the owner any more," MaMa keeps telling us.

Sometimes we waited up until BaBa came home from work. In addition to a table and crates, we had for furniture an ironing board and an army cot, which MaMa unfolded next to the gas stove in the wintertime. While she ironed our clothes, she sang and talked story, and I sat on the cot holding one or two of the babies. When BaBa came home, he and MaMa got into the cot and pretended they were refugees under a blanket tent. He brought out his hardbound brown book with the gray and white photographs of white men standing before a flag, sitting in rows of chairs, shaking hands in the street, hand-signaling from car windows. A teacher with a suit stood at a blackboard and pointed out things with a stick. There were no children or women or animals in this book. "Before you came to New York," he told my mother, "I went to school to study English. The classroom looked like this, and every student came from another country." He read words to my mother and told her what they meant. He also wrote them on the blackboard, it and the daruma, the doll which always rights itself when knocked down, the only toys we owned at that time. The little h's looked like chairs, the e's like lidded eyes, but those words were not *chair* and *eye*. " 'Do you speak English?' " He read and translated. " 'Yes, I am learning to speak English better.' 'I speak English a little.' " " 'How are you?' 'I am fine, and you?' " My mother forgot what she learned from one reading to the next. The words had no crags, windows, or hooks to grasp. No pictures.

The same *a, b, c*'s for everything. She couldn't make out ducks, cats, and mice in American cartoons either.

During World War II, a gang of police demons charged into the gambling house with drawn guns. They handcuffed the gamblers and assigned them to paddy wagons and patrol cars, which lined the street. The wagons were so full, people had to stand with their hands up on the ceiling to keep their balance. My father was not jailed or deported, but neither he nor the owner worked in gambling again. They went straight. Stockton became a clean town. From the outside the gambling house looks the same closed down as when it flourished.

My father brought his abacus, the hole punch, and extra tickets home, but those were the last presents for a while. A dismal time began for him.

He became a disheartened man. He was always home. He sat in his chair and stared, or he sat on the floor and stared. He stopped showing the boys the few kung fu moves he knew. He suddenly turned angry and quiet. For a few days he walked up and down on the sidewalk in front of businesses and did not bring himself to enter. He walked right past them in his beautiful clothes and acted very busy, as if having an important other place to go for a job interview. "You're nothing but a gambler," MaMa scolded. "You're spoiled and won't go looking for a job." "The only thing you're trained for is writing poems," she said. "I know you," she said. (I hated her sentences that started with "I know you.") "You poet. You scholar. You gambler. What use is any of that?" "It's a wife's job to scold her husband into working," she explained to us.

My father sat. "You're so scared," MaMa accused. "You're shy. You're lazy." "Do something. You never do anything." "You let your so-called friends steal your laundry. You let your brothers and the Communists take your land. You have no head for business." She nagged him and pampered him. MaMa and we kids scraped his back with a porcelain spoon. We did not know whether it was the spoon or the porcelain or the massage that was supposed to be efficacious. "Quit being so shy," she advised. "Take a walk through Chinatown and see if any of the uncles has heard of a job. Just ask. You don't even need apply. Go find out the gossip." "He's shy," she explained him to us, but she was not one to understand shyness, being entirely bold herself. "Why are you so shy? People invite you and go out of their way for you, and you act like a snob or a king. It's only human to reciprocate." "You act like a piece of liver. Who do you think you are? A piece of liver?" She did not understand how some of us run down and stop. Some of us use up all our life force getting out of bed in the morning, and it's a wonder we can get to a chair and sit in it. "You piece of liver. You poet. You scholar. What's the use of a poet and a scholar on the Gold Mountain? You're so skinny. You're not supposed to be so skinny in this country. You have to be tough. You lost the New York laundry. You lost the house with the upstairs. You lost the house with the back porch." She summarized, "No loyal friends or brothers. Savings draining away like time. Can't speak English. Now you've lost the gambling job and the land in China."

Somebody—a Chinese, it had to be a Chinese—dug up our loquat tree, which BaBa had planted in front of the house. He or she had come in the middle of the night and left a big hole. MaMa blamed BaBa for that too, that he didn't go track down the tree and bring it back. In fact, a new loquat tree had appeared in the yard of a house around the corner. He ignored her, stopped shaving, and sat in his T-shirt from morning to night.

He seemed to have lost his feelings. His own mother wrote him asking for money, and he asked for proof that she was still alive before he would send it. He did not say, "I miss her." Maybe she was dead, and the Communists maintained a bureau of grandmother letter writers in order to get our money. That we kids no longer received the sweet taste of invisible candy was no proof that she had stopped sending it; we had outgrown it. For proof, the aunts sent a new photograph of Ah Po. She looked like the same woman, all right, like the pictures we already had but aged. She was ninety-nine years old. She was lying on her side on a lounge chair, alone, her head pillowed on her arm, the other arm along her side, no green tints at her earlobes, fingers, and wrists. She still had little feet and a curved-down mouth. "Maybe she's dead and propped up," we kids conjectured.

BaBa sat drinking whiskey. He no longer bought new clothes. Nor did he go to the dentist and come back telling us the compliments on his perfect teeth, how the dentist said that only one person in a thousand had teeth with no fillings. He no longer advised us that to have perfect teeth, it's good to clamp them together, especially when having a bowel movement.

MaMa assured us that what he was looking forward to was when each child came home with gold. Then he or she (the pronoun is neutral in the spoken language) was to ask the father, "BaBa, what kind of a suit do you want? A silk gown? Or a suit from the West? An Eastern suit or a Western suit? What kind of a Western suit do you want?" She suggested that we ask him right now. Go-out-on-the-road. Make our fortunes. Buy a Western suit for Father.

I went to his closet and studied his suits. He owned gray suits, dark blue ones, and a light pinstripe, expensive, successful suits to wear on the best occasions. Power suits. Money suits. Two-hundred-dollars-apiece New York suits. Businessmen-in-the-movies suits. Boss suits. Suits from before we were born. At the foot of the closet arranged in order, order his habit, were his leather shoes blocked on shoe trees. How could I make money like that? I looked in stores at suits and at the prices. I could never learn to sew this evenly, each suit perfect and similar to the next.

MaMa worked in the fields and the canneries. She showed us how to use her new tools, the pitters and curved knives. We tried on her cap pinned with union buttons and her rubber gloves that smelled like rubber tomatoes. She emptied her buckets, thermoses, shopping bags, lunch pail, apron, and scarf; she brought home every kind of vegetable and fruit grown in San Joaquin County. She said she was tired after work but kept moving, busy, banged doors, drawers, pots and cleaver, turned faucets off and on with *ka-chunk*'s in the pipes. Her cleaver banged on the chopping block for an hour straight as she minced pork and steak into patties. Her energy slammed BaBa back into his chair. She took care of everything; he did not have a reason to get up. He stared at his toes and fingers. "You've lost your sense of emergency," she said; she kept up her sense of emergency every moment.

He dozed and woke with a jerk or a scream. MaMa medicated him with a pill that came in a purple cube lined with red silk quilting, which cushioned a tiny black jar; inside the jar was a black dot made out of ground pearls, ox horn, and ox blood. She dropped this pill in a bantam broth that had steamed all day in a little porcelain crock on metal legs. He drank this soup, also a thick beef broth with gold coins in the bottom, beef teas, squab soup, and still he sat. He sat on. It seemed to me that he was getting skinnier.

"You're getting skinny again," MaMa kept saying. "Eat. Eat. You're less than a hundred pounds."

I cut a Charles Atlas coupon out of a comic book. I read all the small print. Charles Atlas promised to send some free information. "Ninety-seven-pound weakling," the cartoon man called himself. "I'll gamble a stamp," he said. Charles Atlas did not say anything about building fat, which was what my father needed. He already had muscles. But he was ninety-seven pounds like the weakling, maybe ninety pounds. Also he kicked over chairs like in the middle panel. I filled in the coupon and forged his signature. I did not dare ask him how old he was, so I guessed maybe he was half as old as his weight: age forty-five, weight ninety. If Charles Atlas saw that he was even skinnier than the weakling, maybe he would hurry up answering. I took the envelope and stamp from BaBa's desk.

Charles Atlas sent pamphlets with more coupons. From the hints of information, I gathered that my father needed lessons, which cost money. The lessons had to be done vigorously, not just read. There seemed to be no preliminary lesson on how to get up.

The one event of the day that made him get up out of his easy chair was the newspaper. He looked forward to it. He opened the front door and looked for it hours before the mailman was due. *The Gold Mountain News* (or *The Chinese Times*, according to the English logo) came from San Francisco in a paper sleeve on which his name and address were neatly typed. He put on his gold-rimmed glasses and readied his smoking equipment: the 1939 World's Fair ashtray, Lucky Strikes, matches, coffee. He killed several hours reading the paper, scrupulously reading everything, the date on each page, the page numbers, the want ads. Events went on; the world kept moving. The hands on the clocks kept moving. This sitting ought to have felt as good as sitting in his chair on a day off. He was not sick. He checked his limbs, the crooks of his arms. Everything was normal, quite comfortable, his easy chair fitting under him, the room temperature right.

MaMa said a man can be like a rat and bite through wood, bite through glass and rock. "What's wrong?" she asked.

"I'm tired," he said, and she gave him the cure for tiredness, which is to hit the inside joints of elbows and knees until red and black dots—the tiredness—appear on the skin.

He screamed in his sleep. "Night sweats," MaMa diagnosed. "Fear sweats." What he dreamed must have been ax murders. The family man kills his entire family. He throws slain bodies in heaps out the front door. He leaves no family member alive; he or she would suffer too much being the last one. About to swing the ax, screaming in horror of killing, he is also the last little child who runs into the night and hides behind a fence. Someone chops at the bushes beside him. He covers his ears and shuts his mouth tight, but the scream comes out.

I invented a plan to test my theory that males feel no pain; males don't feel. At school, I stood under the trees where the girls played house and watched a strip of cement near the gate. There were two places where boys and girls mixed; one was the kindergarten playground, where we didn't go any more, and the other was this bit of sidewalk. I had a list of boys to kick: the boy who burned spiders, the boy who had grabbed me by my coat lapels like in a gangster movie, the boy who told dirty pregnancy jokes. I would get them one at a time with my heavy shoes, on which I had nailed toe taps and horseshoe taps. I saw my boy, a friendly one for a start. I ran fast, crunching gravel. He was kneeling; I grabbed him by the arm and kicked him sprawling into the circle of marbles. I ran through the girls' playground and playroom to our lavatory, where I looked out the window. Sure enough, he was not crying. "See?" I told the girls. "Boys have no feelings. It's some kind of immunity." It was the same with Chinese boys, black boys, white boys, and Mexican and Filipino boys. Girls and women of all races cried and had feelings. We had to toughen up. We had to be as tough as boys, tougher because we only pretended not to feel pain.

One of my girl friends had a brother who cried, but he had been raised as a girl. Their mother was a German American and their father a Chinese American. This family didn't belong to our Benevolent Association nor did they go to our parties. The youngest boy wore girls' dresses with ruffles and bows, and brown-blondish ringlets grew long to his waist. When this thin, pale boy was about seven, he had to go to school; it was already two years past the time when most people started school. "Come and see something strange," his sister said on Labor Day. I stood in their yard and watched their mother cut off his hair. The hair lay like tails around his feet. Mother cried, and son cried. He was so delicate, he had feelings in his hair; it hurt him to have his hair cut. I did not pick on him.

There was a war between the boys and the girls; we sisters and brothers were evenly matched three against three. The sister next to me, who was like my twin, pushed our oldest brother off the porch railing. He landed on his face and broke two front teeth on the sidewalk. They fought with knives, the cleaver and a boning knife; they circled the dining room table and sliced one another's arms. I did try to stop that fight—they were cutting bloody slits, an earnest fight to the death. The telephone rang. Thinking it was MaMa, I shouted, "Help. Help. We're having a knife fight. They'll kill each other." "Well, do try to stop them." It was the owner's wife; she'd gossip to everybody that our parents had lost control of us, such bad parents who couldn't get respectable jobs, mother gone all day, and kids turned into killers. "That was Big Aunt on the phone," I said, "and she's going to tell the whole town about us," and they quit after a while. Our youngest sister snuck up on our middle brother, who was digging in the ground. She was about to drop a boulder on his head when somebody shouted, "Look out." She only hit his shoulder. I told my girl friends at school that I had a stepfather and three wicked stepbrothers. Among my stepfather's many aliases was the name of my real father, who was gone.

The white girls at school said, "I got a spanking." I said we never got spanked. "My parents don't believe in it," I said, which was true. They didn't know about spanking, which is orderly. My mother swung wooden hangers, the thick kind, and brooms. We got trapped behind a door or under a bed and got hit anywhere (except the head). When the other kids said, "They kissed me good night," I also felt left out; not that I cared about kissing but to be normal.

We children became so wild that we broke BaBa loose from his chair. We goaded him, irked him—*gikked* him—and the gravity suddenly let him go. He chased my sister, who locked herself in a bedroom. "Come out," he shouted. But, of course, she wouldn't, he having a coat hanger in hand and angry. I watched him kick the door; the round mirror fell off the wall and crashed. The door broke open, and he beat her. Only, my sister remembers that it was she who watched my father's shoe against the door and the mirror outside fall, and I who was beaten. But I know I saw the mirror in crazy pieces; I was standing by the table with the blue linoleum top, which was outside the door. I saw his brown shoe against the door and his knee flex and the other brothers and sisters watching from the outside of the door, and heard MaMa saying, "Seven years bad luck." My sister claims that same memory. Neither of us has the recollection of curling up inside that room, whether behind the pounding door or under the bed or in the closet.

A white girl friend, whose jobless and drunk father picked up a sofa and dropped it on her, said, "My mother saw him pushing *me* down the stairs, and *she* was watching from the landing. And I remember him pushing *her*, and *I* was at the landing. Both of us remember looking up and seeing the other rolling down the stairs."

He did not return to sitting. He shaved, put on some good clothes, and went out. He found a friend who had opened a new laundry on El Dorado Street. He went inside and chatted, asked if he could help out. The friend said he had changed his mind about owning the laundry, which he had named New Port Laundry. My father bought it and had a Grand Opening. We were proud and quiet as he wrote in gold and black on big red ribbons. The Chinese community brought flowers, mirrors, and pictures of flowers and one of Guan Goong. BaBa's liveliness returned. It came from nowhere, like my new idea that males have feelings. I had no proof for this idea but took my brothers' word for it.

BaBa made a new special place. There was a trap door on the floor inside the laundry, and BaBa looked like a trap-door spider when he pulled it over his head or lifted it, emerging. The basement light shone through the door's cracks. Stored on the steps, which were also shelves, were some rolled-up flags that belonged to a previous owner; gold eagles gleamed on the pole tips.

We children waited until we were left in charge of the laundry. Then some of us kept a lookout while the rest, hanging on to the edge of the hole, stepped down between the supplies. The stairs were steep against the backs of our legs.

The floor under the building was gray soil, a fine powder. Nothing had ever grown in it; it was sunless, rainless city soil. Beyond the light from one bulb the blackness began, the inside of the earth, the insides of the city. We had our flashlights ready. We chose a tunnel and walked side by side into the dark. There are breezes inside the earth. They blow cool and dry. Blackness absorbed our lights. The people who lived and worked in the four stories above us didn't know how incomplete civilization is, the street only a crust. Down here under the sidewalks and the streets and the cars, the builders had left mounds of loose dirt, piles of dumped cement, rough patches of concrete tamping down and holding back some of the dirt. The posts were unpainted and not square on their pilings. We followed the tunnels to places that had no man-made materials, wild areas, then turned around and headed for the lighted section under the laundry. We never found the ends of some tunnels. We did not find elevators or ramps or the undersides of the buckling metal doors one sees on sidewalks. "Now we know the secret of cities," we told one another. On the shelves built against the dirt walls, BaBa had stacked boxes of notebooks and laundry tickets, rubber stamps, pencils, new brushes, blue bands for the shirts, rolls of wrapping paper, cones of new string, bottles of ink, bottles of distilled water in case of air raids. Here was where we would hide when war came and we went underground for gorilla warfare. We stepped carefully; he had set copper and wood rat traps. I opened boxes until it was time to come up and give someone else a chance to explore.

So my father at last owned his house and his business in America. He bought chicks and squabs, built a chicken run, a pigeon coop, and a turkey pen; he dug a duck pond, set the baby bathtub inside for the lining, and won ducklings and goldfish and turtles at carnivals and county fairs. He bought rabbits and bantams and did not refuse dogs, puppies, cats, and kittens. He told a funny story about a friend of his who kept his sweater on while visiting another friend on a hot day; when the visitor was walking out the gate, the host said, "Well, Uncle, and what are those chicken feet wiggling out of your sweater?" One morning we found a stack of new coloring books and follow-the-dot books on the floor next to our beds. "BaBa left them," we said. He buried wine bottles upside down in the garden; their bottoms made a path of sea-color circles. He gave me a picture from the newspaper of redwoods in Yosemite, and said, "This is beautiful." He talked about a Los Angeles Massacre, but I wished that he had not, and pretended he had not. He told an ancient story about two feuding poets: one killed the other's plant by watering it with hot water. He sang "The Song of the Man of the Green Hill," the end of which goes like this: "The disheveled poet beheads the great whale. He shoots an arrow and hits a suspended flea. He sees well through rhinoceros-horn lenses." This was a song by Kao Chi, who had been executed for his politics; he is famous for poems to his wife and daughter written upon leaving for the capital; he owned a small piece of land where he grew enough to eat without working too hard so he could write poems. BaBa's luffa and grapevines climbed up ropes to the roof of the house. He planted many kinds of gourds, peas, beans, melons, and cabbages—and perennials—tangerines, oranges, grapefruit, almonds, pomegranates, apples, black figs, and white figs—and from seed pits, another loquat, peaches, apricots, plums of many varieties—trees that take years to fruit.

Leonard Nathan

Leonard Nathan (1924–), a native of El Monte, is among California's most enduring and honored poets. He has published ten collections of poetry including Carrying On: New and Selected Poems *(1985). In a memoir ("The Center of the Outskirts," published in 1988) Nathan reflected upon a seminal time of his youth when he had been lucky enough to encounter someone who knew that "poetry was not a private enchantment, but the disciplined craft that made enchantment into communication." Nathan has been doing just that ever since. These selections are from* Western Reaches *(1958). Also a translator of note, Leonard Nathan is a longtime professor at the University of California, Berkeley.*

. . . .

CROP DUSTING

He is archaic in air as heroes and his flight
Is strained with wooden wings and toothpick struts;
Strung wire and awkward fuselage resist
All motion, and the desperate engine butts
Ahead and roars unwilling as if height
Thickened and the propeller fought to twist.
Now he banks lower on infected green
To harrow life that kills, though all life dies;
Then, staggering straight, he levels out to dust.
I see him now, his goggles like gross eyes
To take on earth the fix of his machine,
The life and death contraption of his trust.

FIELDS IN LIGHT

I

Last summer the sweet acreage of blue grape
And gentle almond orchards made us rich
So easy to the reach and known as skin
Knows sun where both are nude in leisure noon . . .
Even the work was grace, sober but deep,
To give such pregnant poise to vine and tree
Beyond a bare endurance, that stripped bole
Would wedge its buds again through wintering rind.

So understood this acreage that in sleep
It let you walk its always springing ways,
The lordly stroller through the larded dream,
That waking seemed more of the same sleepwalk
Through green boulevards until yourself
Was the land lighted to its ripening edge,
Easy to vision, easing the will through earth,
The fields sufficient green for their possessor.

II

This winter at the silver shoulder of storm
The fields bristled, troubled by scouting wind;
The lordly stroller windowed and roofed his walk,
Watcher now of the worst, but not the end
Of time disguising its uses in dead weather,
Thinking, "The fields though cold are in my hands."
So we thought and darkening on the glass
The fields answered shuddering through themselves,
A beast you trained but cannot help through pain,

Then flooded the air with such exacting light,
Vine, tree, branch, twig, bud, weed and clod
Were sudden shapes, wild detail in strange fire,
So that the landscape was a world of things
Suddenly out of reach, too hard to feel,
As if always under the spring, earth lay
Suffering false labor of the dying hand,
Possessed though by whoever walked this storm,
Alive, terrible and past all known endurance,
Now fields lived with a light that made the sun
Our *ignis fatuus*, a noonday clown,
Made walking dark as in a fable's cloud.

Thunder buckled the vision, rain flushed out
The dark. The heart beat imprecise and slow.
The window gave us back the shattered self,
Translucent, comic, rattling from the blow.

Cyra McFadden

Cyra McFadden (1937–) wrote her hilarious novel The Serial *in 1976 to parody the terminal California trendiness symbolized by a sybaritic version of Marin County. A longtime newspaper columnist and free-lance writer, McFadden pinpointed the desperation of the "pop" psychology movement that swept the Bay Area during the 1970s: EST, I Ching, rebirthing, reorienting brain hemispheres, channeling the spirits of the dead, etc.—a bouillabaisse of nonsense that McFadden skillfully exposed. Her characters are "into" everything but void of genuine feeling or sense. They confuse psychobabble for reality and are gratingly self-conscious, wear cork sandals, respect whales, mourn Che Guevara, and give everyone "space." In* The Serial, *the author took actual fads to ridiculous ends, as the excerpted chapter that follows illustrates.*

. . . .

DEALING WITH THE WHOLE CHILD

Kate's friend Martha and her husband Bill shared with their Fairfax next-door neighbors a total commitment to the nurturing of the whole child, so they had a lot in common even though Martha was a college dropout while Naomi Maginnis had two master's degrees from Mills, one in sociology and one in batik.

It just went to show that intellectual heavies could be beautiful in spite of all those smarts. Naomi, for instance, was a model mother. Unlike Martha herself, she never shouted at her kids, never blew her cool with them, and never came on like a parent figure. Look at the way she was now persuading her youngest, John Muir Maginnis, to stop swinging on Martha's drapes.

"John-John," Naomi was saying, "I shouldn't engage in that form of activity if I were you. Your actions might be subject to misinterpretation, don't you agree?"

John-John stared at her balefully. "I don' give a shit," he said, and instead began to beat Tamalpa, Martha's four-year-old daughter, over the head with his Playskool carpenter's awl. It was just amazing the way children worked out their hostilities among themselves if you didn't interfere with their natural instincts.

Serving the coffee and her homemade whole-wheat baklava, Martha thought about the way parents in Marin raised their young. The contrast to her own oppressively regimented childhood made her feel truly optimistic about the future of humanity in the hands of Consciousness III. If, like Tamalpa and John-John, she had been permitted as a child to "act out" when she felt like it, Martha was pretty sure she wouldn't have spent all those years in psychoanalysis. Her shrink had told her that her own father, as she'd described him, was practically a casebook example of an anal retentive.

It did worry her, occasionally, that her oldest daughter, Debbie, had gone all through high school in Marin without learning to write a grammatical sentence and without knowing where Europe was. (Debbie got Europe mixed up with Eureka.) But Martha had discussed the whole thing with Debbie's counselor on more than one occasion and had found him terrifically *simpático;* he'd pointed out to her that the written word was on its way out, that what was most important was that Debbie learn to function in the here/now, and that Martha must want her daughter to be happy.

Martha hadn't heard from Debbie since she ran off to Zihuatanejo with a dirt-bike racer, so she didn't know whether Debbie was really, *really* happy or not. But she was glad she had a chance to parent all over again with Tamalpa, Gregor and Che.

She sat down beside Naomi on her new natural linen sofa from McDermott's (Martha was getting back to natural fibers and earthy colors, because your environment was terrifically important to your inner serenity), and started to ask her, as she'd planned to do earlier, about whether or not she should tell Kate about Harvey's new liaison. Naomi was the person to give her the straight dope, because while she didn't know either of the Holroyds, she not only belonged to Mensa but was fantastic at conceptualizing.

But John-John sort of blew it by picking up his father's coffee cup and dumping the scalding French roast methodically down his pant leg, which caused Jason, who usually didn't overreact like that, to scream. So they had to drop everything else for the moment and explain the pleasure/pain principle to him, and Martha had to get a sponge and mop up the coffee from the natural linen, a little nostalgic for the old Naugahyde sofa it had replaced. Of course she wouldn't have plastic in her house anymore, because it was so *synthetic*, but sometimes she missed it.

Jason was superintelligent, too, however (he had a Ph.D. in Medieval Studies from Cornell and was currently teaching night classes in bonehead English at the College of Marin), so he naturally dealt with John-John calmly once he stopped writhing. "John," he said, "I can only surmise that your impulsive gesture, in pouring hot coffee on your father, was the result of some instinctual aversion to the use of stimulants—an admirable course of action in the abstract but a painful one in actuality. I feel we should discuss the question of how one chooses the form of protest he employs as a vehicle for his convictions. It's difficult to entertain an honest difference of opinion on the rational level when one is suffering from third-degree burns, can you understand that?"

John-John gave him the finger, snatched Martha's baklava off her plate and began to pull Gregor's hair. Martha thought it really spoke volumes for the Maginnises that he was so uninhibited.

Finally, although the intrusion of the children continued to be a problem throughout the evening, Martha and Bill brought the conversation around to what Martha should do about Kate. Was it more authentic to tell her that Harvey was getting it on with Carol, whom Kate thought of as her best friend, or just to cop out?

Naomi resolved the issue definitively once she'd gently restrained Gregor from kicking her repeatedly in the calf of her Danskin leotard. "Look, Martha," she said, "while my opinion is necessarily 'off the wall,' as you'd put it, I should think that your dilemma, as you've articulated it, has wider implications. . . . John-John, Mummy finds it unpleasant to be poked in the eye like that. . . . I myself feel that absolute honesty must always take precedence, in an enlightened community, over crasser, more pragmatic considerations. Otherwise we simply recreate the hypocrisy of our times, with all its disastrous and perhaps irrevocable consequences.

"I, for one, would want to know if Jason were betraying me in that particularly squalid fashion . . ." Naomi paused meaningfully . . . "so I could *kill* the son-of-a-bitch."

Martha was just zapped. Naomi *always* got right down to the nitty-gritty. "Wow," she said, "you're right. You're right, you know? Really." As soon as the Maginnises went home, if they ever did, she was determined to call Kate, painful duty though it was, and give her the word. . . .

Wallace Stegner

Wallace Stegner (1909–), a major force in American letters, was born in Iowa, raised in Saskatchewan, Montana, and Utah, and finally settled in California where he has lived for nearly fifty years. His mobility makes him typical of a generation that, especially following World War II, changed the social and literary face of the nation. Stegner was instrumental in establishing the creative writing program at Stanford University as one of the nation's finest. Among his novels are Angle of Repose, *which won the Pulitzer Prize in 1972, and* The Spectator Bird, *winner of the 1977 National Book Award. He won an earlier National Book Award in 1976 for his biography of Bernard DeVoto,* The Uneasy Chair (1974). *As Joseph Flora noted in* A Literary History of the American West, *"Stegner has always conceived of West in broad terms—intent, as it were, not to let westerness limit or hinder his work." It hasn't. Not surprisingly, he has also long been an advocate for the preservation of the natural environment. The essay that follows first appeared in* Sierra, *the magazine of the Sierra Club.*

· ·

OUR COMMON DOMAIN

The present public lands, most of them in the West and Alaska, remain public for a variety of reasons. The national parks are there because they are so spectacular that no country with pride in itself could have resisted preserving them in the public interest. The national forests are there because if we hadn't protected our remaining timberlands, the loggers would have cut them clean from sea to sea. The Bureau of Land Management lands are there because successive resource booms busted and retreated, because the attempt to tame the dry country into family farms withered and died, and because until recently nobody thought they were worth anything—and by the time realization began to dawn, the federal government had had to bite the bullet and accept responsibility for their management. The bureaus that now manage the public lands take a good deal of flak, some of it well deserved. Environmentalists get on them if they don't do their job, stockmen and lumbermen and miners get on them if they do. Local residents resent them as absentee landlords, local interests try to undermine or intimidate them. For a long time the federal government was reluctant to carry out its responsibilities to the public lands. Early in the Depression, Herbert Hoover and his Interior Secretary Ray Lyman Wilbur, got up a plan to give a lot of troublesome land to the states. The states laughed. "Who needs any more desert?" asked Utah's Governor Dern.

But times and minds change. By the mid-1940s the stockmen's associations were finding federal rules too restrictive, and launched legislation aimed at getting Grazing Service and Forest Service range transferred to the states. The states, controlled by the same interests that started the landgrab, would know whom to convey it to. Bernard DeVoto almost singlehandedly broke up that steal, but if he had lived he would have had another chance to fight the same people in the '80s. The Sagebrush Rebellion marched to the same tune, repeated the same slogans, misread law and history, and abused the bureaus in precisely the same way. That bunch will be back, for there are resources in the public lands that tempt the spirit that won the West.

Nevertheless, I see little danger that the million-square-mile public domain, or any part of it, is in serious danger of becoming un-federal. The real danger is that it will be *left* federal, so that the feds can pay the bills for inadequate protection, so that the lands will be open, as they are to some extent now, to be everybody's booty and nobody's responsibility.

The national parks, the best idea we ever had, are the best-protected public lands, though they labor under the excruciating mandate to provide lands for use but without impairment—hard doctrine when annual visitation has passed 300,000,000. In a good many years of association with the parks and the Park Service, I have heard complaints that the system is too small, underfunded, a stepchild on appropriations day; and that as islands in less-protected territory the parks are threatened from without; and that the Park Service and Congress spend too much on maintaining facilities and too little on protecting the land resource; and I have heard exploiters who covet Olympic's timber or Dinosaur's damsites or Yellowstone's geothermal potential. But I never heard anybody, even the parks' enemies, suggest that the parks be sold off or turned over to the states.

How about the Fish and Wildlife Service, whose territory was so enormously enlarged by the Alaska National Interest Lands Conservation Act of 1980? Its lands aren't as safe as the parks, as witness the determination of the last two administrations to drill the Arctic National Wildlife Refuge for oil. President Bush and Interior Secretary Lujan backed off that idea in the wake of the *Exxon Valdez* spill, but they didn't drop it for good. Mr. Lujan has expressed the "hope" that drilling can be revived after the furor has died down. His hope will be realized, too, unless Congress wraps that lovely, pristine, soul-enlarging Artic Eden in the protective blanket of wilderness designation. But it is not likely to be defederalized. Degrading it, breaching its protections, will be enough—under the pretense, in the face of all experience, that we can keep Eden and pump its oil too.

And the Forest Service? Once the most respected of federal bureaus, it has for 30 years been diligently trying to destroy its image as protector of a vital resource. In the view of many environmentalists, including me, it has become the stooge of the timber industry and an enemy of conservation. It talks multiple use and thinks only in board feet. It is not immune to the bureaucratic jealousies that put turf rights ahead of the public good. It resents every chunk of its domain that it loses to the higher protection of the Park Service or the wilderness system. It drags its heels on wilderness study and pushes roads through untouched wilderness in the apparent effort to disqualify it as wilderness and set it up for cutting. It overroads and overcuts, often at a financial loss, at a time when the world should be planting ten trees for every one it cuts down, and perhaps should be cutting no trees at all. Even when it plants, it thinks a tree farm is a forest.

As for the Bureau of Land Management (BLM), it too seems bent on serving the interests it was set up to control. It seems to feel its duty is not to the land, but to the stockmen for whom it drags chains across square miles of piñon, juniper, and sage to clear expensive, subsidized, artificial range for cattle already too numerous on the public lands and dubiously salable in the market. Like the Forest Service with its road-building and below-cost timber sales, the BLM's chaining and fencing subsidize an industry whose expansion, or even continuation at present levels is a threat to the land's health. According to a 1983 report by the Council on Environmental Quality, desertification—the conversion of a viable dryland ecosystem into a barren waste—proceeds faster in the western United States than in Africa. One of the chief villains is overgrazing, which the BLM is supposed to control. It should know, if anyone does, that pastoralism in arid country, unless it learns the two dryland imperatives of sparseness and mobility, is a desert-maker with or without the chaining-off of ground cover.

The land-management bureaus are far from perfect, and many people both inside and outside them would like to see them emancipated from political control and the shortsighted immediate-profit pressures of private interests, and set in their proper purpose of serving the long-term interests of the land. As Marcus Aurelius once remarked, what is bad for the beehive cannot be good for the bee. What destroys the habitat will make itself felt upon people and society.

Nevertheless, imperfect as they are, politicized, corrupted by local pressures and cowed by local threats, the federal bureaus are absolutely essential, the only possible barrier to real disaster in the arid and drought-threatened West where they function. They represent the country's effort, inadequate and faltering, to stand in the way of that good old American spirit of enterprise that according to myth won the West, and according to history half ruined it.

The public domain *must* remain public.

It was not, of course, intended to be. When the American colonies with western land claims relinquished them to the federal government in 1781, in order to get Maryland's agreement to the Articles of Confederation, the public domain thus created was meant to be disposed of, and was. It was granted to individuals and corporations in return for the building of roads, bridges, canals, and railroads; it was sold in wholesale lots to speculators who in turn sold it to settlers. The states between the Alleghenies and the Mississippi were made out of it, and by the outbreak of the Civil War the original "Public Domain" was well on the way to liquidation.

The policy of disposal was not changed by later, enormous additions to the public domain. The Louisiana Purchase took the nation to the crest of the Rockies; the Florida Purchase consolidated the Southeast; the Mexican War and the settlement of the Oregon dispute with Great Britain took us to the Pacific. All of that was federal land. All of it, it was assumed, would someday be in private hands, and the process of disposal would bring in revenue, build up communications, and create the farms and fields that in the booster language of the time are always "smiling," and the towns and cities that are forever "bustling."

Bemused by the vigor of our history, we sometimes forget how much of our territory came by conquest, and how our opportunity and freedom came at the expense of native Americans and through a bullying war with the inheritors of Spain's fading empire. Stolen or not, that free land was the basis of American freedom. It gave opportunity and optimism to settlers; it invigorated the westward movement that is a salient event in our history. The public domain was the very seedbed of the American Dream, and if the country beyond the 98th meridian had been watered instead of dry, the pattern that operated well east of the Missouri would have continued all the way. All the land that now comprises the public domain would be subdivided into private farms, ranches, and town lots. The public domain itself would be no more than a collection of scenic and forested islands— fragments scattered, as Charles Little has said, like jewels in the wake of a fleeing thief.

Instead, forced by aridity, we have retreated from much of the dry country we once tried to occupy. We created an oasis civilization in the West— towns on water, separated by great reaches of arid federal space. As a westerner, I can't think that anything but a blessing. We were prevented by timely land withdrawals and by lack of water from defacing the West completely, and changing it into something man-made. We have had the chance, or the necessity, to preserve space, openness, distance, the natural world, the remnants of a vigorous dryland ecology, and along with that the illusion at least of self-reliance and independence. We have had to learn sparseness and mobility, and though every boom deludes us with the notion of a great permanent increase in the western population, every bust brings us back to sanity, the land reclaims its own, and many of the people get out, leaving the rest the dignity of a tough rareness.

It would not be that way if the federal government had washed its hands of the public domain as Hoover and Wilbur proposed. The days when the public domain was open to mass trespass—when anybody, citizen or not, could do what he wanted with it in a legal and social vacuum—did not last. Thank God and Congress and aridity, not necessarily in that order.

It is customary at political rallies and in faith-promoting history books to celebrate the American Spirit that "won" or "conquered" or "tamed" the West. I do not join in that celebration. The ruthlessness and greed that dominated the frontier seem to me American in the very worst sense of the word. I would rather celebrate another kind of Americanism, quieter, less greedy, more farsighted, more public-spirited.

If we need a celebratory date, we can hardly do better than the day in 1872 when Congress, with enthusiastic public support, voted to create Yellowstone National Park, and thus took the first step toward a permanent public domain in the public interest. We can celebrate the day in 1891 when the General Revision Act opened the door for Presidents Harrison, Cleveland, and Theodore Roosevelt to set aside the "forest reserves" that have become the national forests. (I have just panned the Forest Service, but it must be said that in the beginning it did a marvelous job, and continued doing it until sometime in the 1950s when board feet took over. Fallen or not from its once-high estate, it prevented in the West, until recently, the tree slaughter that desolated Michigan and Wisconsin.) Or we can make a festival of the day in 1903 when Theodore Roosevelt established the first wildlife refuge, to protect Florida birds. Or even that day in 1934 when dust clouds blown all the way from Kansas and Colorado darkened Washington's sky as Congress passed the Taylor Grazing Act that in effect closed the public domain to any further entry.

Those acts, congressional or presidential, were inspired by something higher than American initiative in the raping of resources from a fragile environment. They were the product of a genuine, humane concern with things that make life more than a rat race, a response to natural beauty and grandeur, a solidarity with other creatures, a concern for the rights and pleasures of future generations, a sense of membership in the community of nature and of the family responsibility that derives from that membership.

All the fragile values that our public domain now preserves and protects would have been chewed to bits by the kind of American initiative that Mr. Reagan used to celebrate. Intractable aridity and federal action saved them, and the latter created machinery for their management—and sometimes for the benign hands-off neglect that is better than management.

Relieved from political domination and pressure from local resource interests, the bureaus could provide that management, or that benign neglect. They could learn to operate as an interdependent system rather than as entities competing for territory and appropriations. As for the public that inherits and uses and enjoys the public lands, it might someday learn both respect and responsibility for its priceless inheritance. No other nation on Earth so swiftly wasted its birthright; no other, in time, made such an effort to save what was left. We need to remind ourselves constantly that the land resource itself is what must be saved; that like liberty, democracy, all the freedoms guaranteed by the Constitution, like everything we truly value to the point where we might die for it, the heritage of our public lands is not a fact but a responsibility, an obligation, a task. A pleasure.

The pleasure must be emphasized. I do not mean the pleasure of tearing up the wilderness with ORVs, tote-goats, dune buggies, cross-country motor-bikes, and other implements of the permanently juvenile. Those destructive activities cannot be condoned, and should not be permitted except in special sacrifice areas. I mean the sort of pleasure reported by John Moore, a literate cattle rancher from Miles City, Montana, who took his children out with him onto the range one day and was with them when a hawk labored off with a struggling snake in its talons. "I'm glad they saw that," Moore said. "Not many people anymore see that sort of thing. I'm glad they saw it, and that I was with them when they did."

Moore is struggling to make it, and perhaps failing on 40,000 acres of dry Montana plains. It is not out of the question that his spread will eventually be returned to the public domain, or added to other uneconomic spreads in some larger unit or commons grazed only in alternate years, or every third year, as the buffalo might have grazed. But what matters is that love of the land that he himself feels and that he wants his children to feel. His 40,000 acres, uneconomic or not, are about as close as a private landowner can provide to the public-domain experience—that wide openness, those lilac distances, those wild dust storms, blizzards, thunderstorms, downpours of savage hail, that sense of the largeness, wonder, mystery, danger, of the natural world.

I grew up with that, in and among and around the vast emptinesses of the public domain in the years when we were still trying to domesticate it. I would not trade that experience for any experience of my life. Like Aldo Leopold, who said he would not like to be young again without wild country to be young in, I would feel I had been cheated if I had grown up on concrete and in the tameness of artificial lawns. I grew up knowing the kind of silence that rings in the ears like quinine, knowing the feel of a night wind groping through the spokes of a wagon under which I slept. I grew up hunting, trapping, lamentably killing, the wild creatures of my childhood country; the only good thing about all that is that in killing them I learned to know them, and in knowing them, eventually learned to love them.

Most of all, I was awed, very early and indelibly. I remember winter nights in Saskatchewan when the moon was round as a dollar, the snow dead white, the shadows blue, the stars myriad and icy and distant. The universe was neither hostile nor friendly, simply indifferent to my small, freezing-handed, steam-breathing figure in the white waste. You do not feel that mystery in city canyons or on suburban lawns. What you feel is the specious persuasiveness of human control, human management and organization and rearrangement. You do not know who the ultimate Authority is. Out in the public lands, where the nearest neighbor may be ten miles away and the stars are closer than the nearest town, you do.

That is the best reason I know for keeping the public lands healthy, keeping them as natural as they can be kept, keeping them public. They are indeed the safety valve that they were once called; but the safety valve is there not to keep city mechanics from revolutionary unrest by providing them with land where they can make farms. This safety valve is a safety valve of the spirit, the most precious antidote to the spiritual demoralization that immersion in our industrial culture is likely to breed.

Wilma Elizabeth McDaniel

Wilma Elizabeth McDaniel (1918–   ), called "the biscuits and gravy poet" by writer Eddie Lopez, is a native of Oklahoma who has lived in California's Central Valley throughout her adult life. Her family were sharecroppers who migrated to California in 1936. With little formal training, McDaniel has produced poetry that is both distinct and revealing; critic Cornelia Jessey praised her "dry and burning phraseology" and novelist James D. Houston called her writing "absolutely unique and magical." Collections such as Sister Vayda's Song *(1982),* A Primer for Buford *(1990), and* The Girl from Buttonwillow *(1990) have forged a high reputation for the poet, who is arguably the finest writer produced by the Okie migration. Certainly her verse portraits of rural folks are without peer.*

· ·

BURIED TREASURE

Elbie Hayes ruined his
expensive shoes
squashing around the autumn
desolation
of a sharecrop farm
In Caddo County

Okie boy
turned fifty
searching for anything that
had belonged
to his father
when he was fighting the
Great Depression

Kicked at a lump
behind the caved-in cellar
and uncovered a rusty
Prince Albert tobacco can

Stowed it away
as he would a saint's bones
in his Lincoln Continental
and headed back to Bakersfield

TIMING

Only four years old
Uncle Bailey's twin boys
caught measles and whooping cough

Chub died after five days
with Doc Copley sitting beside
his bed
and him the healthy twin

but Pick
short for toothpick
lay on the cot with his hand
stretched out
on their old collie's head

and lived to die in the
Battle of the Bulge

K-MART SAGE

Dirty Stetson
khaki clothes
cane beside him
on a K-mart bench
I heard the old man say

you know
us men don't have to
look no certain way

like a woman does
or men expect her to look

you take Buck Owens
why he looks just right

if you put that face on
a woman
they'd run her out of town

Hisaye Yamamoto

Hisaye Yamamoto (1924–   ) was born in Redondo Beach. In 1942 she and her family were incarcerated in a so-called internment camp at Poston, Arizona. They would suffer the full tragedy while behind barbed wire in their own country when a brother was killed while fighting for the United States in Italy. Yamamoto, who graduated from Compton College, began writing for the camp newspaper at Poston and continued producing short stories that eventually appeared in prestigious journals such as Partisan Review, Kenyon Review, Arizona Quarterly, Furioso, Carleton Miscellany, *and* Harper's Bazaar. *Her fiction is, according to the editors of* Aiiieeeee!: An Anthology of Asian American Writers *(1974), "remarkable for its range and gut understanding of Japanese America." More than that, her work reflects the complexity and contradictions of post–World War II California. Yamamoto is also acknowledged to be a prose stylist. The story that follows is from* Seventeen Syllables and Other Stories *(1988).*

· ·

YONEKO'S EARTHQUAKE

Yoneko Hosoume became a free-thinker on the night of March 10, 1933, only a few months after her first actual recognition of God. Ten years old at the time, of course she had heard rumors about God all along, long before Marpo came. Her cousins who lived in the city were all Christians, living as they did right next door to a Baptist church exclusively for Japanese people. These city cousins, of whom there were several, had been baptized en masse, and were very proud of their condition. Yoneko was impressed when she heard of this and thereafter was given to referring to them as "my cousins, the Christians." She, too, yearned at times after Christianity, but she realized the absurdity of her whim, seeing that there was no Baptist church for Japanese in the rural community she lived in. Such a church would have been impractical, moreover, since Yoneko, her father, her mother, and her little brother Seigo, were the only Japanese thereabouts. They were the only ones, too, whose agriculture was so diverse as to include blackberries, cabbages, rhubarb, potatoes, cucumbers, onions, and canteloupes. The rest of the countryside there was like one vast orange grove.

Yoneko had entered her cousins' church once, but she could not recall the sacred occasion without mortification. It had been one day when the cousins had taken her and Seigo along with them to Sunday school. The church was a narrow, wooden building mysterious-looking because of its unusual bluish-gray paint and its steeple, but the basement schoolroom inside had been disappointingly ordinary, with desks, a blackboard, and erasers. They had all sung "Let Us Gather at the River" in Japanese. This goes:

> Mamonaku kanata no
> Nagare no soba de
> Tanoshiku ai-masho
> Mata tomodachi to
>
> Mamonaku ai-masho
> Kirei-na, kirei-na kawa de
> Tanoshiku ai-masho
> Mata tomodachi to.

Yoneko had not known the words at all, but always clever in such situations, she had opened her mouth and grimaced nonchalantly to the rhythm. What with everyone else singing at the top of his lungs, no one had noticed that she was not making a peep. Then everyone had sat down again and the man had suggested, "Let us pray." Her cousins and the rest had promptly curled their arms on the desks to make nests for their heads, and Yoneko had done the same. But not Seigo. Because when the room had become so still that one was aware of the breathing, the creaking, and the chittering in the trees outside, Seigo, sitting with her, had suddenly flung his arm around her neck and said with concern, "Sis, what are you crying for? Don't cry." Even the man had laughed and Yoneko had been terribly ashamed that Seigo should thus disclose them to be interlopers. She had pinched him fiercely and he had begun to cry, so she had had to drag him outside, which was a fortunate move, because he had immediately wet his pants. But he had been only three then, so it was not very fair to expect dignity of him.

So it remained for Marpo to bring the word of God to Yoneko, Marpo with the face like brown leather, the thin mustache like Edmund Lowe's, and the rare, breathtaking smile like white gold. Marpo, who was twenty-seven years old, was a Filipino and his last name was lovely, something like Humming Wing, but no one ever ascertained the spelling of it. He ate principally rice, just as though he were Japanese, but he never sat down to the Hosoume table, because he lived in the bunkhouse out by the barn and cooked on his own kerosene stove. Once Yoneko read somewhere that Filipinos trapped wild dogs, starved them for a time, then, feeding them mountains of rice, killed them at the peak of their bloatedness, thus insuring themselves meat ready to roast, stuffing and all, without further ado. This, the book said, was considered a delicacy. Unable to hide her disgust and her fascination, Yoneko went straightway to Marpo and asked, "Marpo, is it true that you eat dogs?", and he, flashing that smile, answered, "Don't be funny, honey!" This caused her no end of amusement, because it was a poem, and she compeletely forgot about the wild dogs.

Well, there seemed to be nothing Marpo could not do. Mr. Hosoume said Marpo was the best hired man he had ever had, and he said this often, because it was an irrefutable fact among Japanese in general that Filipinos in general were an indolent lot. Mr. Hosoume ascribed Marpo's industry to his having grown up in Hawaii, where there is known to be considerable Japanese influence. Marpo had gone to a missionary school there and he owned a Bible given him by one of his teachers. This had black leather covers that gave as easily as cloth, golden edges, and a slim purple ribbon for a marker. He always kept it on the little table by his bunk, which was not a bed with springs but a low, three-plank shelf with a mattress only. On the first page of the book, which was stiff and black, his teacher had written in large swirls of white ink, "As we draw near to God, He will draw near to us."

What, for instance, could Marpo do? Why, it would take an entire, leisurely evening to go into his accomplishments adequately, because there was not only Marpo the Christian and Marpo the best hired man, but Marpo the athlete, Marpo the musician (both instrumental and vocal), Marpo the artist, and Marpo the radio technician:

(1) As an athlete, Marpo owned a special pair of black shoes, equipped with sharp nails on the soles, which he kept in shape with the regular application of neatsfoot oil. Putting these on, he would dash down the dirt road to the highway, a distance of perhaps half a mile, and back again. When he first came to work for the Hosoumes, he undertook this sprint every evening

before he went to get his supper but, as time went on, he referred to these shoes less and less and, in the end, when he left, he had not touched them for months. He also owned a muscle-builder sent him by Charles Atlas which, despite his unassuming size, he could stretch the length of his outspread arms; his teeth gritted then and his whole body became temporarily victim to a jerky vibration. (2) As an artist, Marpo painted larger-than-life water colors of his favorite movie stars, all of whom were women and all of whom were blonde, like Ann Harding and Jean Harlow, and tacked them up on his walls. He also made for Yoneko a folding contraption of wood holding two pencils, one with lead and one without, with which she, too, could obtain double-sized likenesses of any picture she wished. It was a fragile instrument, however, and Seigo splintered it to pieces one day when Yoneko was away at school. He claimed he was only trying to copy Boob McNutt from the funny paper when it failed. (3) As a musician, Marpo owned a violin for which he had paid over one hundred dollars. He kept this in a case whose lining was red velvet, first wrapping it gently in a brilliant red silk scarf. This scarf, which weighed nothing, he tucked under his chin when he played, gathering it up delicately by the center and flicking it once to unfurl it—a gesture Yoneko prized. In addition to this, Marpo was a singer, with a soft tenor which came out in professional quavers and rolled r's when he applied a slight pressure to his Adam's apple with thumb and forefinger. His violin and vocal repertoire consisted of the same numbers, mostly hymns and Irish folk airs. He was especially addicted to "The Rose of Tralee" and the "Londonderry Air." (4) Finally, as a radio technician who had spent two previous winters at a specialists' school in the city, Marpo had put together a bulky table-size radio which brought in equal proportions of static and entertainment. He never got around to building a cabinet to house it and its innards of metal and glass remained public throughout its lifetime. This was just as well, for not a week passed without Marpo's deciding to solder one bit or another. Yoneko and Seigo became a part of the great listening audience with such fidelity that Mr. Hosoume began remarking the fact that they dwelt more with Marpo than with their own parents. He eventually took a serious view of the matter and bought the naked radio from Marpo, who thereupon put away his radio manuals and his soldering iron in the bottom of his steamer trunk and divided more time among his other interests.

However, Marpo's versatility was not revealed, as it is here, in a lump. Yoneko uncovered it fragment by fragment every day, by dint of unabashed questions, explorations among his possessions, and even silent observation, although this last was rare. In fact, she and Seigo visited with Marpo at least once a day and both of them regularly came away amazed with their findings. The most surprising thing was that Marpo was, after all this, a rather shy young man meek to the point of speechlessness in the presence of Mr. and Mrs. Hosoume. With Yoneko and Seigo, he was somewhat more self-confident and at ease.

It is not remembered now just how Yoneko and Marpo came to open their protracted discussion on religion. It is sufficient here to note that Yoneko was an ideal apostle, adoring Jesus, desiring Heaven, and fearing Hell. Once Marpo had enlightened her on these basics, Yoneko never questioned their truth. The questions she put up to him, therefore, sought neither proof of her exegeses nor balm for her doubts, but simply additional color to round out her mental images. For example, who did Marpo suppose was God's favorite movie star? Or, what sound did Jesus' laughter have (it must be like music, she added, nodding sagely, answering herself to her own satisfaction), and did Marpo suppose that God's sense of humor would have appreciated the delicious chant she had learned from friends at school today:

> There ain't no bugs on us,
> There ain't no bugs on us,
> There may be bugs on the rest of you mugs,
> But there ain't no bugs on us?

Or, did Marpo believe Jesus to have been exempt from stinging eyes when he shampooed that long, naturally wavy hair of his?

To shake such faith, there would have been required a most monstrous upheaval of some sort, and it might be said that this is just what happened. For early on the evening of March 10, 1933, a little after five o'clock this was, as Mrs. Hosoume was getting supper, as Marpo was finishing up in the fields alone because Mr. Hosoume had gone to order some chicken fertilizer, and as Yoneko and Seigo were listening to Skippy, a tremendous roar came out of nowhere and the Hosoume house began shuddering violently as though some giant had seized it in his two hands and was giving it a good shaking. Mrs. Hosoume, who remembered similar, although milder experiences, from her childhood in Japan, screamed, "*Jishin, jishin!*" before she ran and grabbed Yoneko and Seigo each by a hand and dragged them outside with her. She took them as far as the middle of the rhubarb patch near the house, and there they all crouched, pressed together, watching the world about them rock and sway. In a few minutes, Marpo, stumbling in from the fields, joined them, saying, "Earthquake, earthquake!", and he gathered them all in his arms, as much to protect them as to support himself.

Mr. Hosoume came home later that evening in a stranger's car, with another stranger driving the family Reo. Pallid, trembling, his eyes wildly staring, he could have been mistaken for a drunkard, except that he was famous as a teetotaler. It seemed that he had been on the way home when the first jolt came, that the old green Reo had been kissed by a broken live wire dangling from a suddenly leaning pole. Mr. Hosoume, knowing that the end had come by electrocution, had begun to writhe and kick and this had been his salvation. His hands had flown from the wheel, the car had swerved into a ditch, freeing itself from the sputtering wire. Later, it was found that he was left permanently inhibited about driving automobiles and permanently incapable of considering electricity with calmness. He spent the larger part of his later life weakly, wandering about the house or fields and lying down frequently to rest because of splitting headaches and sudden dizzy spells.

So it was Marpo who went back into the house as Yoneko screamed, "No, Marpo, no!" and brought out the Hosoumes' kerosene stove, the food, the blankets, while Mr. Hosoume huddled on the ground near his family.

The earth trembled for days afterwards. The Hosoumes and Marpo Humming Wing lived during that time on a natural patch of Bermuda grass between the house and the rhubarb patch, remembering to take three meals a day and retire at night. Marpo ventured inside the house many times despite Yoneko's protests and reported the damage slight: a few dishes had been broken; a gallon jug of mayonnaise had fallen from the top pantry shelf and spattered the kitchen floor with yellow blobs and pieces of glass.

Yoneko was in constant terror during this experience. Immediately on learning what all the commotion was about, she began praying to God to end this violence. She entreated God, flattered Him, wheedled Him, commanded Him, but He did not listen to her at all—inexorably, the earth went on rumbling. After three solid hours of silent, desperate prayer, without any results whatsoever, Yoneko began to suspect that God was either powerless, callous, downright cruel, or nonexistent. In the murky night, under a strange moon wearing a pale ring of light, she decided upon the last as the most plausible theory. "Ha," was one of the things she said tremulously to Marpo, when she was not begging him to stay out of the house, "you and your God!"

The others soon oriented themselves to the catastrophe with philosophy, saying how fortunate they were to live in the country where the peril was less than in the city and going so far as to regard the period as a sort of vacation from work, with their enforced alfresco existence a sort of camping trip. They tried to bring Yoneko to partake of this pleasant outlook, but she, shivering with each new quiver, looked on them as dreamers who refused to see things as they really were. Indeed, Yoneko's reaction was so notable that the Hosoume household thereafter spoke of the event as "Yoneko's earthquake."

After the earth subsided and the mayonnaise was mopped off the kitchen floor, life returned to normal, except that Mr. Hosoume stayed at home most of the time. Sometimes, if he had a relatively painless day, he would have supper on the stove when Mrs. Hosoume came in from the fields. Mrs. Hosoume and Marpo did all the field labor now, except on certain overwhelming days when several Mexicans were hired to assist them. Marpo did most of the driving, too, and it was now he and Mrs. Hosoume who went into town on the weekly trip for groceries. In fact, Marpo became indispensable and both Mr. and Mrs. Hosoume often told each other how grateful they were for Marpo.

When summer vacation began and Yoneko stayed at home, too, she found the new arrangement rather inconvenient. Her father's presence cramped her style: for instance, once when her friends came over and it was decided to make fudge, he would not permit them, saying fudge used too much sugar and that sugar was not a plaything; once when they were playing paper dolls, he came along and stuck his finger up his nose and pretended he was going to rub some snot off onto the dolls. Things like that. So, on some days, she was very much annoyed with her father.

Therefore when her mother came home breathless from the fields one day and pushed a ring at her, a gold-colored ring with a tiny glasslike stone in it, saying, "Look, Yoneko, I'm going to give you this ring. If your father asks where you got it, say you found it on the street." Yoneko was perplexed but delighted both by the unexpected gift and the chance to have some secret revenge on her father, and she said, certainly, she was willing to comply with her mother's request. Her mother went back to the fields then and Yoneko put the pretty ring on her middle finger, taking up the loose space with a bit of newspaper. It was similar to the rings found occasionally in boxes of Crackerjack, except that it appeared a bit more substantial.

Mr. Hosoume never asked about the ring; in fact, he never noticed she was wearing one. Yoneko thought he was about to, once, but he only reproved her for the flamingo nail polish she was wearing, which she had applied from a vial brought over by Yvonne Fournier, the French girl two orange groves away. "You look like a Filipino," Mr. Hosoume said sternly, for it was another irrefutable fact among Japanese in general that Filipinos in general were a gaudy lot. Mrs. Hosoume immediately came to her defense, saying that in Japan, if she remembered correctly, young girls did the same thing. In fact, she remembered having gone to elaborate lengths to tint her fingernails: she used to gather, she said, the petals of the red *tsubobana* or the purple *kogane* (which grows on the underside of stones), grind them well, mix them with some alum powder, then cook the mixture and leave it to stand overnight in an envelope of either persimmon or sugar potato leaves (both very strong leaves). The second night, just before going to bed, she used to obtain threads by ripping a palm leaf (because real thread was dear) and tightly bind the paste to her fingernails under shields of persimmon or sugar potato leaves. She would be helpless for the night, the fingertips bound so well that they were alternately numb or aching, but she would grit her teeth and tell herself that the discomfort indicated the success of the operation. In the morning, finally releasing her fingers, she would find the nails shining with a translucent red-orange color.

Yoneko was fascinated, because she usually thought of her parents as having been adults all their lives. She thought that her mother must have been a beautiful child, with or without bright fingernails, because, though surely past thirty, she was even yet a beautiful person. When she herself was younger, she remembered, she had at times been so struck with her mother's appearance that she had dropped to her knees and mutely clasped her mother's legs in her arms. She had left off this habit as she learned to control her emotions, because at such times her mother had usually walked away, saying, "My, what a clinging child you are. You've got to learn to be a little more independent." She also remembered she had once heard someone comparing her mother to "a dewy, half-opened rosebud."

Mr. Hosoume, however, was irritated. "That's no excuse for Yoneko to begin using paint on her fingernails," he said. "She's only ten."

"Her Japanese age is eleven, and we weren't much older," Mrs. Hosoume said.

"Look," Mr. Hosoume said, "if you're going to contradict every piece of advice I give the children, they'll end up disobeying us both and doing what they very well please. Just because I'm ill just now is no reason for them to start being disrespectful."

"When have I ever contradicted you before?" Mrs. Hosoume said.

"Countless times," Mr. Hosoume said.

"Name one instance," Mrs. Hosoume said.

Certainly there had been times, but Mr. Hosoume could not happen to mention the one requested instance on the spot and he became quite angry. "That's quite enough of your insolence," he said. Since he was speaking in Japanese, his exact accusation was that she was *nama-iki,* which is a shade more revolting than being merely insolent.

"*Nama-iki, nama-iki?*" said Mrs. Hosoume. "How dare you? I'll not have anyone calling me *nama-iki!*"

At that, Mr. Hosoume went up to where his wife was ironing and slapped her smartly on the face. It was the first time he had ever laid hands on her. Mrs. Hosoume was immobile for an instant, but she resumed her ironing as though nothing had happened, although she glanced over at Marpo, who happened to be in the room reading a newspaper. Yoneko and Seigo forgot they were listening to the radio and stared at their parents, thunderstruck.

"Hit me again," said Mrs. Hosoume quietly, as she ironed. "Hit me all you wish."

Mr. Hosoume was apparently about to, but Marpo stepped up and put his hand on Mr. Hosoume's shoulder. "The children are here," said Marpo, "the children."

"Mind your own business," said Mr. Hosoume in broken English. "Get out of here!"

Marpo left, and that was about all. Mrs. Hosoume went on ironing, Yoneko and Seigo turned back to the radio, and Mr. Hosoume muttered that Marpo was beginning to forget his place. Now that he thought of it, he said, Marpo had been increasingly impudent towards him since his illness. He said just because he was temporarily an invalid was no reason for Marpo to start being disrespectful. He added that Marpo had better watch his step or that he might find himself jobless one of these fine days.

And something of the sort must have happened. Marpo was here one day and gone the next, without even saying good-bye to Yoneko and Seigo. That was also the day the Hosoume family went to the city on a weekday afternoon, which was most unusual. Mr. Hosoume, who now avoided driving as much as possible, handled the cumbersome Reo as though it were a nervous stallion, sitting on the edge of the seat and hugging the steering wheel. He drove very fast and about halfway to the city struck a beautiful collie which had dashed out barking from someone's yard. The car jerked with the impact, but Mr. Hosoume drove right on and Yoneko, wanting suddenly to vomit, looked back and saw the collie lying very still at the side of the road.

When they arrived at the Japanese hospital, which was their destination, Mr. Hosoume cautioned Yoneko and Seigo to be exemplary children and wait patiently in the car. It seemed hours before he and Mrs. Hosoume returned, she walking with very small, slow steps and he assisting her. When Mrs. Hosoume got in the car, she leaned back and closed her eyes. Yoneko inquired as to the source of her distress, for she was obviously in pain, but she only answered that she was feeling a little under the weather and that the doctor had administered some necessarily astringent treatment. At that, Mr. Hosoume turned around and advised Yoneko and Seigo that they must tell no one of coming to the city on a weekday afternoon, absolutely no one, and Yoneko and Seigo readily assented. On the way home, they passed the place of the encounter with the collie, and Yoneko looked up and down the stretch of road but the dog was nowhere to be seen.

Not long after that, the Hosoumes got a new hired hand, an old Japanese man who wore his gray hair in a military cut and who, unlike Marpo, had no particular interests outside working, eating, sleeping, and playing an occasional game of *goh* with Mr. Hosoume. Before he came Yoneko and Seigo played sometimes in the empty bunkhouse and recalled Marpo's various charms together. Privately, Yoneko was wounded more than she would admit even to herself that Marpo should have subjected her to such an abrupt desertion. Whenever her indignation became too great to endure gracefully, she would console herself by telling Seigo that, after all, Marpo was a mere Filipino, an eater of wild dogs.

Seigo never knew about the disappointing new hired man, because he suddenly died in the night. He and Yoneko had spent the hot morning in the nearest orange grove, she driving him to distraction by repeating certain words he could not bear to hear: she had called him Serge, a name she had read somewhere, instead of Seigo; and she had chanted off the name of the tires they were rolling around like hoops as Goodrich Silver-TO-town, Goodrich Silver-TO-town, instead of Goodrich Silvertown. This had enraged him, and he had chased her around the trees most of the morning. Finally she had taunted him from several trees away by singing "You're a

Yellow-streaked Coward," which was one of several small songs she had composed. Seigo had suddenly grinned and shouted, "Sure!", and walked off, leaving her, as he intended, with a sense of emptiness. In the afternoon, they had perspired and followed the potato-digging machine and the Mexican workers, both hired for the day, around the field, delighting in unearthing marblesized, smooth-skinned potatoes that both the machine and the men had missed. Then, in the middle of the night, Seigo began crying, complaining of a stomach ache. Mrs. Hosoume felt his head and sent her husband for the doctor, who smiled and said Seigo would be fine in the morning. He said it was doubtless the combination of green oranges, raw potatoes, and the July heat. But as soon as the doctor left, Seigo fell into a coma and a drop of red blood stood out on his underlip, where he had evidently bit it. Mr. Hosoume again fetched the doctor, who was this time very grave and wagged his head, saying several times, "It looks very bad." So Seigo died at the age of five.

Mrs. Hosoume was inconsolable and had swollen eyes in the morning for weeks afterwards. She now insisted on visiting the city relatives each Sunday, so that she could attend church services with them. One Sunday, she stood up and accepted Christ. It was through accompanying her mother to many of these services that Yoneko finally learned the Japanese words to "Let Us Gather at the River." Mrs. Hosoume also did not seem interested in discussing anything but God and Seigo. She was especially fond of reminding visitors how adorable Seigo had been as an infant, how she had been unable to refrain from dressing him as a little girl and fixing his hair in bangs until he was two. Mr. Hosoume was very gentle with her and when Yoneko accidentally caused her to giggle once, he nodded and said, "Yes, that's right, Yoneko, we must make your mother laugh and forget about Seigo." Yoneko herself did not think about Seigo at all. Whenever the thought of Seigo crossed her mind, she instantly began composing a new song, and this worked very well.

One evening, when the new hired man had been with them a while, Yoneko was helping her mother with the dishes when she found herself being examined with such peculiarly intent eyes that, with a start of guilt, she began searching in her mind for a possible crime she had lately committed. But Mrs. Hosoume only said, "Never kill a person, Yoneko, because if you do, God will take from you someone you love."

"Oh, that," said Yoneko quickly, "I don't believe in that, I don't believe in God." And her words tumbling pell-mell over one another, she went on eagerly to explain a few of her reasons why. If she neglected to mention the test she had given God during the earthquake, it was probably because she was a little upset. She had believed for a moment that her mother was going to ask about the ring (which, alas, she had lost already, somewhere in the flumes along the canteloupe patch).

Gerald Locklin

Gerald Locklin (1941–   ), raised in New York State, has lived in Southern California since the early 1960s and is a fixture in the literary scene there. He is, in a sense, a prototypical migrant to a state that is full of migrants, explaining, "I became a different writer, a different person, after moving here." He is among the most widely published poets of his generation and is a noted teacher of creative writing at California State University, Long Beach. Charles Bukowski is a fan of Locklin's writing: asked to explain why, Bukowski says simply, "He swings from the hip." Locklin's verse, frequently autobiographical, is also frequently brilliant, as the examples which follow illustrate. He has also had novels and stories published that explore the contemporary southland.

. . . .

WEIGHTLIFTING

twice a week i meet my friend
in his garage, which we have turned into a gym
we stretch, hang, do our hated sit-ups, jog a mile
along the ashen alamitos bay—then hit the weights.

we've rigged a makeshift bench-press.
this is our special love.
we're straining at three hundred twenty pounds, which is all
our bowed, beleaguered, rusting bar will take.

when we were young, involved in sports, with indefatigable lungs,
we couldn't bench the half of that.
of course we weighed a lot less also, but it's nice,
in one's thirties, to be able to do *something* better.

we do not rush our workouts.
there's time to speak of nixon, king lear, women.
it is the best part of the week. we've something there,
in our ramshackle gym, that many do not have.

THE BEST YEAR OF HER LIFE

When my two-year-old daughter
sees someone come through the door
whom she loves, and hasn't seen for a while,
and has been anticipating,

she literally shrieks with joy.

I have to go into the other room
so that no one will notice the tears in my eyes.

Later, after putting my daughter to bed,
I say to my wife,
"She will never be this happy again,"
and my wife gets angry and snaps,
"Don't you dare communicate your negativism to her!"

And, of course, I won't, if I can possibly help it,

and, of course I fully expect her

to have much joy in her life,
and, of course, I hope to be able to contribute to that joy—
I hope that she'll always
be happy to see me come through the door—

but why kid ourselves—she, like every child,
has a life of great suffering ahead of her,
and while joy will not go out of her life,

she will one of these days cease to actually,
literally, jump and shriek for joy.

HAPPY HOUR

i like to call my girl at five on thursdays
when she gets home from work
and meet her for the happy hour
at seaport village on the marina in seal beach.

our first stop is the steak house
for cut-rate harvey wallbangers, a primary
source of vitamin c. then, at the jolly roger,
double gin-and-tonics for a buck, and each half-hour

they roll out a steaming buffet
of chicken, shrimp, and cheeses.
later we wash down enchiladas at hungry joe's
with a couple of volcanic margaritas.

it's a pleasant ritual,
reminiscent of the free lunches of the depression,
and of cheap pub fare, but infinitely more edible
than many a sheep-dip pie.

meanwhile the sailboats glide as wistfully
as forfeited ambitions,
and the waitresses move in-and-out
of onanistic half-worlds.

my students scorn the seaport village
as a capitalistic scheme, which it is,
and as an apotheosis of plastic,
which of course it is . . .

but was there any chance it would remain
a stolid carapace for indigent fishermen,
or that small businesses would lease space for arts
and crafts authentic as the vanished sea bass?

i wishy-washily will make the best of things:
tanqueray martinis, yachts beyond my means,
and women that may not be.
i will be happy at the happy hour.

Luis Valdez

Luis Valdez (1940–) was born in Delano and graduated from San Jose State College before joining the United Farm Workers' strike in his native Kern County in the 1960s. There he organized El Teatro Campesino *(the Farmworkers' Theater) and employed drama as a weapon against recalcitrant growers. Eventually he emerged as a leader in innovative theater; his full-length drama* Zoot Suit *(1978) became recognized as one of the state's finest, and his screenplay for the movie* La Bamba *(1988) was an award winner. Not only is he one of California's first distinguished dramatists, he is also America's first major playwright of Mexican extraction. Valdez and his* teatro *are now located in San Juan Bautista.* Soldado Razo *was first presented by El Teatro Campesino on April 3, 1971, in Fresno at the Chicano (Vietnam War) Moratorium.*

• •

SOLDADO RAZO

MUERTE (*enters singing*): Me voy de soldado razo, voy ingresar a las filas . . . con los valientes muchachos que dejan madres queridas, que dejan novias llorando, llorando, llorando su despedida. Ajua! Pos que a toda madre para mi que hay guerra. Quihubo pues, Raza. Yo soy la muerte. Que nuevas, no? Bueno, no se escamen porque I didn't come to take anybody away, I came to tell you a story. Simon, the story of the Soldado Razo. Maybe you knew him, eh? He was killed not too long ago in Vietnam.

JOHNNY *enters adjusting his uniform.*

MUERTE: This is Johnny, El Soldado Razo. He's leaving for Vietnam in the morning, but tonight—bueno, tonight he's going to enjoy himself, verdad? Look at his face. Know what he's thinking? He's thinking (JOHNNY *moves his lips.*) "Ahora si, I'm a man!"

MAMA *enters.*

MUERTE: This is his jefita. Pobrecita. She's worried about her son, como todas las madres. "Bendito sea dios," she's thinking: (MAMA *moves mouth.*) "Ojala y no le pase nada a mijo." (MAMA *touches* JOHNNY *on the shoulder.*)

JOHNNY: Ya esta la cena, jefa?

MAMA: Si, hijo, ya merito. Pero porque te vestiste asi? No te vas hasta mañana.

JOHNNY: Pos ya sabe. Va venir Cecilia y todo.

MAMA: Ay, que mijo. Me traes mil novias pero nunca te casas.

JOHNNY: Pos a ver cuando le caigo con un surprise, 'ama. (*He kisses her forehead. Embraces her.*)

MUERTE: Orale! Que picture de tenderness, no? Pero watcha la jefita. Listen to what she's thinking. "Ahora si, mijo es hombre. Se mira tan simpatico en ese uniforme."

JOHNNY: Bueno, jefita, it's getting late. Al rato vuelvo con Cecilia, eh?

MAMA: Si, hijo, vuelve pronto. (*He leaves.*) Dios te cuide, corazon de tu madre.

JOHNNY *re-enters and begins to walk.*

MUERTE: Out in the street, Johnny begins to think about his family, his girl, his barrio, his life.

JOHNNY: Chihuahua, pobre jefita. Mañana va ser muy duro para ella. Tambien pa' mi. It was pretty hard when I went to bootcamp, pero ahora? Vietnam! 'To cabron, man. El jefito tabien. I'm not going to be here to help him out. No me estaba haciendo rico en el jale, but it was something. Una livianda si quiera. El carnalillo no puede trabajar todavia porque esta en la escuela. I hope he stays there tambien. And finishes. A mi nunca me cayo ese jale, but I know the carnalillo digs it. He's smart too—maybe he'll even go to college. One of us has got to make it in this life. Me—I guess I'll just get married con Cecilia and have a bola de chavalos. I remember when I first saw her at the Rainbow. I couldn't even dance with her porque me habia hechado mis birrias. The next week was perty good, though. Desde entonces. How long ago was that? June . . . no, Julio. Four months. Ahora me quiero ranar con ella. Her parents don't like me, I know. They think I'm a vago. Maybe they'll feel different when I come back from Nam. Simon, el War Veteran! Maybe I'll get wounded and come back con un chingatal de medals. I wonder how the vatos around here are going to think about that? Pinche barrio—I've lived here all my life. Now I'm going to Vietnam. (*Taps and drum.*) Va estar cabron, man. I might even get killed. If I do, they'll bring me back here in a box, covered with the flag . . . military funeral like they gave Pete Gomez . . . everybody crying . . . la jefita . . . (*He stops.*) What the fuck am I thinking, man? Pinche loco! (*He freezes.*)

MUERTE: Loco pero no pendejo, eh? He knew the kind of funeral he wanted and he got it. Military coffin, muchas flores, American flag, mujeres llorando, and a trumpet playing taps with a rifle salute at the end. Or was it goodbye? No hay pedo, you know what I mean. It was first class all the way. Orale pues, next scene.

JOHNNY *goes on to* CECILIA's *and exits.*

MUERTE: Back en la casa, his jefito is just getting home.

EL PAPA *enters.*

PAPA: Vieja? Ya vine. Ya esta la cena?

MAMA *enters.*

MAMA: Si, viejo. Esperate nomas que llegue Juan. Que compraste?
PAPA: Un sixpack de Coors.
MAMA: Cerveza?
PAPA: Pues porque no? Mira—si esta es la ultima noche de mijo, que.
MAMA: Como que ultima noche? No hables asi, hombre.
PAPA: Digo que la ultima noche en la casa, mujer. Tu me comrendes—hip.
MAMA: Andas tomado, verdad?
PAPA: Y si ando, que te importa? Nomas me heche unas cuantas eladas con mi compadre y es todo. Pos mira . . . ? Ahora si pario la burra seca hombre. Mijo se va a la guerra, y no quieres que tome. Si hay que celebrar, mujer!
MAMA: Celebrar que?
PAPA: Que mijo ya es hombre! Y bien macho el cabron. Asi es que no me alegues. Traime de que cenar.
MAMA: Esperate que venga Juan.
PAPA: Donde esta? No esta aqui? Que salio de vago el desgraciado? Juan? Juan?
MAMA: Te digo que se fue a traer a Cecilia, que va cenar con nosotros. Y por

favor no hables tantas cochinadas, hombre. Que dira la muchacha si te oye hablar asi?

PAPA: Con una jodia, mujer! Pos de quien es esta pinche casa? No soy yo el que paga la renta? El que compra la comida? No me hagas enojar, eh? O te va muy mal. No le hace que ya tengas un hijo de soldado.

MAMA: Por favor, viejo. Te lo pido por tu hijo, eh? Calmate. (She exits.)

PAPA: Ba? Calmate! Nomas asi quiere que me calme. Y quien me va callar el hocico? Mijo el soldado? Mijo . . .

MUERTE: The jefito's thoughts are racing back a dozen years to a warm afternoon in July. Johnny, eight years old, is running toward him between the vines, shouting: " 'Apaaa, ya pizque 20 tablas, papaaa."

PAPA: Huh. Veinte tablas. Mocoso.

EL HERMANO *enters*.

HERMANO: 'Apa, is Johnny here?

MUERTE: This is Johnny's carnalito.

PAPA: Y tu de donde vienes?

HERMANO: Alla andaba en Polo's house. Tiene un motor scooter nuevo.

PAPA: Tu nomas te la llevas jugando, no?

HERMANO: Yo no hise nada.

PAPA: No me resongues.

HERMANO (*shrugs*): Ya vamos a cenar?

PAPA: Yo no se. Ve preguntale a tu madre.

HERMANO *exits*.

MUERTE: Looking at his younger son, the jefito se pone a pensar de el. His thoughts spin around in the usual hopeless cycle of defeat, undercut by more defeat.

PAPA: Ese muchacho ya debe de andar trabajando. Ya tiene su catorce años cumplidos. Yo no se porque la ley las obliga que vayan a la escuela hasta lo diez y seis. Alcabo no va llegar a ser nada. Mejor que se meta a trabajar conmigo pa' que ayude a la familia.

MUERTE: Simon, se sale de la escuela y en three or four years, I take him the way I took Johnny, although not in Vietnam but in Latin America, where he will be sent to defend American investments. Que loco, no Raza?

JOHNNY *returns with* CECILIA.

JOHNNY: Buenas noches, 'apa.

PAPA: Hijo! Buenas noches. Ay pos mira, ya andas de soldado otra vez?

JOHNNY: Traje a Cecilia a cenar con nosotros.

PAPA: Pos que entre, que entre.

CECILIA: Muchas gracias.

PAPA: Que bien se mira mijo, verdad?

CECILIA: Si, señor.

PAPA: Pos si. Ya se nos va de soldado razo. (*Pause.*) Bueno, vamos a ver . . . uh, hijo, no gustas una cervecita?!

JOHNNY: Si, señor, pero no hay una silla primero? Para Cecilia?

PAPA: Como no? Si aqui tenemos de todo. Dejame traer. Vieja? Ya llego la visita! (*He exits.*)

JOHNNY: How you doing?

CECILIA: Okay. Te quiero.

MUERTE: This, of course, is Johnny's novia. Fine, eh? Too bad he'll never get to marry her. Oh, he proposed tonight y todo—and she accepted, but she doesn't know what's ahead. Listen to what she's thinking. (CECILIA *moves her mouth.*) "When we get married I hope Johnny still has his uniform. We'd look so good together. Me in a wedding gown and him like that. Chihuahua, I wish we were getting married tomorrow!"

JOHNNY: Que estas pensando?

CECILIA: Nothing.

JOHNNY: Come on.

CECILIA: Really.

JOHNNY: Chale, I saw your eyes. Now come on, dime que estabas pensando.

CECILIA: It was nothing.

JOHNNY: Are you scared?

CECILIA: About what?

JOHNNY: My going to Vietnam.

CECILIA: No! I mean . . . yes, in a way, but I wasn't thinking that.

JOHNNY: What was it?

CECILIA (*pause*): I was thinking I wish the boda was tomorrow.

JOHNNY: Really?

CECILIA: Yes.

JOHNNY: Sabes que? I wish it was too. (*He embraces her.*)

MUERTE: And, of course, now he's thinking too. But it's not what she was thinking. Que Raza!

EL PAPA *and the* HERMANO *enter with four chairs.*

PAPA: Aqui vienen las sillas. No que no? (*To the* HERMANO): A ver tu, aydame a mover la mesa, andale.

JOHNNY: Necesita ayuda 'apa?

PAPA: No, hijo, yo y tu hermano la movemos. (*He and the* HERMANO *move imaginary table into place.*) Ahi 'ta. Y dice tu 'ama que ya se vayan sentando porque ya esta la cena. Hiso tamales, fijate!

JOHNNY: Tamales?

HERMANO: They're Taco Bell, eeehh.

PAPA: Tu callate el hocico! Mira . . . no le haga caso, Cecilia, este cabron, uh, este guerco siempre anda con sus babozadas, uh, tonterias. Sientense.

MAMA (*entering with imaginary bowl*): Aqui vienen los tamales! Cuidado porque la olla esta caliente, eh? Oh, Cecilia, buenas noches, hija.

CECILIA: Buenas noches, señora. Le puedo aydar en algo?

MAMA: No, no, ya esta todo listo. Sientese por favor.

JOHNNY: 'Ama, how come you made tamales?

MAMA: Pos ya se como te gustan tanto, hijo.

MUERTE: A thought flashes across Johnny's mind: "Too much, man. I should go to war every day." Over on this side of the table, the carnalillo is thinking: "What's so hot about going to war—tamales?"

HERMANO: I like tamales.

PAPA: Quien te dijo que abrieras la boca? Gustas una cerveza, hijo?

JOHNNY (*nods*): Gracias, jefe.

PAPA: Y Ud., Cecilia?

CECILIA (*surprised*): No, señor, uh, gracias.

MAMA: Juan, hombre, no seas tan imprudente. Cecilia no tiene la edad pa' tomar. Que diran sus padres? Hice Kool-Aid, hija, ahorita traigo el pichel. (*She exits.*)

MUERTE: You know what's going through the carnalito's mind? He is thinking: "He offered her a beer! She was barely in the eighth grade three years ago. When I'm seventeen I'm going to join the service and get bien pedo."

PAPA: Cuantos años tienes, Cecilia?

CECILIA: Diez y ocho.

MUERTE: She lied, of course.

PAPA: Oh pos que caray, si ya eres mujer! Andale, hijo, no dejes que se te escape.

JOHNNY: I'm not.

MAMA (*re-entering*): Aqui esta el Kool-Aid y los frijoles.

JOHNNY: 'Ama, I got an announcement to make. Se quiere sentar por favor?

MAMA: Que es?

PAPA (*to* HERMANO): Dale tu silla a tu mama.

HERMANO: What about my tamale?

MAMA: Dejalo que cene.

PAPA (*to* HERMANO): Quitate!

JOHNNY: Sientese, 'ama.

MAMA: Que es hijo? (*She sits down.*)

MUERTE: Funny little games que juega la gente, no? The mother asks, but she already knows what her son is going to say. So does the father. And even the little brother. They are all thinking: "He is going to say: 'Yo y Cecilia nos vamos a casar!' "

JOHNNY: Yo y Cecilia nos vamos a casar!

MAMA: Ay, mijo!

PAPA: No, hombre!

HERMANO: Really?

MAMA: Cuando, hijo?

JOHNNY: When I get back from Vietnam.

MUERTE: Suddenly a thought is crossing everybody's mind: *y si no regresa?* But they shove it aside.

MAMA: Ay, mija! (*She hugs* CECILIA.)

PAPA: Felicitaciones, hijo. (*He hugs* JOHNNY.)

MAMA (*hugging* JOHNNY): Hijo de mi alma! (*She cries.*)

JOHNNY: Eh, jefa, wait a minute. Save that for tomorrow. Ya pues, 'ama.

PAPA: Hija. (*He hugs* CECILIA *properly.*)

HERMANO: Heh, Johnny, why don't I go to Vietnam and you stay here for the wedding? I'm not afraid to die.

MAMA: Porque dices eso, muchacho?

HERMANO: Se me salio.

PAPA: Ya se te salio mucho, no crees?

HERMANO: I didn't mean it! (HERMANO *exits.*)

JOHNNY: It was an accident, 'apa.

MAMA: Si pues, fue accidente. Por favor, viejito, vamos a cenar en paz, eh? Mañana se va Juan.

MUERTE: The rest of the cena pasa sin ningun problema. They discuss the wedding, the tamales, and the weather. Then it's time to go to the party.

PAPA: Que va haber party?

JOHNNY: A small dance nomas, alla en la casa del Sapo.

MAMA: A cual Sapo, hijo?

JOHNNY: Sapo, mi amigo.

PAPA: No te vayas a enborrachar, eh?

JOHNNY: Chale, jefe, va ir la Cecilia conmigo.

PAPA: Ya le pediste permiso a sus padres?

JOHNNY: Si señor. She's got to be home by eleven.

PAPA: Esta bien. (JOHNNY *and* CECILIA *rise.*)

CECILIA: Gracias por la cena, señora.

MAMA: Ay, hija, no hay de que.

CECILIA: The tamales were really good.

JOHNNY: Si,'ama, estuvieron a todo dar.

MAMA: Si, hijo? Te gustaron?

JOHNNY: They were great. (*He hugs her.*) Gracias, eh?

MAMA: Como que gracias? Eres mijo. Vayanse pues, que se hace tarde.

PAPA: No quieres usar la troquita, hijo?

JOHNNY: No, gracias, 'pa. Ya traigo el carro de Cecilia.

CECILIA: Not mine. My parents' car. They loaned it to us for the dance.

PAPA: Parece que dejaste buena impresion, eh?

CECILIA: He sure did. They say he's more responsible now that he's in the service.

MUERTE (*to audience*): Did you hear that? Listen to her again.

CECILIA (*repeats sentence, exactly as before*): They say he's more responsible now that he's in the service.

MUERTE: Asi me gusta!

PAPA: Que bueno. Entonces nomas nos queda ir a pedirles la mano de Cecilia, no vieja?

MAMA: Si dios quiere.

JOHNNY: We're going pues.

CECILIA: Buenas noches.

PAPA: Buenas noches, hija.

MAMA: Cuidado en el camino, hijos.

JOHNNY: Don't worry, jefa. Be back later.

CECILIA: Bye!

JOHNNY *and* CECILIA *exit. The* MAMA *stands at the door.*

PAPA (*sitting down again*): Pues, si, viejita, ya se nos hiso hombre el Juanito. Que pronto pasan los años, no?

MUERTE: The jefito is thinking about the Korean War. Johnny was born about that time. He wishes he had some advice, some consejos, to pass on to him about la guerra. But he never went to Korea. The draft skipped him, and somehow, he never got around to enlisting. (MAMA *turns around.*)

MAMA (*sees* LA MUERTE): Valgame dios!

MUERTE (*ducking down*): Shit! I think she saw me. (MUERTE *exits.*)

PAPA: Que te pasa? (MAMA *is standing frozen looking toward the spot where* MUERTE *was standing.*) Contestame pues, que traes? (*Pause.*) Oyes, pos si no estoy aqui pintado. Hablame!

MAMA (*solemnly*): Acabo de ver a la Muerte.

PAPA: Muerte? Estas loca.

MAMA: Es cierto. Salio Juan ahorita, voltie y alli estaba La Muerte parada— sonriendose! (PAPA *moves away from the spot inadvertently.*) Ave Maria Purisima, si acaso le pasa algo a Juan.

PAPA: Ya callate el hocico! Que no vez que es mala suerte?

They exit. MUERTE *re-enters.*

MUERTE: The next day, Johnny goes to the Greyhound Bus Depot. His mother, his father, and his novia go with him to say goodbye. The bus depot is full of soldiers and sailors and old men. Here and there, a wino is passed out on the benches. Then there's the announcements: THE LOS ANGELES BUS IS NOW RECEIVING PASSENGERS AT GATE TWO, FOR KINGSBURG, TULARE, DELANO, BAKERSFIELD, AND LOS ANGELES, CONNECTIONS IN LA FOR POINTS EAST AND SOUTH.

JOHNNY, PAPA, MAMA, *and* CECILIA *enter.* CECILIA *clings on to* JOHNNY.

PAPA: Ya hace muchos años que no me he pasiado en el esteche.

MAMA: Tienes tu tiquete, hijo?

JOHNNY: Ay no, I got to buy it.

CECILIA: I'll go with you.

PAPA: Traes dinero, hijo?

JOHNNY: Si 'apa, I got it.

JOHNNY *and* CECILIA *walk over to* LA MUERTE.

JOHNNY: One ticket, please.
MUERTE: Where to?
JOHNNY: Vietnam. I mean, Oakland.
MUERTE: Round trip or one way?
JOHNNY: One way.
MUERTE: Right. One way.

JOHNNY *gets his ticket and he and* CECILIA *start back toward his parents.* JOHNNY *stops abruptly and glances back at* LA MUERTE, *who has already shifted positions.*

CECILIA: What's wrong?
JOHNNY: Nothing. (*They join the parents.*)
MUERTE: For a half an hour then, they exchange small talk and trivialities, repeating some of the things that have been said several times before. Cecilia promises Johnny she will be true to him and wait until he returns. Then it's time to go: THE OAKLAND-VIETNAM EXPRESS IS NOW RECEIVING PASSENGERS AT GATE NUMBER FOUR. ALL ABOARD PLEASE.
JOHNNY: That's my bus.
MAMA: Ay, mijito.
PAPA: Cuidate mucho pues, eh hijo?
JOHNNY: No se apure, jefe.
CECILIA: I love you, Johnny. (*She embraces him.*)
MUERTE: THE OAKLAND-VIETNAM EXPRESS IS IN THE FINAL BOARDING STAGES. PASSENGERS WITH TICKETS, ALL ABOARD PLEASE. AND THANKS FOR GOING GREYHOUND.
JOHNNY: Ya me voy!

Embraces all around, weeping, last goodbyes, etc. JOHNNY *exits. Then parents exit.* MAMA *and* CECILIA *are crying.*

MUERTE (*sings*): Adios, Adios
           Lucero de mis noches
           Dijo unsoldado al pie de una ventana
           Me voy, me voy
           Pero no llores, angel mia
           Que volvere mañana. . . .

So Johnny left for Vietnam, never to return. He didn't want to go and yet he did. It never crossed his mind to refuse. How can he refuse the gobierno de los estados unidos? How could he refuse his family? Besides, who wants to go to prison? And there was always the chance he'd come back alive . . . wounded maybe, but alive. So he took a chance—and lost. But before he died he saw many things in Vietnam; he had his eyes opened. He wrote his mother about them.

JOHNNY *and* LA MAMA *enter at opposite sides of the stage.* JOHNNY *is in full battle gear.*

JOHNNY: Dear jefita.

MAMA: Querido hijo.

JOHNNY: I am writing this letter.

MAMA: Recibi tu carta.

JOHNNY: To tell you I'm okay.

MAMA: Y doy gracias a los cielos que estas bien.

JOHNNY: How's everybody over there?

MAMA: Pos aqui todos estamos bien tambien, gracias a dios.

JOHNNY: 'Ama, there's a lot happening here that I didn't know about before. I don't know if I'm allowed to write about it, pero voy hacer la lucha. Yesterday we attacked a small village near some rice paddies. We had orders to kill everybody because they were supposed to be VCs, communistas. We entered the small pueblito and my buddies comenzaron a disparar. I saw one of them kill an old man and an old lady. My sergeant killed a small boy about seven years old, then he shot his mother or some woman that came running up crying. Blood was everywhere. I don't remember what happened after that but my sergeant ordered me to start shooting. I think I did. May God forgive me for what I did, but I never wanted to come over here. They say we have to do it to defend our country.

MAMA: Hijo, me da tristeza con lo que nos escribes. Hable con tu padre y tambien se puso muy triste, pero dice que asi es la guerra. Te recuerda que estas peleando con communistas. Tengo una vela prendida y todos los dias le pido a diosito santo que te cuide mucho alla por donde andas y que te regrese a nuestros brazos bueno y sano.

JOHNNY: 'Ama, I had a dream la otra noche. I dreamed I was breaking into one of the hooches, asi le decimos a las casas de los Vietnameses. I went in firing my M-16 porque sabia que el village estaba controlado por los gooks. I killed three of them right away, but when I looked down it was mi 'apa, el carnalillo, and you, jefita. I don't know how much more I can stand. Please tell Sapo and all the vatos how it's like over here. Don't let them . . .

LA MUERTE *fires a gun, shooting* JOHNNY *in the head. He falls.* LA MAMA *screams without looking at* JOHNNY.

MUERTE: Johnny was killed in action November, 1965, at Chuy Lai. His body lay in the field for two days and then it was taken to the beach and placed in a freezer, a converted portable food locker. Two weeks later he was shipped home for burial.

LA MUERTE *straightens out* JOHNNY's *body, takes his helmet, rifle, etc.* EL PAPA, LA MAMA, *the* HERMANO, CECILIA *file past and gather around the body. Taps play.*

Wanda Coleman

Wanda Coleman (1946–) is a former welfare mother, dancer, typist, and waitress, who eventually became an award-winning writer of both poetry and prose. She, along with writers such as Joyce Carol Thomas, Ed Bullins, Sherley Anne Williams, and J. California Cooper, is a leader in the contemporary flowering of writing by Afro-Americans in this state. Her books include Mad Dog Black Lady *(1979),* Imagoes *(1983), and* Heavy Daughter Blues *(1987), which collects her poetry and prose from 1968 until 1986. Coleman is a fixture of contemporary Southern California's literary scene and a highly regarded performance reader of poetry and prose.*

. . . .

THE SCREAMER

Goodness gracious!

Linda looked up from the book. The bizarre scream rode through her on a chill, arousing prickles on the nape of her neck. What was it? Where was it coming from?

She had been hearing it daily for over a week. Sometimes it was so loud it seemed to come from within her.

She set the book open, face down on the cluttered, paint-splotched desk before her. She tilted her bulk over it, and peered out that portion of the plate glass window that was not plastered over with advertisements. There was no one along either side of the long commercial block.

Business in the blackening neighborhood was sparse as the white population fled west, taking economic prosperity with it. This was Linda's first job and she was glad to have it. No one in the real business world was eager to hire an eighteen-year-old high school graduate, black, female and very pregnant. But Mr. Sims had hired her on the spot.

Linda sat all day long. She seldom saw anyone except old man Sims who came in to lock up at the end of the day. Or when he came to pay her the few little dollars he had promised. Or when he came in with nothing but the promise to pay—tomorrow or the day after—or the coming week. And she needed the money—the desperate little money.

She had started her job three months into her pregnancy. It didn't seem very demanding, physically. All she did was sit. Yet each day she found it more and more difficult to motivate herself to get up, get breakfast for her husband, Rupert, get the bus the half mile to the shop, and walk the half block from the bus stop.

Her working conditions were not much of an incentive. The shop was musty and stank of old paint. And it was poorly lit.

The nature of her work was boring beyond anything Linda had ever known. She had taken the summer job to get experience as a receptionist. There were always plenty of newspaper wantads for that calling. But there was rarely anyone in the shop on whom she could ply even that vague trade.

Occasionally the phone rang.

"Hello, may I help you?"

"He isn't in."

"Would you like to leave a message?"

Too frequently the caller was a dunner, angrily demanding payment. Angrily insistent with threats of lawsuits, threats of violence. It upset her, at first, to have to convey these messages to the old man. He took them without a ripple of emotion in his placid chocolate mask, thanked her and said he'd take care of it.

And the dunners would call back even angrier demanding satisfaction from her. She would stammer that she knew nothing. Had no information, could not help them, and would, most certainly, convey the message again. On two occasions the phone service had been terminated due to lack of payment. But in some mysterious way old Mr. Sims managed to come up with the money.

"House painting is a good business," he would say to her occasionally, smiling at her from beneath one of his protective paper caps. "People always need a good house painter." She would watch him drive away alone, the ladders clattering in the rear of his old paint-splotched truck—hardly secured by the threadbare ropes—the multicolored cans of paint sealed tightly, knocking against each other as the truck sputtered off.

Occasionally, for bigger jobs, he took on a helper. Young black men between employments, students, or old ghetto hardcores—winos and the indigent. She could smell the youth and inexperience on the young ones—

their eagerness to learn (like her own); their belief in old man Sims; their desire to help; their gratefulness at a chance to prove and improve themselves. All the more grateful because he too was a black man. And she could smell the destitution and the self-disgust on the others—as aromatic as the stench of the grape. She could also smell their impermanence—all of them moved on—shadows against a darkening vista of white wall. Painted over by pain and disappointment.

I too am a shadow.

Yet she persisted. Time was coming when she'd have to leave the shop. The twinges in her distended belly came more and more frequently. She worried about the effects paint fumes might have on her baby-about-to-be. What would she do if it started to come while she sat there in that cold, dismal, dank little paint shop with its colder, rugless cement floors, and its teensy toilet beyond any possible sanitation no matter how much elbow grease and cleanser she applied? She was so horrified by its nastiness that she held her water as long as possible out of fear of somehow contaminating the fetus.

Now was such a moment. Feeling her bladder about to burst, she bolted the front door and scuttled around back to the hamburger shack next door. There the motherly, sympathetic fry cook allowed her to relieve herself.

"You need to quit that place, chile!" The brown-skinned woman observed, as Linda wobbled out of the restroom. "You 'bout near ready to pop!"

Sometimes the woman would give her a free hamburger, saying "This one here didn't turn out so good. I don't dare serve it to a customer." She had one bagged and ready and gave it to Linda as she left. Linda thanked her timidly, seized the little brown bag, and scurried back to the shop.

She was barely able to keep from gulping down the burger in two ecstatic bites. She never bothered to notice that it was, as always, fast food perfect.

Linda was grateful for any kindness that came her way. She could not afford to buy lunch, and occasionally brought a piece of fruit or a peanut butter and jelly sandwich from home. It was all she and Rupert could afford. And Rupert didn't like her working at all, but his janitor's job barely made rent and utilities. With the baby coming, they needed every cent that could be scrounged.

"Did you tell the old man you leavin'?"

"Not yet."

"When you gonna tell him?"

"I'll tell him Friday, after he pay me."

"Well, he better this time or I'm coming down there and make him."

"Don't—I mean—you don't have to. I'll see to it."

"Better. I don't want my baby ruint cause you ain't gettin' proper rest."

She was six months—maybe seven, she guessed. Movement was more and more difficult with each hour, it seemed.

She leaned back in the chair to savor the taste of the hamburger as it lingered in her mouth. She was seized by a sudden and overwhelming nausea. Her head began to throb and her heart jittered fiercely. She sat upright and grabbed hold of the desk, hoping the feeling would pass, leaning into it, fighting off the urge to vomit.

In her struggle to maintain equilibrium, she became aware of that murderous wail. Its shrillness penetrated her discomfort as she clamped her teeth, willing her body to obey. Finally it abated, and the nausea also began to subside.

Linda eased herself out of the chair and walked slowly to the toilet at the back of the shop. She stood in the door of the closet and looked down at the stool blackened with layers of dirt, grease, paint and the remnants of urine and feces. Her head began to ache as the nausea returned. She jerked forward, opening her mouth. Nothing came up except a yellow-green bile-tasting fluid. She spat it into the toilet bowl. She turned to the sink, turned on the cold water tap and ran her cupped hands under the faucet. She rinsed her mouth out and dabbed a little of the tepid liquid on her face. She wished she had something to drink other than the lukewarm water from the sink which was nearly as nasty as the toilet. She stood at the sink taking gasps of stale odorous air until she felt better.

When she returned to her desk, the scream met her, crescendoed, then vanished. This time she was certain it came from outside the building. But from where was still a mystery. She opened the front door and took another, more thorough look. She saw a half dozen passersby, all of them going quite normally about their business.

She eased back into the swivel chair. It groaned under her increasing weight. She was only five-two and the pregnancy had taken her weight up over one-fifty. She was beginning to resemble a gigantic rum ball.

She turned the book face up and yawned. She had found it the day before under a stack of papers at the bottom of one of the desk drawers. Her search had been motivated by stultifying boredom. She had to do *something*—if only read a book. She had discovered it under scores of bounced checks and bank notices demanding coverage. She marveled that the old man had written so much bad paper and yet escaped prosecution.

Again she took up the book. Again she was disturbed by that terrible half screech, half groan. She bounced up from the chair, determined to catch sight of the source. The ungodliness of it left sweat icing on her scalp, beneath her mop of thick kinky brown hair.

But there was no one.

What was it?

She sat down to the book again, forcing herself to focus on it. The story was about a young Englishman on his first holiday "on the Continent" and took place in the late 1800s. His ofay travels and adventures among Europe's wealthy were only a momentary escape. It was a meager getaway, only a bit less numbing than the job. One out of every ten or fifteen words eluded her. A search of the shop had not turned up anything vaguely resembling a dictionary. The French phrases were especially troublesome. She tried to guess meanings by rereading a sentence or paragraph a half dozen times, hoping meaning would somehow jump out at her. It was a tedious process with little success.

And the screamer would not let go of her thoughts.

Who is it? Why that hideous holler? Must be somebody sick—somebody insane. What could've happened to make them banshee so?

She tried to imagine all sorts of horrors. But the limits of her imaginings reflected her avid taste in television: A junky. A spy tortured for information. A cripple maimed by fire. The death of a loved-one in an auto crash. Beyond video banalities she could not conjure. Then the phone rang.

"I told that old cheat he'd better have my money today!"

"He's not in."

"You lyin'."

"Me? No, Sir."

"I'm coming down there and see for myself."

The angry click resonated in her ear. She looked up and was startled to see the old man standing there, his eyes smiling at her.

"Did I get any calls?"

"There," she handed him the neat stack of a dozen little pink slips. "And some man just called real mad. He said he wants his money. He's on his way here."

"Did he leave his name?"

"No."

"Well, I've got to go over to the courthouse, now."

She wondered if this was the right moment and decided there was no better moment under the circumstances.

"Could you pay me today, please, Mister Sims?"

"Of course, Linda. When I get back."

He's not comin' back. He'll expect me to lock up with the spare key in the desk. "Now," she lied. "I wants to run next door and get me some lunch."

"Well—all right."

She watched the dark old man pat his body, searching the paint-stained white coveralls for the wallet hidden in his street clothes underneath. He located it, slowly unzipped the front, reached in across his thick chest, and slipped it out. He opened it and a wad of business cards fell to the floor. He stooped over, slowly picked up the cards, went over to the desk, opened it up in the dimness, and peered into its leathery recesses.

"All I got is this twenty," he pulled out the thin limp bill and waved it toward her reluctantly.

"That's what you owe me for last week."

"Well—all right. Take it." He handed it to her. It smelled of turpentine.

He slipped the wallet back into his coveralls and rezipped them.

"When that guy comes in, get his name."

"I will."

She watched him ease out the back door. Moments later she heard the sputter of the truck backing out the driveway along the side of the building. She listened till the sound of the truck disappeared. Then she examined the twenty and smiled, relieved. She wouldn't go home empty-handed. She reached under the desk where she kept her purse. She plucked out her wallet and laid the twenty in the empty bill section.

You still ain't told him you quittin'.

As she tucked her purse away, the door rattled violently.

A tall, well-dressed, honey-skinned man in his late thirties stomped through it in expensively shod feet. "I called a little while ago!" he announced, surprised to see the young woman so grossly pregnant. He glared uncomfortably at her belly.

"You jes' missed him. I told him you was comin'. You didn't give me your name. He had to go to the courthouse. He said for me to get your name."

"*Hmph!*" He walked past her and went around in the back of the shop to see for himself. He returned to the desk greatly upset. There was a strangely vacant look in his eyes as he turned to her, leaning across the desk.

"Tell him his boy was lookin' for him—the oldest." He turned and stomped out, slamming the door.

At the noise, Linda felt a twinge in her belly. It was so strong she let out a little moan and leaned back in the swivel chair to get her breath. And then she heard it. That resonant agony, laboring in its manifestation. Goose bumps rose on her skin. Hairs tingled at the nape of her neck. She sat still and listened as the scream gradually waned into silence.

Linda bolted upright in the chair, dropped the book, grabbed the message pad and scrawled a note: "Dear Mr. Sims. My husband, Rupert say I have to quit cuz the baby 'bout to come. I left the key with the burger lady next door. Sorry. Linda."

She propped the pad against the phone so he would be sure to see it.

She felt a second twinge as she took the key from the top drawer in the desk, grabbed her purse, and waddled over to the front door and bolted it. She hurried as fast as she could through the shop, past scaffolding, canvas, rolls of poster paper, and old cans of paint and thinner, to the rear door. She pulled it shut behind her and struggled to secure the lock.

There it was again. That scream. She cocked her head and listened. It seemed to surround her. She stood listening until it faded, giving way to the cacophony of traffic and the muffled sounds of the world at work. She clutched the key firmly in her right hand and made her escape.

Leonard Gardner

Leonard Gardner's (1936–   ) novel Fat City *(1969)—from which the following chapter is excerpted—is a contemporary classic. He was born and raised in Stockton, California, the "fat city" of the novel's title. The harsh view of life on skid row that characterizes his novel—a kind of neo-naturalism—was successfully transposed to the screen when he wrote the script for John Huston's critically acclaimed film* Fat City. *Gardner is an ex-boxer and field laborer who graduated from the creative writing program at San Francisco State College. He is also the winner of a James D. Phelan Award and a Guggenheim Fellowship. He resides in Mill Valley.*

. . . .

THE TOMATO FIELD

Wearing a new straw hat, Billy Tully crawled for seven days in the onion fields, then he was back on the dark morning street among crowds of men left behind by the buses, acridly awake with nothing to do at the impossible hour of 5 a.m. The men grumbled about workers from Mexico, talked of the canneries hiring, passed bottles, knelt in doorways for furtive games of crap, and in the blue light of dawn dwindled away, up Main and Market, along Center and El Dorado, back to the hotels, the lawn and shade of Washington Square, to Chinese and Mexican cafés and to the bars whose doors again were opening.

After reading the paper over coffee and eggs, Tully went back to his room, slept awhile on top of the covers, then took a bus across town. In a crowd of several hundred he stood in the sweet-sour stench of stewing peaches outside a cannery. Trucks passed laden with peach lugs and can-filled cartons. On a vast paved area behind a Cyclone fence, yellow forklifts were stacking lugs into piles the size of barns. Amid the hum of machinery, gleaming empty cans clattered constantly down a conveyor from a boxcar where a man was unstacking and feeding them to the belt with a wooden pitchfork.

Blocking the steps to the office, an aged watchman armed with a billy club and a large revolver, his pants hiked above his belly and dewlaps quivering over his buttoned and tieless collar, warned the crowd to keep back from the building.

"Are you hiring or not?" Tully demanded, sweating and irritable now that the sun had cleared the roof.

"You'll just have to wait and hear from them inside."

"It don't do them no good us standing here. Why can't they come out and say if they don't want us?"

"I wouldn't know nothing about that."

"Then let me go in and ask somebody."

"Keep back. No one's going in that office."

"Why not? Who the hell you think you're talking to?"

"I'm just doing what they told me. They told me don't let nobody in the office and nobody's going through that door as long as I'm here. It's none of my doing."

"They're hiring all right," said a man at Tully's side. "I was out here yesterday and they said come back today."

Tully pushed to the front of the crowd and stood with his hands on his hips to prevent anyone from pushing around him. One of the big corrugated steel doors was open; visible in the gloom of the cannery were lines of aproned women. Inside the doorway a forklift had set down a pallet stacked with full lugs, and now a man left the crowd, stepped into the doorway and came back with two peaches. Several men and women followed, returning with handfuls of fruit before the watchman arrived and took the peaches from one final, grinning, capitulating pilferer. At that moment two Negro women sat down on the office steps. The guard ran belligerently back, neck and pelvis forward, squared chin bony from the downward abandonment by its flesh. Arguing, the women rose, and his head turned from them to the open door, from which one more man slipped back to the crowd with a handful of peaches.

"Well, you old fart, are they hiring or not?" shouted Tully.

"Not your kind. You can go home right now."

A whistle blew, the cans stopped rolling from the boxcar, the women inside the building left the line, and the office door was opened by a youthful, sober-faced man in a white short-sleeve shirt with a striped tie.

"The cannery won't be hiring any more personnel at the present time," he announced from the porch. "We've got our full crews for peaches. Come back when the tomatoes are ripe."

A peach banged against the corrugated metal wall several yards to his side—a loud juiceless thump.

"Who did that?" shouted the watchman. He was answered with snickers. The man on the porch stated that throwing peaches would not get anybody a job, and he went back into the office. The crowd fragmented, people walking off down the sides of the street, some running to parked cars, some remaining in the yard as if not believing the announcement. Tully went over to the open cannery door.

"Not hiring!" yelled the watchman.

Nearby in the immense dim room, a girl in jeans and workshirt was seated on a pallet eating a sandwich, her neck round and sloping, with short black curls at the nape.

The watchman arrived wheezing. "Not hiring. Come back when the tomatoes are ripe. Don't take any of that fruit."

Tully took a peach and walked past him into the sunlight. The small chunk he managed to bite away he spit out. When he threw the peach against the front door of a house, it struck with the hardness of stone. Along the sides of the street green peaches lay in the weeds.

The next morning he went out with a busload of tomato thinners. It was a day haul he had many times been warned against, but it paid ninety cents an hour. There was no talk on the ride out of town. The men slept; those with seats to themselves lay down on them. By sunrise they were in the delta.

Preceded by another, the bus jolted down a dirt road to a field bordered by irrigation ditches. With a few groans but mostly in silence, the men climbed out into the sparkling air and selected short-handled hoes from the bed of a pickup truck. Then they jumped a ditch, a foreman already yelling on the other side, and they ranged over the field to continue the previous day's weeding. Bent double, chopping with hoes half a yard long, crossing and uncrossing their legs, they stepped sideways along the rows.

Tully glanced around, saw what was being done, and began chopping, trying to leave an isolated tomato plant every width of a hoe blade. Engulfed by new weeds, grass and dandelion, they were seedlings growing in a double line down each row.

"What the hell kind of weeding you call that?"

Tully turned to a pair of legs in clean khaki. Straightening, he confronted a black mustache on a face he assumed, from its displeasure, was a foreman's. Then he turned to the ground he had cleared: long, leafless gaps, interrupted by infrequent plants, several of which appeared now not to be tomatoes.

"Shape up and get your ass in gear or you can spend the day in the bus."

"Tough shit. A lot I care. Big deal," Tully whispered at the departing back, wanting to hurl his hoe at it. He stooped lower, gripped the handle closer to the blade and hacked on. Instead of spaced plants, for a yard of mounting anxiety he left nothing at all. Sliding his hand all the way down to the blade, he meticulously scraped around the next plant, cutting down grass and weeds in a closer and closer square, plucking with his free hand until the tomato with its two jagged leaves and an adjacent red-rooted weed stood alone; and then in one final minuscule nick both were down. Guiltily, he peered around before propping the tomato plant upright between two clods. Already his back was hurting. The pain began at his waist, spread down the backs of his thighs to the tendons behind the knee joints and up the spine to the shoulders and the back of the neck. A tractor came up his row pulling a disk harrow, and when Tully straightened and moved aside for it to roar past, plowing under the chopped weeds, tiny transparent specks quivered before his eyes. He was falling behind. Soon he was the last stooped man moving across the field, and the foreman, stepping in long strides over the rows, again came threatening dismissal. Tully chopped on with desperate imprecision, dismayed by the lowness of the sun, which seemed to hang stationary. He doubted his back could last, and it was not the loss of the money, a day-long wait or the hitchhiking back he feared. It was the disgrace, for all around him were oaths, moans, bellowed complaints, the brief tableaux of upright wincing men, hoes dangling, their hands on the small of their backs, who were going on under the same torment—some of them winos, donut and coffee men, chain smokers, white-bread eaters, maybe none ever athletes yet all moving steadily on while he fell farther and farther behind, hacking in panic over the desertion of his will. He could not resign himself to the inexorable day; he would have to quit, and the others, he felt, were fools in their enduring. Including himself, only three men out of two busloads were white.

He could resolve no more than to clear the next six inches before throwing down his hoe. He straightened up with difficulty and stared hazily at the blue sky that was scrawled with the familiar floating patterns etched for so long now on his eyes. He breathed deeply, stretched, bent back over the row, crouched, knelt, crawled, scrambled up, and all the while the ache in his back continued. He lasted until noon, until the unbelievable half hour of relief. Ten minutes of it he spent waiting in line at a pickup truck to buy bean and potato filled tortillas and a Pepsi-Cola.

"Jesus Christ, you don't care where you eat, do you?" asked one of the two white men passing him where he lay under a pepper tree among a humming profusion of green-glinting flies whose source of delight, he noticed now, lay directly beside him. He had thought the odor was coming from his lunch. With a twinge of embarrassment he rose and entered a bus—sweltering and full of Negroes—and sat next to a man reeking of Sloan's liniment.

Tully was falling asleep while he finished eating, but already the men were hobbling out of the bus and taking up their hoes. Following, he found himself off with the Negroes at one end of the field. Bloated, aching, he again bent over a row. Shuffling sideways, his legs crossing and uncrossing, the short hoe rising and falling, he labored on in the despondency of one condemned, the instrument of his torture held in his own hand. Of all the hated work he had ever done, this was a torment beyond any, almost beyond belief, and so it began to seem this was his future, that this was Work, which he had always tried to evade and would never escape now that his wife was gone and his career was over. And it was as if it were just, as if he deserved no better for the mess he had made of his life. Yet he also felt he could not go on even another hour. He felt his existence had come to a final halt, with no way open to him anywhere. Hand on his back, straightening, he gazed with bleary eyes at all the stooped men inching down the rows, and he felt being white no longer made any difference. His life was being swept in among those countless lives lost hour by captive hour scratching at the miserable earth.

"You call this a living?"

"Uh hum," responded the man he had lunched beside, who, though young, appeared to have lost all his teeth and whose scent of liniment was periodically wafted to Tully's nose.

"How long's it take to get use to this shit, anyway?" Tully asked, and was nettled by gleeful forlorn laughter from the chopping and shuffling men.

"What a man want, what a man need, is a woman with a good job."

"I had that," Tully said. "But she left."

Again there was that irritating laughter. Tully hoed on in silence, listening to a bantering discussion of divorce, which everyone around him seemed to have undergone.

The wind came up; some of the men across the field masked themselves with bandannas, like bandits, and those who had come with goggles around the crowns of their straw hats drew them over their eyes. The peat dust blew in trails across the field and the blue of the sky was obscured by a gray haze through which the sun shone dully like the lid of a can. Tully forced himself on and the others drew steadily away. Dizzy, the tendons at the back of his knee joints swollen and stiff, he stood upright, watching the foreman. He stumbled across the clods to the water can on the back of a jeep that moved slowly up the rows and idled among the men, and he drank a long time from the sticky tin cup. Rebuked for lingering, he limped back cursing. Even his eyes ached in the downward strain of stooping. He trailed farther and farther behind, the Negroes' voices growing faint, blown by the wind.

The sun sloped down the sky, the bent men moved on across the black earth. Tully was hardly thinking now, his mind fixed on pain and chopping and a vision of quitting time. Seeing a man go to the edge of the field, he rose and went to the foreman, who was suspicious but gave his permission. In the tall grass beside an irrigation ditch, Tully squatted a peaceful moment.

When a white sedan arrived, raising a long trail of dust, Tully was lying in the dirt, propped on one arm, doggedly chopping. He did not understand that its appearance signified the end of the day until some of the crew began leaping over the rows and incredibly racing to the car, where a man now stood at the fender with a small green strongbox.

"Who wants to make a store stop?" the driver asked on the road back to Stockton. So empty cans and bottles clanked along the floor when the bus arrived with its silent motionless passengers in the sunlit town.

"You'll never see me again," declared Tully, and he swayed, leaning oddly backwards, up the street to his hotel, straw cowboy hat cocked forward, his fingers discovering new mounds of muscle in the small of his agonized back.

But the pay was ninety cents an hour, and two days later he was again gripping a short-handled hoe.

Gary Soto

Gary Soto (1952–), one of the most honored of Fresno Poets and Chicano poets, has actually escaped labels—he is regarded simply as a major writer. He is nonetheless a Fresno native, proudly Hispanic, who remembers having been an uninspired student—"I went to school, as my mother put it, 'to eat my lunch'." He soon discovered the Fresno Public Library, though, "which I consider a great gift to the poor." Eventually, he graduated from Fresno State and the University of California, Irvine. In 1976 The Elements of San Joaquin *established Soto as an emerging force in American poetry, and he hasn't looked back since. Today he is widely anthologized, has won numerous awards, and worked successfully in both prose and verse. His sketches in books like* A Summer Life *(1990) or* Lesser Evils *(1988) complement the poetry of* Who Will Know Us? *(1990) or* Home Course in Religion *(1991). Soto lives in Albany and teaches at the University of California, Berkeley.*

. . . .

THINKING LIKE A KID

It was suffering that I couldn't stab
Like a bug and stop. Russia
Was cheating us out of rain,
China out of air.
In bed disease scared me—
People woke up and it was there,
Like a baseball under the skin,
A vest of darker blood.

I worried myself into thinner clothes.
I prayed, walked with fear,
Jumped when I saw a retarded woman

Drool big gobs on her shoes,
Her eyes so loose they couldn't follow
A leaf seesawing from a tree.
At dinner I asked mother, who passed the butter
And said, It's Life. The nuns said prayers.
The priest made bell sounds and raised a chalice.
As far as I knew the earth didn't trouble
With me—earth smug with its toothy alps,
Five continents, a river so long
Egyptians could stand on the bank,
Hold hands, and never reach the sea.

This left me scared, and more scared
When at choir practice
—Catholics in green sweaters
Singing above the organ's squeeze
Of noise—I saw a girl from
My class drool on a high note,
Just a little, like a broken shoelace.
Disease, I thought, starts small
—string in the mouth—
And goes and goes until you're like that woman,
A noisy one with shadows in the head.
And now my classmate, two rows
To the left of me and years
Ahead in math. She's got it.
I made my eyes big, sang loud, sang
In the streets to keep the world from
Pushing into my third grade life with all its worry.

MAGNETS

I click the plastic faces of kewpie dolls
Together—they want to kiss but can't.
The magnets behind their heads have died
Out, and wouldn't pull up iron filings
From the loosest dirt, let alone show
Affection, smack lips or clunk heads
And make my bashful nephew say,
Ah, that's for sissies.
                  They stare at each other,
Shyly with hands behind their backs,
Black lash of youth, pink cheeks of first time.
But it's over for them. The magnets
Have died out. I drink my coffee
And think of old girlfriends,
How we too clunked heads together,
Kissed and clunked until that pull of love
Stopped and we just looked.

Sometimes the magnets fall from our heads,
Settle in our hips. Beds are ruined
This way. Books tumble from crowded shelves
When couples clunk waists together,
With the women looking at ceilings,
Men at loose hair on pillows,
And then it's the other way around.
But magnets die out. They grow heavy,
These stones that could sharpen knives
Or bring faces together for one last kiss.

For years I thought iron lived forever,
Certainly longer than love. Now I have doubts.
The kewpie dolls, set on starched doilies
On my grandmother's television,
Smile but don't touch. The paint is flaking,
Dust is a faint aura of loss. Grandmother loved

Her husband for five decades, and still does,
Poor grandpa who is gone. They worked
Side by side in fields, boxed raisins,
Raised children in pairs. Now grandmother
Wants to die but doesn't know how.
Her arms are frail, her eyes of cataract
Can't hold a face. Hijo, hijo,
She says, and looks over my shoulder.
It's blinding wisdom to see her on the edge
of her couch. The magnet is in her feet,
Ready to gather up the earth.

A RED PALM

You're in this dream of cotton plants.
You raise a hoe, swing, and the first weeds
Fall with a sigh. You take another step,
Chop, and the sigh comes again,
Until you yourself are breathing that way
With each step, a sigh that will follow you into town.

That's hours later. The sun is a red blister
Coming up in your palm. Your back is strong,
Young, not yet the broken chair
In an abandoned school of dry spiders.
Dust settles on your forehead, dirt
Smiles under each fingernail.
You chop, step, and by the end of the first row,
You can buy one splendid fish for wife
And three sons. Another row, another fish,
Until you have enough and move on to milk,
Bread, meat. Ten hours and the cupboards creak.
You can rest in the back yard under a tree.
Your hands twitch on your lap,
Not unlike the fish on a pier or the bottom
Of a boat. You drink iced tea. The minutes jerk
Like flies.
              It's dusk, now night,
And the lights in your home are on.
That costs money, yellow light
In the kitchen. That's thirty steps,
You say to your hands,
Now shaped into binoculars.
You could raise them to your eyes:
You were a fool in school, now look at you.
You're a giant among cotton plants,
The lung-shaped leaves that run breathing for miles.
Now you see your oldest boy, also running.
Papa, he says, it's time to come in,

You pull him into your lap
And ask, What's forty times nine?
He knows as well as you, and you smile.
The wind makes peace with the trees,
The stars strike themselves in the dark.
You get up and walk with the sigh of cotton plants.
You go to sleep with a red sun on your palm,
The sore light you see when you first stir in bed.

T. Coraghessan Boyle

T. Coraghessan Boyle (1948–), a native of Peekskill, New York, lives in the San Fernando Valley and teaches at the University of Southern California. Says Gary Soto, "Somehow Boyle has created a quirky, absolutely true vision of the L.A. area, something no local writer has, or probably could, do. He's got both the distance and the familiarity." Boyle's books such as The Descent of Man *(1979),* Water Music *(1981), and* If the River Was Whiskey *(1989), from which the following story has been excerpted, have won him a long list of literary awards.*

. . . .

THE HUMAN FLY

Just try to explain to anyone the art of fasting!
  —Franz Kafka, "A Hunger Artist"

In the early days, before the press took him up, his outfit was pretty basic: tights and cape, plastic swim goggles and a bathing cap in the brightest shade of red he could find. The tights were red too, though they'd faded to pink in the thighs and calves and had begun to sag around the knees. He wore a pair of scuffed hightops—red, of course—and the cape, which looked as if it had last been used to line a trash can, was the color of poached salmon. He seemed to be in his thirties, though I never did find out how old he was, and he was thin, skinny, emaciated—so wasted you worried about his limbs dropping off. When he limped into the office that first afternoon, I didn't know what to think. If he brought an insect to mind, it was something spindly and frail—a daddy longlegs or one of those spidery things that scoot across the surface of the pool no matter how much chlorine the pool man dumps in.

"A gentleman here to see you," Crystal sang through the intercom.

My guard was down. I was vulnerable. I admit it. Basking in the glow of my first success (ten percent of a walk-on for Bettina Buttons, a nasally inflected twelve-year-old with pushy parents, in a picture called *Tyranno-*

saurus II—no lines, but she did manage a memorable screech) and bloated with a celebratory lunch, I was feeling magnanimous, large-spirited, and saintly. Of course, the two splits of Sangre de Cristo, 1978, might have had something to do with it. I hit the button on the intercom. "Who is it?"

"Your name, sir?" I heard Crystal ask, and then, through the crackle of static, I heard him respond in the peculiar unmodulated rumble he associated with speech.

"Pardon?" Crystal said.

"La Mosca Humana," he rumbled.

Crystal leaned into the intercom. "Uh, I think he's Mexican or something."

At that stage in my career, I had exactly three clients, all inherited from my predecessor: the aforementioned Bettina; a comic with a harelip who did harelip jokes only; and a soft-rock band called Mu, who believed they were reincarnated court musicians from the lost continent of Atlantis. The phone hadn't rung all morning and my next (and only) appointment, with Bettina's mother, grandmother, acting coach, and dietician, was at seven. "Show him in," I said grandly.

The door pushed open, and there he was. He drew himself up with as much dignity as you could expect from a grown man in a red bathing cap and pink tights, and hobbled into the office. I took in the cap, the cape, the hightops and tights, the slumped shoulders and fleshless limbs. He wore a blond mustache, droopy and unkempt, the left side of his face was badly bruised, and his nose looked as if it had been broken repeatedly—and recently. The fluorescent light glared off his goggles.

My first impulse was to call security—he looked like one of those panhandling freaks out on Hollywood Boulevard—but I resisted it. As I said, I was full of wine and feeling generous. Besides, I was so bored I'd spent the last half-hour crumpling up sheets of high-fiber bond and shooting three-pointers into the wastebasket. I nodded. He nodded back. "So," I said, "what can I do for you, Mr., ah—?"

"Mosca," he rumbled, the syllables thick and muffled, as if he were trying to speak and clear his throat at the same time. "La Mosca Humana."

"The Human Fly, right?" I said, dredging up my high-school Spanish.

He looked down at the desk and then fixed his eyes on mine. "I want to be famous," he said.

How he found his way to my office, I'll never know. I've often wondered if it wasn't somebody's idea of a joke. In those days, I was nothing—I had less seniority than the guy who ran the Xerox machine—and my office was the smallest and farthest from the door of any in the agency. I was expected to get by with two phone lines, one secretary, and a workspace not much bigger than a couple of good-sized refrigerator boxes. There were no Utrillos or Demuths on my walls. I didn't even have a window.

I understood that the man hovering over my desk was a nut case, but there was more to it than that. I could see that he had something—a dignity, a sad elemental presence—that gave the lie to his silly outfit. I felt uneasy under his gaze. "Don't we all," I said.

"No, no," he insisted, "you don't understand," and he pulled a battered manila envelope from the folds of his cape. "Here," he said, "look."

The envelope contained his press clippings, a good handful of them, yellowed and crumbling, bleached of print. All but one were in Spanish. I adjusted the desk lamp, squinted hard. The datelines were from places like Chetumal, Tuxtla, Hidalgo, Tehuantepec. As best I could make out, he'd been part of a Mexican circus. The sole clipping in English was from the "Metro" section of the *Los Angeles Times*: MAN ARRESTED FOR SCALING ARCO TOWER.

I read the first line—"A man known only as 'The Human Fly' "—and I was hooked. What a concept: *a man known only as the Human Fly!* It was priceless. Reading on, I began to see him in a new light: the costume, the limp, the bruises. This was a man who'd climbed twenty stories with nothing more than a couple pieces of rope and his fingernails. A man who defied the authorities, defied death—my mind was doing backflips; we could run with this one, oh, yes, indeed. Forget your Rambos and Conans, this guy was the real thing.

"Five billion of us monkey on the planet," he said in his choked, moribund tones, "I want to make my mark."

I looked up in awe. I saw him on Carson, Letterman, grappling his way to the top of the Bonaventure Hotel, hurtling Niagara in a barrel, starring in his own series. I tried to calm myself. "Uh, your face," I said, and I made a broad gesture that took in the peach-colored bruise, the ravaged nose and stiffened leg, "what happened?"

For the first time, he smiled. His teeth were stained and ragged; his eyes flared behind the cracked plastic lenses of the goggles. "An accident," he said.

As it turned out, he wasn't Mexican at all—he was Hungarian. I saw my mistake when he peeled back the goggles and bathing cap. A fine band of skin as blanched and waxen as the cap of a mushroom outlined his ears, his hairline, the back of his neck, dead-white against the sun-burnished oval of his face. His eyes were a pale watery blue and the hair beneath the cap was as wispy and colorless as the strands of his mustache. His name was Zoltan Mindszenty, and he'd come to Los Angeles to live with his uncle when the Russian tanks rolled through Budapest in 1956. He'd learned English, Spanish, and baseball, practiced fire-eating and tightrope-walking in his spare time, graduated at the top of his high-school class, and operated a forklift in a cannery that produced refried beans and cactus salad. At the age of nineteen he joined the Quesadilla Brothers' Circus and saw the world. Or at least that part of it bounded by California, Arizona, New Mexico, and Texas to the north and Belize and Guatemala to the south. Now he wanted to be famous.

He moved fast. Two days after I'd agreed to represent him he made the eyewitness news on all three major networks when he suspended himself in a mesh bag from the twenty-second floor of the Sumitomo Building and refused to come down.

Terrific. The only problem was that he didn't bother to tell me about it. I was choking down a quick lunch—avocado and sprouts on a garlic-cheese croissant—already running late for an audition I'd set up for my harelipped comedian—when the phone rang. It was a Lieutenant Peachtree of the LAPD. "Listen," the lieutenant hissed, "if this is a publicity stunt . . ." and he trailed off, leaving the threat—heavy ire, the violation of penal codes, the arcane and merciless measures taken to deal with accessories—unspoken.

"Pardon?"

"The nutball up on the Sumitomo Building. Your client."

Comprehension washed over me. My first thought was to deny the connection, but instead I found myself stammering, "But, but how did you get my name?"

Terse and efficient, a living police report, Peachtree gave me the details. One of his men, hanging out of a window on the twenty-first floor, had pleaded with Zoltan to come down. "I am the Human Fly," Zoltan rumbled in response as the wind snapped and the traffic sizzled below, "you want to talk to me, call my agent."

"Twenty minutes," Peachtree added, and his tone was as flat and unforgiving as the drop of a guillotine, "I want you down here. Five minutes after that I want this clown in the back of the nearest patrol car—is that understood?"

It was. Perfectly. And twenty minutes later, with the help of an Officer Dientes, a screaming siren, and several hundred alert motorists who fell away from us on the freeway like swatted flies, I was taking the breeze on the twenty-first floor of the Sumitomo Building. Two of Peachtree's men gripped my legs and eased my torso out onto the slick glassy plane of the building's façade.

I was sick with fear. Before me lay the immensity of the city, its jaws and molars exposed. Above was the murky sky, half a dozen pigeons on a ledge, and Zoltan, bundled up like a sack of grapefruit and calmly perusing a paperback thriller. I choked back the remains of the croissant and cleared my throat. "Zoltan!" I shouted, the wind snatching the words from my lips and flinging them away. "Zoltan, what are you doing up there?"

There was a movement from the bag above me, Zoltan stirring himself like a great leathery fruit bat unfolding its wings, and then his skinny legs and outsized feet emerged from their confinement as the bag swayed gently in the breeze. He peered down at me, the goggles aflame with the sun, and gave me a sour look. "You're supposed to be my agent, and you have to ask me that?"

"It's a stunt, then—is that it?" I shouted.

He turned his face away, and the glare of the goggles died. He wouldn't answer. Behind me, I could hear Peachtree's crisp, efficient tones: "Tell him he's going to jail."

"They're going to lock you up. They're not kidding."

For a long moment, he didn't respond. Then the goggles caught the sun again and he turned to me. "I want the TV people, Tricia Toyota, 'Action News,' the works."

I began to feel dizzy. The pavement below, with its toy cars and its clots of tiny people, seemed to rush up at me and recede again in a pulsing wave. I felt Peachtree's men relax their grip. "They won't come!" I gasped, clutching the windowframe so desperately my fingers went numb. "They can't. It's network policy." It was true, as far as I knew. Every flake in the country would be out on that ledge if they thought they could get a ten-second clip on the evening news.

Zoltan was unimpressed. "TV," he rumbled into the wind, "or I stay here till you see the white of my bone."

I believed him.

As it turned out, he stayed there, aloft, for two weeks. And for some reason—because he was intractable, absurd, mad beyond hope or redemption—the press couldn't get enough of it. TV included. How he passed the time, what he ate, how he relieved himself, no one knew. He was just a presence, a distant speck in a mesh sack, the faintest intrusion of reality on the clear smooth towering face of the Sumitomo Building. Peachtree tried to get him down, of course—harassing him with helicopters, sending a squad of window cleaners, firemen, and lederhosen up after him—but nothing worked. If anyone got close to him, Zoltan would emerge from his cocoon, cling to the seamless face of the building, and float—float like a big red fly—to a new position.

Finally, after the two weeks were up—two weeks during which my phone never stopped ringing, by the way—he decided to come down. Did he climb in the nearest window and take the elevator? No, not Zoltan. He backed down, inch by inch, uncannily turning up finger- and toe-holds where none existed. He sprang the last fifteen feet to the ground, tumbled like a sky diver, and came up in the grip of a dozen policemen. There was a barricade up, streets were blocked, hundreds of spectators had gathered. As they were hustling him to a patrol car, the media people converged on him. Was it a protest? they wanted to know. A hunger strike? What did it mean?

He turned to them, the goggles steamed over, pigeon feathers and flecks of airborne debris clinging to his cape. His legs were like sticks, his face nearly black with sun and soot. "I want to be famous," he said.

"A DC 10?"

Zoltan nodded. "The bigger, the better," he rumbled.

It was the day after he'd decamped from the face of the Sumitomo Building and we were in my office, discussing the next project. (I'd bailed him out myself, though the figure was right up there with what you'd expect for a serial killer. There were fourteen charges against him, ranging from trespassing to creating a public nuisance and refusing the reasonable request of a police officer to indecent exposure. I had to call in every favor that was ever owed me and go down on my knees to Sol Bankoff, the head of the agency, to raise the cash.) Zoltan was wearing the outfit I'd had specially made for him: new tights, a black silk cape without a wrinkle in it, a pair of Air Jordan basketball shoes in red and black, and most important of all, a red leather aviator's cap and goggles. Now he looked less like a geriatric at a health spa and more like the sort of fearless daredevil/superhero the public could relate to.

"But Zoltan," I pleaded, "those things go five hundred miles an hour. You'd be ripped to pieces. Climbing buildings is one thing, but this is insane. It's suicidal."

He was slouched in the chair, one skinny leg thrown over the other. "The Human Fly can survive anything," he droned in his lifeless voice. He was staring at the floor, and now he lifted his head. "Besides, you think the public have any respect for me if I don't lay it all on line?"

He had a point. But strapping yourself to the wing of a DC 10 made about as much sense as taking lunch at a sidewalk café in Beirut. "Okay," I said, "you're right. But you've got to draw the line somewhere. What good's it going to do you to be famous if you're dead?"

Zoltan shrugged.

"I mean already, just with the Sumitomo thing, I can book you on half the talk shows in the country. . . ."

He rose shakily to his feet, lifted his hand, and let it drop. Two weeks on the face of the Sumitomo Building with no apparent source of nourishment hadn't done him any good. If he was skinny before, he was nothing now—a shadow, a ghost, a pair of tights stuffed with straw. "Set it up," he rumbled, the words riding up out of the depths of his sunken abdomen, "I talk when I got something to talk about."

It took me a week. I called every airline in the directory, listened to a lifetime's worth of holding jingles, and talked to everyone from the forklift operator at KLM to the president and CEO of Texas Air. I was met by scorn, hostility, disbelief, and naked contempt. Finally I got hold of the schedules manager of Aero Masoquisto, the Ecuadorian national airline. It was going to cost me, he said, but he could hold up the regular weekly flight to Quito for a few hours while Zoltan strapped himself to the wing and took a couple passes round the airport. He suggested an airstrip outside Tijuana, where the officials would look the other way. For a price, of course.

Of course.

I went to Sol again. I was prepared to press my forehead to the floor, shine his shoes, anything—but he surprised me. "I'll front the money," he rasped, his voice ruined from forty years of whispering into the telephone, "no problem." Sol was seventy, looked fifty, and he'd had his own table in the Polo Lounge since before I was born. "If he bags it," he said, his voice as dry as a husk, "we got the rights to his life story and we'll do a paperback/ miniseries/action-figure tie-in. Just get him to sign this, that's all." He slid a contract across the table. "And if he makes it, which I doubt—I mean I've seen some crazies in my time, but this guy is something else—if he makes it, we'll have a million and a half offers for him. Either way, we make out, right?"

"Right," I said, but I was thinking of Zoltan, his brittle limbs pressed to the unyielding metal, the terrible pull of the G-forces, and the cyclonic blast of the wind. What chance did he have?

Sol cleared his throat, shook a few lozenges into his fist, and rattled them like dice. "Your job," he said, "is to make sure the press shows up. No sense in this nimrod bagging it for nothing, right?"

I felt something clench in my gut.

Sol repeated himself. "Right?"

"Right," I said.

Zoltan was in full regalia as we boarded the plane at LAX, along with a handful of reporters and photographers and a hundred grim-looking Ecua- dorians with plastic bags full of disposable diapers, cosmetics, and pen- light batteries. The plan was for the pilot to announce a minor problem— a clogged air-conditioning vent or a broken handle in the flush toilet; we didn't want to panic anybody—and an unscheduled stop to repair it. Once on the ground, the passengers would be asked to disembark and we'd offer them free drinks in the spacious terminal while the plane taxied out of sight and Zoltan did his thing.

Problem was, there was no terminal. The landing strip looked as if it had been bombed during the Mexican Revolution, it was a hundred degrees in- side the airplane and 120 out on the asphalt, and all I could see was heat haze and prickly-pear cactus. "What do you want to do?" I asked Zoltan.

Zoltan turned to me, already fumbling with his chin strap. "It's per- fect," he whispered, and then he was out in the aisle, waving his arms and whistling for the passengers' attention. When they quieted down, he spoke to them in Spanish, the words coming so fast you might have thought he was a Mexican disc jockey, his voice riding on a current of emotion he never approached in English. I don't know what he said—he could have been exhorting them to hijack the plane, for all I knew—but the effect was dramatic. When he finished, they rose to their feet and cheered.

With a flourish, Zoltan threw open the emergency exit over the wing and began his preparations. Flashbulbs popped, reporters hung out the door and shouted questions at him—Had this ever been attempted before? Did he have his will made out? How high was he planning to go?—and the passengers pressed their faces to the windows. I'd brought along a TV crew to capture the death-defying feat for syndication, and they set up one camera on the ground while the other shot through the window.

Zoltan didn't waste any time. He buckled what looked like a huge leather truss around the girth of the wing, strapped himself into the pouch attached to it, tightened his chin strap a final time, and then gave me the thumbs-up sign. My heart was hammering. A dry wind breathed through the open window. The heat was like a fist in my face. "You're sure you want to go through with this?" I yelled.

"One hundred percent, A-OK," Zoltan shouted, grinning as the reporters crowded round me in the narrow passageway. Then the pilot said something in Spanish and the flight attendants pulled the window shut, fastened the bolts, and told us to take our seats. A moment later the big engines roared to life and we were hurtling down the runway. I could barely stand to look. At best, I consider flying an unavoidable necessity, a time to resurrect forgotten prayers and contemplate the end of all joy in a twisted howling heap of machinery; at worst, I rank it right up there with psychotic episodes and torture at the hands of malevolent strangers. I felt the wheels lift off, heard a shout from the passengers, and there he was—Zoltan—clinging to the trembling thunderous wing like a second coat of paint.

It was a heady moment, transcendent, the cameras whirring, the passengers cheering, Zoltan's greatness a part of us all. This was an event, a once-in-a-lifetime thing, like watching Hank Aaron stroke his seven hundred fifteenth homer or Neil Armstrong step out onto the surface of the moon. We forgot the heat, forgot the roar of the engines, forgot ourselves. He's doing it, I thought, he's actually doing it. And I truly think he would have pulled it off, if—well, it was one of those things no one could have foreseen. Bad luck, that's all.

What happened was this: just as the pilot was coming in for his final approach, a big black bird—a buzzard, somebody said—loomed up out of nowhere and slammed into Zoltan with a thump that reverberated throughout the plane. The whole thing took maybe half a second. This black bundle appears, there's a thump, and next thing Zoltan's goggles are gone and he's covered from head to toe in raw meat and feathers.

A gasp went through the cabin. Babies began to mewl, grown men burst into tears, a nun fainted. My eyes were riveted on Zoltan. He lay limp in his truss while the hot air sliced over the wing and the jagged yellow mountains, the prickly pear, and the pocked landing strip rushed past him like the backdrop of an old movie. The plane was still rolling when we threw open the emergency exit and staggered out onto the wing. The copilot was ahead of me, a reporter on my heels. "Zoltan!" I cried, scared and sick and trembling. "Zoltan, are you all right?"

There was no answer. Zoltan's head lolled against the flat hard surface of the wing and his eyes were closed, sunk deep behind the wrinkled flaps of his lids. There was blood everywhere. I bent to tear at the straps of the aviator's cap, my mind racing, thinking alternately of mouth-to-mouth and the medical team I should have thought to bring along, when an urgent voice spoke at my back. "Perdóneme, perdóneme, I yam a doaktor."

One of the passengers, a wizened little man in Mickey Mouse T-shirt and Bermudas, knelt over Zoltan, shoving back his eyelids and feeling for his pulse. There were shouts behind me. The wing was as hot as the surface of a frying pan. "Jes, I yam getting a pulse," the doctor announced and then Zoltan winked open an eye. "Hey," he rumbled, "am I famous yet?"

Zoltan was right: the airplane stunt fired the imagination of the country. The wire services picked it up, the news magazines ran stories—there was even a bit on the CBS evening news. A week later the *National Enquirer* was calling him the reincarnation of Houdini and the *Star* was speculating about his love life. I booked him on the talk-show circuit, and while he might not have had much to say, he just about oozed charisma. He appeared on the Carson show in his trademark outfit, goggles and all, limping and with his arm in a sling (he'd suffered a minor concussion, a shoulder separation, and a fractured kneecap when the bird hit him). Johnny asked him what it was like out there on the wing and Zoltan said: "Loud." And what was it like spending two weeks on the face of the Sumitomo Building? "Boring," Zoltan rumbled. But Carson segued into a couple of airline jokes ("Have you heard the new slogan for China Airlines?" Pause. "You've seen us drive, now watch us fly") and the audience ate it up. Offers poured in from promoters, producers, book editors, and toy manufacturers. I was able to book David Mugillo, my harelipped comedian, on Zoltan's coattails, and when we did the Carson show we got Bettina Buttons on for three minutes of nasal simpering about *Tyrannosaurus II* and how educational an experience it was for her to work with such a sensitive and caring director as so-and-so.

Zoltan had arrived.

A week after his triumph on "The Tonight Show" he hobbled into the office, the cape stained and torn, tights gone in the knees. He brought a distinctive smell with him—the smell of pissed-over gutters and fermenting dumpsters—and for the first time I began to understand why he'd never given me an address or a phone number. ("You want me," he said, "leave a message with Ramón at Jiffy Cleaners.") All at once I had a vision of him slinging his grapefruit sack from the nearest drainpipe and curling up for the night. "Zoltan," I said, "are you okay? You need some cash? A place to stay?"

He sat heavily in the chair across from me. Behind him, on the wall, was an oil painting of an open window, a gift from Mu's bass player. Zoltan waved me off. Then, with a weary gesture, he reached up and removed the cap and goggles. I was shocked. His hair was practically gone and his face was as seamed and scarred as an old hockey puck. He looked about a hundred and twelve. He said nothing.

"Well," I said, to break the silence, "you got your wish. You made it." I lifted a stack of correspondence from the desk and waved it at him. "You're famous."

Zoltan turned his head and spat on the floor. "Famous," he mocked. "Fidel Castro is famous. Irving Berlin. Evel Knievel." His rumble had turned bitter. "Peterbilt," he said suddenly.

This last took me by surprise. I'd been thinking of consolatory platitudes, and all I could do was echo him weakly: "Peterbilt?"

"I want the biggest rig going. The loudest, the dirtiest."

I wasn't following him.

"Maine to L.A.," he rumbled.

"You're going to drive it?"

He stood shakily, fought his way back into the cap, and lowered the goggles. "Shit," he spat, "I ride the axle."

I tried to talk him out of it. "Think of the fumes," I said, "the road hazards. Potholes, dead dogs, mufflers. You'll be two feet off the pavement, going seventy-five, eighty miles an hour. Christ, a cardboard box'll tear you apart."

He wouldn't listen. Not only was he going through with it, but he wanted to coordinate it so that he ended up in Pasadena, for the swap meet at the

Rose Bowl. There he would emerge from beneath the truck, wheel a motor-cycle out of the back, roar up a ramp, and sail over twenty-six big rigs lined up fender to fender in the middle of the parking lot.

I asked Sol about it. Advance contracts had already made back the money he'd laid out for the airplane thing ten times over. And now we could line up backers. "Get him to wear a Pirelli patch on his cape," Sol rasped, "it's money in the bank."

Easy for Sol to say, but I was having problems with the whole business. This wasn't a plastic dinosaur on a movie lot or a stinko audience at the Improv, this was flesh and blood we were talking about here, a human life. Zoltan wasn't healthy—in mind or body. The risks he took weren't healthy. His ambition wasn't healthy. And if I went along with him, I was no better than Sol, a mercenary, a huckster who'd watch a man die for ten percent of the action. For a day or two I stayed away from the office, brooding around the kitchen in my slippers. In the end, though, I talked myself into it— Zoltan was going to do it with or without me. And who knew what kind of bloodsucker he'd wind up with next?

I hired a PR firm, got a major trucking company to carry him for the goodwill and free publicity, and told myself it was for the best. I'd ride in the cab with the driver, keep him awake, watch over Zoltan personally. And of course I didn't know how it was going to turn out—Zoltan *was* amazing, and if anyone could pull it off, he could—and I thought of the Sumitomo Building and Aero Masoquisto and hoped for the best.

We left Bangor in a cold drizzle on a morning that could have served as the backdrop for a low-budget horror picture: full-bellied clouds, gloom, mist, nose-running cold. By the time we reached Portland the drizzle had begun to crust on the windshield wipers; before we reached New Hampshire it was sleet. The driver was an American Indian by the name of Mink—no middle name, no surname, just Mink. He weighed close to five hundred pounds and he wore his hair in a single braided coil that hung to his belt loops in back. The other driver, whose name was Steve, was asleep in the compart-ment behind the cab. "Listen, Mink," I said, the windshield wipers beating methodically at the crust, tires hissing beneath us, "maybe you should pull over so we can check on Zoltan."

Mink shifted his enormous bulk in the seat. "What, the Fly?" he said. "No sweat. That guy is like amazing. I seen that thing with the airplane.

He can survive that, he's got no problem with this rig—long's I don't hit nothin'."

The words were barely out of his mouth when an animal—a huge brown thing like a cow on stilts—materialized out of the mist. Startled, Mink jerked the wheel, the truck went into a skid, there was a jolt like an earthquake, and the cow on stilts was gone, sucked under the front bumper like a scrap of food sucked down a drain. When we finally came to a stop a hundred yards up the road, the trailer was perpendicular to the cab and Mink's hands were locked to the wheel.

"What happened?" I said.

"Moose," Mink breathed, adding a soft breathless curse. "We hit a fuckin' moose."

In the next instant I was down and out of the cab, racing the length of the trailer, and shouting Zoltan's name. Earlier, in the cold dawn of Bangor, I'd watched him stretch out his mesh bag and suspend it like a trampoline from the trailer's undercarriage, just ahead of the rear wheels. He'd waved to the reporters gathered in the drizzle, ducked beneath the trailer, and climbed into the bag. Now, my heart banging, I wondered what a moose might have done to so tenuous an arrangement. "Zoltan!" I shouted, going down on my knees to peer into the gloom beneath the trailer.

There was no moose. Zoltan's cocoon was still intact, and so was he. He was lying there on his side, a thin fetal lump rounding out of the steel and grime. "What?" he rumbled.

I asked him the question I always seemed to be asking him: was he all right?

It took him a moment—he was working his hand free—and then he gave me the thumbs-up sign. "A-OK," he said.

The rest of the trip—through the icy Midwest, the wind-torn Rockies, and the scorching strip between Tucson and Gila Bend—was uneventful. For me, anyway. I alternately slept, ate truckstop fare designed to remove the lining of your stomach, and listened to Mink or Steve—their conversation was interchangeable—rhapsodize about Harleys, IROC Camaros, and women who went down on all fours and had "Truckers' Delite" tattooed across their buttocks. For Zoltan, it was business as usual. If he suffered from the cold, the heat, the tumbleweeds, beer cans, and fast-food containers that ricocheted off his poor lean scrag of a body day and night, he never mentioned it. True to form, he refused food and drink, though I suspected he must have had something concealed in his cape, and he never climbed down out of his cocoon, not even to move his bowels. Three days and three nights after we'd left Maine, we wheeled the big rig through the streets of Pasadena and into the parking lot outside the Rose Bowl, right on schedule.

There was a fair-sized crowd gathered, though there was no telling whether they'd come for the swap meet, the heavy-metal band we'd hired to give some punch to Zoltan's performance, or the stunt itself, but then who cared? They were there. As were the "Action News" teams, the souvenir hawkers and hotdog vendors. Grunting, his face beaded with sweat, Mink guided the truck into place alongside the twenty-five others, straining to get it as close as possible: an inch could mean the difference between life and death for Zoltan, and we all knew it.

I led a knot of cameramen to the rear of the truck so they could get some tape of Zoltan crawling out of his grapefruit bag. When they were all gathered, he stirred himself, shaking off the froth of insects and road grime, the scraps of paper and cellophane, placing first one bony foot and then the other on the pavement. His eyes were feverish behind the lenses of the goggles and when he lurched out from under the truck I had to catch his arm to prevent him from falling. "So how does it feel to conquer the roadways?" asked a microphone-jabbing reporter with moussed hair and flawless teeth. "What was the worst moment?" asked another.

Zoltan's legs were rubber. He reeked of diesel fuel, his cape was in tatters, his face smeared with sweat and grease. "Twenty-six truck," he rumbled. "The Human Fly is invincible."

And then the band started in—smokebombs, megadecibels, subhuman screeches, the works—and I led Zoltan to his dressing room. He refused a shower, but allowed the makeup girl to sponge off his face and hands. We had to cut the old outfit off of him—he was too exhausted to undress himself—and then the girl helped him into the brand-new one I'd provided for the occasion. "Twenty-six truck," he kept mumbling to himself, "A-OK."

I wanted him to call it off. I did. He wasn't in his right mind, anybody could see that. And he was exhausted, beat, as starved and helpless as a refugee. He wouldn't hear of it. "Twenty-six truck," he rumbled, and when I put through a frantic last-minute call to Sol, Sol nearly swallowed the phone. "Damn straight he's going for it!" he shouted. "We got sponsors lined up here. ABC Sports wants to see the tape, for christsake." There was an outraged silence punctuated by the click of throat lozenges, and then Sol cut the connection.

Ultimately, Zoltan went for it. Mink threw open the trailer door, Zoltan fired up the motorcycle—a specially modified Harley Sportster with gas shocks and a bored engine—and one of our people signaled the band to cut it short. The effect was dynamic, the band cutting back suddenly to a punchy drum-and-bass thing and the growl of the big bike coming on in counterpoint . . . and then Zoltan sprang from the back of the trailer, his cape stiff with the breeze, goggles flashing, tires squealing. He made three circuits of the lot, coming in close on the line of trucks, dodging away from the ramp, hunched low and flapping over the handlebars. Every eye was on him. Suddenly he raised a bony fist in the air, swerved wide of the trucks in a great arcing loop that took him to the far end of the lot, and made a run for the ramp.

He was a blur, he was nothing, he was invisible, a rush of motion above the scream of the engine. I saw something—a shadow—launch itself into the thick brown air, cab after cab receding beneath it, the glint of chrome in the sun, fifteen trucks, twenty, twenty-five, and then the sight that haunts me to this day. Suddenly the shadow was gone and a blemish appeared on the broad side panel of the last truck, the one we'd taken across country, Mink's truck, and then, simultaneous with it, there was the noise. A single booming reverberation, as if the world's biggest drum had exploded, followed by the abrupt cessation of the motorcycle's roar and the sad tumbling clatter of dissociated metal.

We had medical help this time, of course, the best available: paramedics, trauma teams, ambulances. None of it did any good. When I pushed through the circle of people around him, Zoltan was lying there on the pavement like a bundle of broken twigs. The cape was twisted round his neck, and his limbs—the sorry fleshless sticks of his arms and legs—were skewed like a doll's. I bent over him as the paramedics brought up the stretcher. "Twenty-five truck next time," he whispered, "promise me."

There was blood in his ears, his nostrils, his eye sockets. "Yes," I said, "yes. Twenty-five."

"No worries," he choked as they slid the stretcher under him, "the Human Fly . . . can survive . . . anything."

We buried him three days later.

It was a lonely affair, as funerals go. The uncle, a man in his seventies with the sad scrawl of time on his face, was the only mourner. The press stayed away, though the videotape of Zoltan's finale was shown repeatedly over the air and the freeze-frame photos appeared in half the newspapers in the country. I was shaken by the whole thing. Sol gave me a week off and I did some real soul-searching. For a while I thought of giving up the entertainment business altogether, but I was pulled back into it despite myself. Everybody, it seemed, wanted a piece of Zoltan. And as I sat down to sort through the letters, telegrams, and urgent callback messages, the phone ringing unceasingly, the sun flooding the windows of my new well-appointed and highflown office, I began to realize that I owed it to Zoltan to pursue them. This was what he'd wanted, after all.

We settled finally on an animated series, with the usual tie-ins. I knew the producer—Sol couldn't say enough about him—and I knew he'd do quality work. Sure enough, the show premiered number one in its timeslot and it's been there ever since. Sometimes I'll get up early on a Saturday morning just to tune in, to watch the jerky figures move against a backdrop of greed and corruption, the Human Fly ascendant, incorruptible, climbing hand over hand to the top.

Kate Braverman

Kate Braverman (1950–), a Southland native and a graduate of U.C.L.A. and Sonoma State University, has written novels, short stories, and poems of note. Much of her early work was a literature exploring excess and addiction, charting lives out of control. Storm Warnings *(1987), from which the following poems are drawn, is typical of Braverman's sharp language. She is a noted performance poet. Her more recent prose has examined Latinas in the Los Angeles area (*Palm Latitudes, *1988) and the consequences of an addictive society in an ostensible land of plenty (*Squandering the Blue, *1990), illustrating her continuing growth as an artist. Braverman lives in Beverly Hills and teaches at California State University, Los Angeles.*

. . . .

10 PM

How many women lay in darkness
in Tangier or Los Angeles,
Mexico City or Paris
considering their marriages
with the dresser mirror thus
and the fading roses
in a blue vase thus.
Through half-drawn blinds
street sounds rise
like a smoke that chokes.

No vocabulary can define this poison.
The man across the alley coughing.
The student downstairs singing opera.
The couple fighting in Spanish.
This is a death by implication.

How many women lay in their separate
and identical darkness
surveying the damage
beneath an intense moon.

Mother, it is all so frail.
Mother, I am terrified.
Hour of the ghost,
the lost drunken husband,
the ambulance siren.
Hour of the bullet that ricochets.
Hour of the rosary that lies.

How many women with their histories
bare, naked.
Not their flesh, which is easy,
but their secrets.
How many women making a list
of the chances they missed.
How many acres of skin creased
by heat-stained sheets.
How many women drifting
in the August night.
How many women burying
themselves at sea.

YOU ASK ABOUT MADNESS

A wrong door is opened
by accident.
You enter the vat kingdom.
It is waveless and deep
as a poisoned well.

Asbestos will not save you,
diligence or vaccinations.
Night is a tunnel
for your fist.
The sky disappears.
You hear the pin pulled
on the hand grenade
in your head.

Your legs poise at the oily
waste ink black high tide,
the full count,
the last unspeakable edge
when sleepless and exhausted
you hate each garden
fence slat,
each black blade of grass.

You sense a crowd of scales,
amphibian breaths
and a persistent chill.
Night callouses,
glacial in impact
and you are sheeted,
a pond under ice where rocks
are tossed and lost stars fall
jaded and degenerate,
burning to death.

Sleep brings no deliverance.
Your dreams are small zoos.

You fear the drain of morning,
affliction of sparrows and sun.
You repeat your sins, one by one.
The black dog rears
and breaks his slender chain.
The bloodless slain return
on their accord.

Survival is absolutely random.

SOFTENINGS

When you have lost everything
the world softens.
Your youth is barricaded
on an impassable avenue
in a city you barely remember
where the architecture aggressively
asserts a premise you cannot comprehend.
The birds assault you from trees
you do not recognize.
The passersby are of another race.
The young men you loved
have died at war or drowned.
It is over.

You learn by trial and fire
your petty abilities
and limits.
You buy illusions,
defend nonexistent borders.
You swing with the arcs
of style and fashion
and know the leap
the hanging man takes.
It means nothing.

When you have exhausted the masks
of betrayer and victim,
girl of the dancing slippers
and slasher,
the world softens.
You know nights when the saints call
And the nights when they are silent.
The process remains hooded,
inexplicable and random.

The music is finite,
the roses, the moon, love
and your personal hourglass,
the monsters under the bed
and all your tumultuous follies,
transitory and arbitrary.
When you know you are unnecessary
the world softens, quiets, dissolves
like the smoke from a worn-out spell.

Gerald Haslam

Gerald Haslam (1937–   ) was born in Bakersfield, raised in Oildale, and educated at San Francisco State College, Washington State University, and Union Graduate School. Like many Central Valley natives, his background includes farm labor and oil-field work—blue-collar roots—and those experiences were reflected in Okies *(1973), a short-story collection that was his breakthrough book. He is noted for short fiction and essays—especially personal essays—set in this state's rural or small-town regions. Critic David Fine observed in a* Westways *article, "He writes with tolerance about intolerance, with a sense of justice about injustice and with humor that doesn't stoop to condescension." Another critic, David Peck, writing in* The Californians, *called him "the quintessential California writer." Haslam lives in rural Penngrove and teaches at Sonoma State University.*

. . . .

UPSTREAM

That morning my Uncle Arlo Epps stalked out from the cabin buck naked and declared, "I'm a unsheathed soul!" Then he dove right into the Kern River and swam, angling kinda upstream to fight the current so that, whenever he finally turned directly into it, he just hung in that swift water, about halfway across, straight out from where I stood watching him.

"A unsheathed soul?" I asked myself.

He sure picked a terrible place to swim, the river right there, just below where Kern Canyon opened into the Southern Sierra, because that water it was snow melt straight from the high country, and it come down fast and freezing. Directly above where Uncle Arlo took to swimming, there was these rapids couldn't no boat get through and, at the canyon's mouth, this cataract was boiling.

At first I just stood there and watched him, stunned I guess. Once Uncle

Arlo got turned into the current, though, and chugged into a rhythm that held him even with me—slipping back, then pulling forward again—I hollered at him, "Uncle Arlo! Uncle Arlo!"

"Leave the ol' fool alone," snapped my Aunt Mazie Bee leaning on the cabin's doorway. "He's just a-tryin' to attract attention." She disappeared back into the darkness, talking to herself.

Me, I spent most of that morning watching my uncle surge, slip back, then surge again, as he tried to hold even with the cabin. You know, I'd never even seen him naked before, let alone acting so crazy, so I didn't know what to do. A couple times I asked Aunt Mazie Bee if we shouldn't try to help him some way.

"Help him?" she finally huffed. "Arlo Epps is a growed man. He can just take care a hisself."

"But he might get drownded," I insisted.

"Hah!" was all she said.

I wasn't surprised at her acting so hateful toward him. They'd had an argument that morning as usual. I'd heard 'em rumbling at one another through the walls. It went on longer than most and I'd begun to wonder if there'd be any breakfast at all, then he'd jumped into the river. As a matter of fact, there wasn't no breakfast, but I never really noticed because I was so worried about Uncle Arlo.

Come midafternoon, me avoiding chores to watch him fight that current, still figuring him to collapse any second, I determined to rescue my uncle. Without asking permission, I pulled our boat, the Packard Prow Special, out from the shed and dragged her to the river's bank.

The Special was this old wooden dinghy that Uncle Arlo he'd took as pay for a dowsing job years before. She'd never looked too great but, in spite of her one-lung'd motor, my uncle'd been able to use her on that river without no trouble. What give the Special class, though, was that Packard hood ornament Uncle Arlo'd wired to her prow. He'd traded for it at this yard sale and he kept it all the time shined, something that really ate at Aunt Mazie Bee. She said it just showed how foolish he was.

Anyways, I launched the boat and managed to put it into position next to my uncle, that bright ornament pointed upstream toward the canyon. I leaned over to talk to him, and was I shocked by how he looked. He was so *white*. I'd always seen his arms from the elbow down, and his face, all real tan, but the rest of him—the part his clothes hid—was the color of a trout's belly, and it seemed like he shimmered in that clear water like some kinda ghost. It was scary. "Uncle Arlo," I finally called, "please come in. You'll get drownded for sure."

My uncle he just kept on cruising, his face out of the water every other stroke. His eyes they looked real big and white, but I couldn't tell if he recognized me. "Shall I bring you some dinner?" I yelled. "You gotta eat." He never answered, but those two-tone arms kept stretching, those white eyes turning.

Then he done something that surprised me. This fat stonefly it come bouncing down the water toward him. Just before it reached his face, he twisted his body and snatched the big insect into his mouth. "Crime-inently!" I gasped. I surely wasn't gonna mention *that* to Aunt Mazie Bee.

When I chugged the Packard Prow back to shore, I hurried to the cabin and faced down my aunt. "You gotta *do* something," I insisted. "Uncle Arlo'll get drownded for sure."

"He'll no such a thang," she snorted. "Arlo Epps won't act his age is what he won't. He jest wants attention, but what he needs is to brang in some money and stop his durn dreamin'."

"But Aunt Mazie Bee . . ."

"No buts! Now do yer chores!"

Well, I stayed up all night, or tried to—I reckon I mighta dozed some leaning against the Special there on the bank. Not much, though, 'cause in the moonlight I could see him out there, holding against the current, that white body flashing like a fishing lure, never still. Just about dawn, I snuck in the cabin and brewed some coffee, then filled the old thermos bottle. I knew my uncle had to be froze by then and I was determined to force some hot coffee down him. I carried it to the Special, then bucked the river's swirl out to Uncle Arlo and directed the boat right next to him. He didn't pay me no mind. "You gotta drink some coffee," I urged. "Uncle Arlo, pleeease." He kept pulling against that rushing water, nipping at the morning's hatch of mayflies. I finally give up.

That afternoon a reporter and a photographer from the Bakersfield newspaper showed up. My aunt'd called them. "I thought you wasn't gonna give Uncle Arlo no attention," I hissed to her out the corner of my mouth.

"Hesh up," she snapped, "or I'll peench a chunk outta you. Besides, I'm not a-givin' him the kind he wants, I'll tell you that much. We gotta live some way, don't we?"

That reporter he was a stout gent that chewed on a unlit cigar. His partner was a little weasel lugging his big, giant camera and with a fat bag hanging from one shoulder.

After my aunt got done telling her story, that reporter just closed his notebook and put his stub pencil away. "Lady," he said real rough, "you must think we were born yesterday. Nobody could do what you claim your old man's done. We weren't born yesterday, right, Earl?"

"Right," agreed the photographer.

"Ask the boy," replied Aunt Mazie Bee, unwilling to back down.

The reporter wiggled his wet cigar at her, then he turned to face me. "Well, boy?" he demanded.

I looked at the ground. "It's true. Honest."

We was standing on the river's bank, maybe a hundred feet from where Uncle Arlo worked against the current. The reporter he stared at that pale form that the rushing water made look like a torpedo, then he asked, "What's that guy wearing?"

I looked at my aunt and she looked at me. "Well, he left in a big hurry," she finally said.

"Yeah, but what's he wearing?"

"Nothin'," she choked.

"Nothing? You mean he's bare-assed?"

"Yeah," I gulped, and my aunt she looked away.

"For Chrissake, Earl, get a picture of that nut!"

"Right," said the photographer.

"What'd you say his name was?" asked the reporter, and Aunt Mazie Bee she smiled.

The story with a picture was in that next day's paper, and the crowds begun arriving before lunch. My aunt was ready for 'em.

She stationed herself at the gate in a warped wooden lawn chair we'd salvaged years before from the river. She also had me set up our old card table—that we got cheap at a yard sale—and she put on it a cigar box to hold all the money she planned to collect, plus a empty soup can to spit snuff juice into. Across her lap she laid our old single-shot .410 that Uncle Arlo'd swapped for way back when. Finally, she tied on her good sunbonnet and waited. "Ever'body pays, buster," she told the first arrival. "That'll be two bits." Then she shot a stream into the can—*Ptui!*—and give me a I-told-you-so grin.

What a buncha jokers turned out. While my uncle was struggling in that water, pickups and jalopies and hot rods sped to the fence and out spilled the darndest specimens I ever seen: mostly young studs with more tattoos per square mile than the state pen. All colors and shapes, sucking on toothpicks and sleeves rolled up, gals parading in bathing suits and shorts, giggling and pointing while boyfriends scowled at each other.

"Hell, I could swim 'er easy," claimed one old boy that had a pack of cigarettes rolled into a sleeve of his T-shirt, and the crowd cheered. A minute later he was into a fight with another guy that had his sleeves rolled up too, and the crowd surged and tugged for a minute, then cheered some more.

Aunt Mazie Bee hardly seemed to notice the goings-on. She sat counting quarters and filling that spit can. Once she called, "No rock-throwin', buster," and she gestured with her scattergun. The old boy quit flinging stones at Uncle Arlo right now.

A little later, after she'd sold a couple old tires for a dollar and this beat-up bike seat for thirty cents, a great big potbellied devil without no shirt on swaggered up to the doorway of our cabin, but my aunt never blinked: "Nothin' fer sale in there, buster, but you about to buy this .410 shell." She clicked back the hammer, and he lost interest in the cabin real quick. A hour later she sold the lawn chair to a Mexican man for seventy-five cents and took to accepting bids on the card table. I never liked the way she took to eyeing the Packard Prow Special.

It was about dark, the crowd finally drifting off, when that Cadillac swooped up to the gate. Out of the driver's seat come this big, tough-looking guy in a suit and tie that went and opened a back door. A short, fat guy—in a suit and tie but with a hat too—he squeezed out. The two of them they paid my aunt—by now she was sitting on a nail keg—then they trooped through what was left of the picnickers and beer drinkers, the crowd kinda opening and staring real quiet as them two passed because they looked like they'd showed up at the wrong place.

On the point closest to Uncle Arlo, they stood for a long time, not talking to one another that I could see, their eyes on them two-tone arms, on that two-tone head and on that ghost of a body in the current. Finally, the fat man called to my aunt in this high-pitched voice: "Lady, you got a boat we can use?"

Aunt Mazie Bee's eyes narrowed. "Fer what?"

"For five bucks."

He was speaking my aunt's language, so even before she answered I was trudging to the Special. I knew I'd be ferrying the fat guy. There wasn't room for three, so only me and the fat guy we chugged out, the current jerking and pushing us around till I got that hood ornament pointed upstream and we moved toward Uncle Arlo. That big shot he clung to the boat's sides tight as he could, and I was half-tempted to dump us both just to keep him away from my uncle because there was something real rank about him.

When we finally arrived alongside Uncle Arlo, the fat guy he raised one hand, signaling me to stop, then grabbed the boat's sides again right now. He watched the swimmer for a long time, then rasped to me, "How long you say he's been at it, boy?"

"Two days nearly."

"Two days without stopping?"

"Uh-huh."

"Take me back," he ordered. "I seen enough."

Soon as we hit shore, the fat man and his pal joined Aunt Mazie Bee in the cabin after she give me the .410 along with orders to make sure nobody got in without paying and not to take less than twenty cents for the nail keg. She carried the cigar box with her.

Half an hour later, my aunt walked the fat man and his pal to that Cad, shook hands, then come back to the gate as they drove away. "Well, I sold him," she announced, her hands on her hips, her chin out, grinning.

"Huh?"

"Your uncle. I sold him to that there Mr. Rattocazano of Wide World Shows. Your uncle's a-gonna be famous and we're a-gonna be rich," she told me real proud.

"But you can't *sell* Uncle Arlo," I protested. "You can't do that!"

"I can so!" she asserted. "Besides, I never exactly sold *him*, I jest sold that Mr. Rattocazano the right to exhibit him. Course, we gotta git him declared crazy first, but Mr. Rattocazano says his lawyer'll take care a that in no time. They'll brang him and the sher'ff out tomorra."

"The sher'ff?"

"To declare Arlo Epps nuts and take him. He's been crazier'n a bedbug for years. Now he can finally support us."

"But Aunt Mazie Bee . . ." I complained.

"Jest hesh!" she snapped. "This here's growed-up's business."

Tired as I was, I couldn't sleep that night for worrying about my uncle that never hurt a soul being declared nuts and took to the nuthouse or stuck in some kinda freak show. No sir, was all I could think, not to my uncle you don't. It seemed to me like Aunt Mazie Bee was the one gone crazy.

Before dawn I crept out to the Packard Prow Special and hit the river. Soon as the engine coughed me out alongside Uncle Arlo—him not looking any different than he had that first morning, arms reaching for the water in front of him, head turning regular to breathe—I hollered at him, hoping the river's growl would cover my voice. "You gotta come back, Uncle Arlo," I pleaded. "The sher'ff's gonna come and take you away. They say you've went nuts." His movements never changed, so I added, "I brung a towel."

His face kept turning, his arms pulling, but I noticed his eyes roll in my direction: He seen me. We seen each other. A real look. So I told him again: "You gotta come in. The sher'ff's coming today, and a lawyer too. They'll take you to the nuthouse or the sideshow, one." I extended that towel.

His body just shimmered in the hurried water, and his arms kept up their rhythm, but the look on his face changed. Then, sure as anything, he winked at me. That was when I noticed that the Special was gradually falling behind him. I thought for a second that the sick old motor was giving up but, no, it sounded the same as always. Then I realized he was moving upstream, real slow but moving, toward the rapids and that cataract.

I opened the throttle of the Special and caught Uncle Arlo, but not for long. We was getting close to those rapids, and he was moving faster all the time. Them two-tone arms they was churning faster, and his two-tone face hardly seemed to be sucking air as he dug in. The Special was wide-open but it was lagging farther and farther behind, so I throttled back the engine to hold even in the current, not wanting to get into the rapids.

Up ahead, I sighted my uncle slide into them, kinda bounce but keep swimming, around curling whirlpools, up swooshing runs, over hidden boulders, not believing what I was seeing with my own eyes, until pretty soon he reached the boiling edge of that cataract. I couldn't hardly breathe.

For what seemed like a long, long time he disappeared in the white water and I was scared he'd finally drownded. Then I seen this pale shape shoot up outta the water, looking less like a man at that distance than some fair fish. The current it drove him back, but a second later he come outta that froth again, farther this time, almost over the worst of it, but not quite, and he fell back into that terrible foam. I figured him a goner for sure, and I squeezed my eyes closed, not wanting to see what happened. A second later, I couldn't resist squinting 'em open. "Come on, Uncle Arlo," I heard myself rooting, "*make* it!"

Then he exploded, a ghost that popped from the cataract like . . . well, almost like a unsheathed soul, smack into the smooth water above. I couldn't believe it, but I cheered, "Yaaaay!"—my heart pumping like sixty. Whenever I rubbed my eyes and shook my head, he was stroking up there outta sight into the canyon.

I plopped in the wiggling Special, breathing real heavy, and I wiped my own face with the towel I'd brung for Uncle Arlo. He was away and I was exhausted, so I pointed the Packard Prow toward the bank. Whenever I got to shore, Aunt Mazie Bee come out from the cabin. "Where's your uncle at?" she demanded, her eyes searching the river.

"He drownded," I replied.

She glanced from me to the stream and back, made a clucking sound with her mouth, then said, "He *would*."

Charles Bukowski

Charles Bukowski (1920–), labeled by some as the most outrageous writer in California—perhaps in the nation—has also been called one of the two most influential poets in the United States. He was born in Germany and raised in Los Angeles after migrating with his family at the age of three. He spent a significant part of his life as a barfly, drinking and fighting in waterfront dives, and that rough life informed most of his early writing. He crisscrossed the country during the 1940s and wrote a stream of short stories that led to a stream of rejection slips. He was twenty-four when Story, *a prestigious literary magazine, published one of his tales. In the mid-1950s he began to write and developed a readership. When his column, "Notes of a Dirty Old Man," appeared in a Los Angeles alternative newspaper called* Open City, *his audience expanded considerably. As critic Eric Tomb explains, "Like Simon Rodia, who worked daily for decades fitting pieces of apparent junk onto his Watts Tower, Bukowski has learned how to make a ceremony of self-regard." The poems that follow, all published during the 1980s, illustrate the recent direction of Bukowski's work. His more than forty books included the inspiration for the movie* Barfly, *for which he wrote the script. He lives in San Pedro.*

. . . .

A RADIO WITH GUTS

it was on the 2nd floor on Coronado Street
I used to get drunk
and throw the radio through the window
while it was playing, and, of course,
it would break the glass in the window
and the radio would sit out there on the roof
still playing

313

and I'd tell my woman,
"Ah, what a marvelous radio!"

the next morning I'd take the window
off the hinges
and carry it down the street
to the glass man
who would put in another pane.

I kept throwing that radio through the window
each time I got drunk
and it would sit out there on the roof
still playing—
a magic radio
a radio with guts,
and each morning I'd take the window
back to the glass man.

I don't remember how it ended exactly
though I do remember
we finally moved out.
there was a woman downstairs who worked in
the garden in her bathing suit
and her husband complained he couldn't sleep nights
because of me
so we moved out
and in the next place
I either forgot to throw the radio out the window
or I didn't feel like it
anymore.
I do remember missing the woman who worked in the
garden in her bathing suit,
she really dug with that trowel
and she put her behind up in the air
and I used to sit in the window
and watch the sun shine all over that thing

while the music played.

THE RED PORSCHE

it feels good
to be driven about in a red
porsche
by a woman better-
read than I
am.
it feels good
to be driven about in a red
porsche
by a woman who can explain
things about
classical
music to
me.

it feels good
to be driven about in a red
porsche
by a woman who buys
things for my refrigerator
and my
kitchen:
cherries, plums, lettuce, celery,
green onions, brown onions,
eggs, muffins, long
chilis, brown sugar,
Italian seasoning, oregano, white
wine vinegar, pompeiian olive oil
and red
radishes.

I like being driven about
in a red porsche
while I smoke cigarettes in
gentle languor.

I'm lucky. I've always been
lucky:
even when I was starving to death
the bands were playing for
me.
but the red porsche is very nice
and she is
too, and
I've learned to feel good when
I feel good.

it's better to be driven around in a
red porsche
than to own
one. the luck of the fool is
inviolate.

EULOGY TO A HELL OF A DAME—

some dogs who sleep at night
must dream of bones
and I remember your bones
in flesh
and best
in that dark green dress
and those high-heeled bright
black shoes,
you always cursed when you
drank,
your hair coming down you
wanted to explode out of
what was holding you:
rotten memories of a
rotten
past, and
you finally got
out
by dying,
leaving me with the
rotten
present;
you've been dead
28 years
yet I remember you
better than any of
the rest;
you were the only one
who understood
the futility of the
arrangement of
life;
all the others were only
displeased with
trivial segments,

carped
nonsensically about
nonsense;
Jane, you were
killed by
knowing too much.
here's a drink
to your bones
that
this dog
still
dreams about.

Ella Leffland

Ella Leffland (1931–), a native of Martinez, has developed a major reputation as a novelist. Love Out of Season *(1979) is set in the Bay Area during the turbulent late 1960s.* Rumors of Peace *(1979), traces life in her hometown (called "Mendoza") from 1941–45 and is among the finest California books dealing with that period. In 1990 she won the Bay Area Book Reviewers' Award for* The Knight, Death and the Devil, *a novel about Herman Goering. Gifted with a complex vision, Leffland explains that she refused to create totally evil stereotypes of Nazis in her novel: "There are almost no people like that. People who perpetuate evil are much like everyone else." And that simple remark illustrates what much of this Bay-Area native's fiction reveals—breaking through cliches and expectations in order to reveal truth. The story that follows is from her lone collection of short fiction,* Last Courtesies *(1980). She lives in San Francisco.*

. . . .

THE LINDEN TREE

In the early years there had been passion, but now they were just a couple who had grown old together. The last twenty years they had owned a rooming house, where they lived contentedly on the ground floor with their cat, Baby.

Giulio was a great putterer. You could always see him sweeping the front steps or polishing the doorknobs, stopping to gossip with the neighbors. He was a slight, pruny man of sixty-eight, perfectly bald, dressed in heavy trousers, a bright sports shirt with a necktie, and an old man's sweater-jacket, liver-colored and hanging straight to the knees. He had a thick Italian accent and gesticulated wildly when he was excited.

George was quite different. Everything about him was slow and solid, touched by grandeur. Though he was a Negro from the Midwest, he spoke with an accent that sounded British, yet not exactly. He was seventy-four, but looked much younger, with a hard body and a hard face with only a few deep fissures in it. Giulio was a neat dresser, but George was attired. His perfectly creased trousers, his crisp white shirt, smoothly knotted tie, and gray sleeveless sweater seemed out of place in the stuffy little flat.

A home is usually the wife's creation, and so it was in their case. The doilies, the vases with their wax flowers, the prints of saints hanging among gaudy floral calendars—all these were Giulio's. George's contribution was less concrete but more important. He made their life possible, dealing with the rents and taxes, attending to the heavy chores, ousting tenants who drank or brawled. If Giulio were to run the building he would soon come to grief, for he had no real sense of work, and as for the rents, it was all he could do to add two digits together. In addition, he was fussy and faultfinding, so that he often took a dislike to perfectly good tenants, yet countenanced glib bullies.

They were a nicely balanced couple, and for years had been happy. When they were young they had had their troubles—living quarters had been hard to find not only because of George's color, but because of their relationship. In those days Giulio had had fetching ways, too obvious to be ignored. But gradually he passed into a fussy dotage, and now people thought of the pair merely as two lonely old men who lived together. George's color no longer presented problems now that he had proved what was not necessarily de-manded of those who asked for proof: that he was a responsible man, an asset to the neighborhood. His building was the best kept on the block, his rents reasonable, his tenants, for the most part, permanent. He would not rent to the fly-by-night element that was slowly invading the district.

The tenants consisted of a pair of raddled, gadabout sisters, a World War I veteran with one leg, and a few clerks and students. Giulio regaled George with facts about these people he gleaned by snooping through their rooms in their absence, and George put him down for this, even threatened him, but it did no good. And in any case, the tenants did not seem to care; there was something so simple about Giulio that his spying was like that of a mouse or a bird. They called him Aunty Nellie (his last name being Anto-nelli), and the younger ones sometimes invited him into their rooms so that his teeth might be enjoyed. These were ill-fitting, too large for his mouth, and clicked through his speech. When he grew excited, they slipped out of place, at which he would pause in a natural, businesslike way to jam them back in before going on.

Giulio was forever dragging the carpet sweeper up and down the halls, looking for an ear to gossip in. George, on the other hand, talked very little. Only tenants who had lived there a long time got to know him at all, when, once in a great while, he would invite them in for a glass of sherry when they came to pay the rent.

In his flat, the tenants found George to be a different man, less aloof and forbidding. Sitting there with Giulio and Baby, the cat, he had something patient, indulgent, altogether loving in his face. Giulio looked with pride at him, glancing now and then at the guest, as though to say: Isn't he wonderful? Sometimes he would go so far as to confess, "I no good at the paper work, but George, George, he *smart*." Or, "We live together fifty years, never a yell, always happy." And George would give him a look to show him that he was saying too much, and then Giulio would sulk and refuse to rejoin the conversation. But the next day he would be the same as ever, whirling creakily around the steps with his broom, or around his garden with a green visor clamped to his head.

He had a shrine in the garden, with statues of the saints standing in sun-blanched profusion. He was an ardent Catholic, and there was no one with a greater collection of religious objects—rosaries and crosses and vestments, which he kept in his bureau drawer and brought out to enjoy their varied glass, wooden, and satin richness. But religious as he was, he would not divest his beloved garden of one fresh bloom for his saints. It was a skimpy garden, heavily bolstered with potted geraniums, and he was so proud of each green shoot that struggled through the hard ground, and attended its subsequent flowering with such worried care, that it was only when a flower had finally begun to wither on the stem that he would pluck it as an offering to his statues.

George understood this attitude and was properly grateful when once a year on his birthday he received a sacrifice of fresh daisies and marigolds. He was amused by Giulio's niggardliness toward the saints. He himself did not care about them. He, too, was a Catholic, but had become one only so that he and Giulio might be buried together. Two fully paid-for plots, side by side, awaited them under a linden tree in Our Lady of Mercy Cemetery just outside town. Whoever was the first to go, George because he was older, Giulio because he was frailer, the other would join him in due time. Giulio had vague visions of an afterlife. The older man did not. He had had a good life, everything considered, and he would be content to die and be done with when the time came, and have his bones rest by his friend's forever. Sometimes he thought of the linden tree and gave a satisfied nod.

But lately George had noticed something strange about Giulio. His large red ears seemed to have grown less red.

"Giulio," he said one day, "your ears don't seem to be as red as they used to be."

Giulio touched his ear. When he was young he had been sensitive about their largeness. "Nothing wrong with my ears," he said defensively.

"I'm not criticizing you, Giulio. I think it's just strange." And now he realized that some definite change had been taking place in his friend, but he could not put his finger on it. It was as though he were a little smaller. The jacket seemed to hang lower than it had.

Ah, well, he thought, we're both getting old.

A few days later, as Giulio was raking the leaves in the garden, he complained to George of shortness of breath, and there was the faintest touch of blue in his lips.

"Why don't you go to the doctor for a checkup?" George asked as casually as he could.

Giulio shook his head and continued his raking.

That night, as Giulio was turning on the television set, he suddenly stepped back and dropped into a chair with his hand spread across his chest. "Help!" he shouted into the air. "Help!" and when his friend ran to his side, he gasped, "I gotta pain. Here! Here!" And his hand clutched at his heart so hard that the knuckles were white.

The next day George took him to the doctor, and sat by his side through all the tests. Giulio was terrified, but when it was all over and they came out of the doctor's office he seemed restored.

"See," he said, "I'm okay. The doctor he say no worry."

George's face did not reflect Giulio's good spirits. "I know he says not to worry, but . . ."

"He say no worry," Giulio repeated cheerfully.

But from then on Giulio was visited frequently by the paralyzing pains. He would stop what he was doing and crouch over, his eyes darting frenziedly in their sockets. If George was there he would hurry to his friend's side, but at these moments Giulio seemed totally alone even though his hand grasped George's arm. When it was over he would be stripped of his little ways; he would wander slowly around the room or stand for long moments looking at nothing. Patiently George would wait, and eventually the old Giulio returned. Uneasily, fretfully, he would say, "I no understand. Looka me, I never hurt a fly in all my life, and this pain, he come and scare me. It's not right."

"Well," George would venture soothingly, "if you'd just eat fewer starches and stop worrying, these pains would go away. You've got plenty of years ahead of you . . ."

"Plenty years?" Giulio would break in sharply. "I *know,* I *know* I got plenty years ahead. This pain, he no *important,* he just *scare* me."

In an effort to distract him, George broke a lifelong precedent and invited Myrna and Alice Heppleworth, the two aging sisters who lived on the third floor, down to the flat for the evening. He himself did not like women, but Giulio did, in a way that George could not understand. Giulio loved to gossip with them, and afterward delighted in describing their clothes and manners, which he usually found distressing. He was more interested in the Heppleworth sisters than in anyone else in the building, and always pursed his lips when he saw them going out with their rheumy escorts, and could never forget that he had once found a bottle of gin in a dresser drawer ostensibly given over to scarves and stockings.

The Heppleworth sisters came, drank all their wine, and turned the television set up as high as it would go. George grew rigid; Giulio went to bed. The sisters were not asked again.

It seemed to George that Giulio failed daily. His ears were as pale as his face, and this seemed particularly significant to George. He found himself suddenly looking at his friend to check his ears, and each time they looked whiter. He never discussed this with Giulio, because Giulio refused to speak about his fears, as though not daring to give them authority by acknowledging them.

And then one morning Giulio gave up this pretense. As he was getting out of bed he had an attack, and when he recovered this time he let out a piercing wail and began to weep, banging his head from side to side. The rest of the day he spent immobile, wrapped from head to foot in a patchwork quilt.

Toward evening George made him get up and walk in the garden with him. George pointed to the flowers, praising them, and gently turned his friend's face to the shrine. The white plaster faces looked peaceful. Even he, George, felt it, and he realized that for weeks he had been in need of some comfort, something outside himself.

"Look," he said, and that was all, fearing to sound presumptuous, because the statues belonged to Giulio and the church—he himself understood nothing of them.

Giulio looked without interest, and then, forgetting them, he took George's arm and his eyes swam with tears. "What can I do?" he asked. "What will happen?"

As they walked slowly back to the house he drew his lips back from his big false teeth and whispered, "I'm gonna die."

"No, no, don't think that way," George soothed, but he felt helpless, and resentful that his friend must go through this terror. And now that Giulio had said the words, his terror would grow, just as the pain of a bad tooth grows when you finally acknowledge the decay and are plunged into a constant probing of it with your tongue.

When they came back inside Giulio went straight to bed. George stood in the kitchen and looked at his face in the little mirror that hung on the wall. He feared Giulio would die this very minute in the bedroom as he was removing his carpet slippers, and he wanted with every muscle to run to him. But it would not do to become as hysterical as Giulio, and he stood still. Presently the sound of the bedsprings released a sigh from his throat. The flat was silent. He looked again at his face in the mirror. It was as though he were one person and the reflection another, and he was uneasy and embarrassed, and yet could not look away. He felt deeply aware of himself standing there, staring, and it seemed he was out of place, lost. He whirled around, catching his breath. He had felt entirely alone for the first time in fifty years.

The next day he decided to call for Father Salmon, the young priest from the neighborhood church Giulio attended. Father Salmon dropped in for friendly chats now and then, and Giulio liked him very much, so much, in fact, that the priest often had to silence him when he got carried away with intimate gossip.

A few days later the priest knocked on the door. He was horsefaced, with thinning hair and rimless glasses, and he was quiet and pleasant.

Giulio was wrapped up in his quilt in the armchair. He did not greet the priest with his usual beam of pleasure; he did not even smile.

"Well, Giulio," the priest said, "how are you feeling? I haven't seen you at church lately."

Giulio said at once, "Father, I'm dying."

"What is the trouble?" the priest asked gently.

"It's my heart," Giulio shot back, his hand scrounging around his shirt-front and fumbling with the buttons until it was clutching his bare chest. He looked as though he were prepared to pull the heart out for inspection. His eyes pleaded with the priest to set it right. The priest sat down next to him.

"What does your doctor say?" he asked.

"Oh, Father," Giulio moaned, "the doctor is a stupid. He never tell me one real thing. In and out and all around, around the bush. He no understand, but *I* understand—this heart, he gonna kill me. You think so, Father? What do you think? You think so?"

"Surely, Giulio," the priest replied, "you must accept the doctor's word. If he says there's no reason to fear . . ."

Giulio looked away, black with melancholy.

The priest sat silently for a moment, then began again. "Giulio, death is as natural as birth. Think of your flowers out there in the garden, how they grow from little seeds and then fade and fall—what could be more natural? God has been with you all your life, and He will not forsake you now . . ."

But Giulio, his eyes shutting tighter and tighter as the priest spoke, got up from his chair and crept into the bedroom, dragging his quilt behind him.

Afterward he said to George, "I no wanna see Father Salmon again."

"Father Salmon is trying to help," George told him.

Giulio shook his head, his fingers rubbing the area of his heart.

What a strange person he is, George thought, looking at him closely. All these years he has been immersed in the church, and now, suddenly, the church means nothing to him. He recalled a conversation he had overheard a few days ago as he was fixing a faulty burner in the second floor kitchen. Two of the students were going down the hall, talking. One had commented on Giulio's bad health. The other had replied, "Don't worry, Aunty Nellie could never do anything so profound as to die."

George had bristled, as he always did whenever anyone made fun of his friend—but it was true that Giulio was not profound. He liked pretty things, and the church gave him its rich symbols; he liked intimate conversation, and the church gave him patient Father Salmon; he liked the idea of an afterlife, and the church gave him that, too. He loved the church, but when you came right down to it, he believed only what he could see with his two eyes, and he could see only his blue lips and wasted face in the mirror. This oddly realistic attitude explained his stinginess toward the saints; they were, after all, only plaster. And yet when Baby had once jumped up on the shrine and relieved himself on St. Francis's foot, Giulio had screamed at the animal until the neighbors hung from the windows.

All these amiable contradictions in Giulio had been known to George for fifty years, and he had always believed that they would sustain his friend through everything. Now the contradictions were gone. All that was left in Giulio was the certainty of death. It made George feel forlorn, on the outside. He sensed that nothing could be set right, that Giulio would live consumed by fear until he died consumed by fear, and the linden tree would not mark two intertwined lives, but forever cast its shadow between two strangers.

They had met for the first time in front of the Minneapolis train station in the first decade of the century. George sat in the driver's seat of a Daimler, in his duster and goggles. His employer had gone inside to meet one Giulio Antonelli, just arrived from Calabria, nephew of the head gardener. When he emerged he had in tow a thin boy of eighteen dressed in a shabby suit and carrying a suitcase that looked like a wicker basket. He wore cherry-colored cigar bands on his fingers, and had a shoot of wilted wild flowers stuck through the buttonhole of his jacket. His eyes were red-rimmed; apparently he had been crying all the way from Calabria. Delicate and terrified, his cigar bands glittering hectically in the sunlight, he crawled into the Daimler and collapsed in a corner.

George had worked as a chauffeur and handyman on his employer's estate for five years, but was originally from an isolated Finnish farming community where God knows what fates had conspired to bring his parents, a bitter, quarreling, aloof, and extremely poor black couple. George became friends with only one thing native to that cold country, the stones that littered the fields. He could not say what attracted him to them, but he felt a great bond with them. When he was ten he built a wall of the stones. It was only a foot high and not very long, and there was nothing in the world for it to guard there in the middle of the empty field, but he knew he had discovered the proper use of the stones, and all his life he had the feeling he was that wall.

In Minneapolis, on the estate, he kept to himself. He liked the Daimler, which he drove with authority, and the appearance of which on the streets caused people to gawk with admiration. He picked up his employer's speech habits, and this, combined with the Finnish accent he had absorbed, gave a peculiar, unplaceable ring to his words, which he relished, because it was his alone.

The Calabrian boy turned out to be a poor gardener, not because he was listless with homesickness, for that soon passed, but because he made favorites of certain flowers and would have nothing to do with the others. The tulips, for instance, he apparently considered stout and silly-looking, and he made disparaging faces at them. He liked the wild flowers that cropped up in odd corners.

George was fascinated by Giulio, although he did not like him. He reminded him of a woman. Women had never respected George's wall, at least a certain type of woman had not—the bold Finnish farm girls, some of the hired women here on the estate. He was well favored, and maybe there was something in his coloring, too, that attracted women, something tawny, reminiscent of the sun, here, where everyone else looked like a peeled banana. In any case, they were always after him. He was not flattered. He felt they were not interested in him as he knew himself, proud and valuable, but in some small part of him that they wanted for their own use, quickly, in a dark corner.

But Giulio, though girlish, had no boldness in him. He would leave the garden and lean against the garage door where George was polishing the Daimler. "*Bella, bella,*" he would murmur, and his face shone with a kind of radiant simplemindedness. There was no calculation in him—sometimes you could see him cocking his head and singing before the wild flowers in the garden. Watching George, the boy spoke foreign words rich in their tones of admiration, and his quick, glittering fingers—he had bought flashy rings with his pay—seemed anxious to catch the sun and make a present of it to the tall, mute figure in the gloom of the garage.

Two months after his arrival Giulio was fired. George, filled with fear for himself, feeling a great chasm opening before him, quit his job, and the two of them, with hardly a word between them, took the train to San Francisco, where Giulio had another uncle. All during the trip George asked himself: "Why am I doing this? Why am I going with him? I don't even like him. He's a silly, ridiculous person; there's something the matter with him."

They got off at the San Francisco depot, and before George was even introduced to the uncle, who stood waiting, he picked up his baggage and, without a word of farewell to Giulio, walked quickly away from him.

First he found odd jobs, and finally he wound up on Rincon Hill with another Daimler. On his half day off each week he would wander around

the city, looking at the sights. Whenever he saw a quick, thin figure that reminded him of Giulio his heart would pound, and he would say to himself,
"Thank God it's not Giulio, I don't want to see him again." And then he
found that what had begun as a casual walk around the city was turning
into a passionate weekly search. The day he caught sight of Giulio sadly and
ineffectively constructing a pyramid of cabbages in a vegetable market, he
had to restrain himself from throwing his arms around him.

Giulio's face had blanched with surprise when he looked up, and then his
eyes had filled with a dazzling welcome, and he had extended his hand to
his returned friend with a tenderness George never forgot.

They were together from then on. In time they bought a vegetable stand,
and as a result of George's frugality and common sense he was able to save
in spite of Giulio's extravagances. They worked and invested, and in thirty
years they were able to buy, for cash, the old apartment building they now
lived in. Life had always been strangely easy for them. They had been incapable of acknowledging affronts, even when they were refused lodgings
or openly stared at on the street, and the last twenty years in the security of
their own flat had been free from problems, satisfying in all ways.

Now Giulio moaned, "Oh, I gotta pain, I gotta pain."

George would take his hand and say, "I'm here, Giulio, I'm here."

But Giulio would look through him, as though he did not exist.

"Don't we *know* each other?" George finally exploded one day, causing
Baby to speed under a table with his ears laid back. "Are we strangers after
all these years?"

Giulio closed his eyes, involved with his fear.

George sighed, stroking his friend's hand, thin and waxy as a sliver of
soap. "What are you thinking about now, this very minute, Giulio? You
must tell me."

"I'm thinking of my dog," Giulio said, after a silence.

"What dog was that?" George asked softly.

"I had him in Nocera."

"And what about him?"

"He died, and my father he dug a hole and put him in." His lips turned
down. "I dug him up later, I was lonely for him."

"What a foolish thing to do, my poor Giulio."

"His own mother wouldn'a wanted him. Bones and worms . . ."

"Hush, Giulio."

"Gonna happen to me."

"But your soul . . ."

"What's my soul look like?" Giulio asked quickly.

"Like you, Giulio . . . it's true . . ."

Giulio cast him a look of contempt George would not have thought him capable of.

"The little hole, the bones and worms," Giulio moaned.

"But you've *had* a life!" George suddenly cried with exasperation. "Do you want to live forever?"

"Yes," Giulio said simply.

From then on George felt a fury. In the past all Giulio's little fears had been bearable because he, George, could exorcise them, like a stevedore bearing a small load away. But this final cowardice excluded him. And there was nothing, no one he could turn to. He went halfheartedly to church, but got nothing from it. He began making small overtures to his tenants, but his sociability was stiff with rust. He looked with curiosity at the black people on the street, and thought there were more of them than there used to be. When a young black couple stopped him on a corner one day he listened attentively as they talked of civil rights. He accepted a pamphlet from them and read it thoroughly. But afterward he threw it out. He felt no connection with the problems it presented.

He cursed Giulio as he had cursed him fifty years ago when he had walked away from him at the train depot, and he wished for the oneness with himself that he had known in the empty fields of his youth.

In the daytime he was angrily helpful, like a disapproving orderly, but at night, as they sat in the small living room with Baby flicking his tail back and forth across the blank television screen, he went to Giulio and mutely pleaded with him. Giulio sighed abstractedly; he seemed far away, deep inside himself, listening to every heartbeat, counting every twinge, with a deep frown line between his eyes.

George moved the twin beds together, and Giulio allowed his hand to be held through the night. From then on they slept that way, hand in hand. George slept lightly, waking often. It was almost as if he wished to be awake, to enjoy the only hours of closeness he had with his friend as he held his hand. And also, in the back of his mind was the fear that if he drifted off, Giulio would be released into the arms of death. And so he lay quietly, listening to Giulio's breathing, to the wind in the trees.

Then gradually the bedroom window would turn from black to gray, and the breeze that ruffled the curtain carried in the scent of early morning. Dawn brought him sleep; the rising sun gave him a sense of security. Bad things never happened in the daytime—at least one felt that way. And so his fingers grew lax in Giulio's hand as he trusted his friend to the kindness of the dawning day.

But when he awoke later it would be with a sharp sense of foreboding. Quickly he would turn to look at Giulio, his eyes narrowed against the possible shock. But Giulio would be breathing evenly, his bluish lips parted over his gums, his teeth grinning from a water glass on the bureau. Giulio's clothes were neatly laid out, his liver-colored jacket hung over the back of a chair. How lifeless the jacket looked. George would shut his eyes, knowing that the sight of that empty jacket would be unbearable when Giulio was gone. He shook the thought from his head, wondering if life could be more painful than this. Then Giulio's eyes would open, George's face take on a formal nonchalance. And so another night had passed. Their hands parted.

"How do you feel?" George would ask shortly.

Giulo would sigh.

They took their breakfast. The sun shone through the kitchen window with a taunting golden light. George snapped at Giulio. Giulio was unmoved.

One summer morning George persuaded Giulio to sit outside in the backyard. He hoped that watching him work in the garden, Giulio might be persuaded to putter around again. He settled his friend into a chair and picked up the rake, but as the minutes wore on and he moved around the garden in the hot sun, raking the leaves together, Giulio showed no sign of interest. George stopped and put the rake down. Not knowing if he wished to please Giulio or anger him, he suddenly broke off the largest marigold in the garden and held it out.

Giulio shaded his watering eyes with his hand; then his eyes drifted away from the flower like two soap bubbles in the air. George flung the flower to the ground, staring at Giulio, then strode to the shrine and stood there with his hands in fists, blindly determined to do something that would shake his friend open, break him in two if need be. He grabbed the arm of the Virgin Mary and lifted the statue high, and heard Giulio's voice.

"George."

"That's right," George growled, replacing the statue and breathing threateningly through his nostrils, "I would have smashed it to bits!"

"Smash what?" Giulio asked indifferently, and George saw that under the awning of his thin hand his eyes were closed.

"Were your eyes closed?" George thundered. "Didn't you *see* me?"

"You no care that I can't open my eyes—this sun, he hurt them. You *mean*, George, make me sit out here. Too hot. Make me feel sick. I wanna go inside."

"I was going to smash your Virgin Mary!" George cried.

Giulio shrugged. "I wanna go inside."

And then George's shoulders hunched, his face twisted up, and he broke into a storm of tears. Turning his head aside with shame, he made for the back door; then he turned around and hurried back, glancing up at the windows, where he hoped no one stood watching him cry. He put his arm around Giulio and helped him up from his chair, and the two old men haltingly crossed the garden out of the sun.

"Humiliating," George whispered when they were inside, shaking his head and pressing his eyes with a handkerchief. He slowly folded the handkerchief into a square and replaced it in his pocket. He gave a loud sniff and squared his shoulders, and looked with resignation at his distant friend.

Giulio was settling himself into the armchair, plucking the patchwork quilt around him. "Time for pills," he muttered, reaching next to him, and he poured a glass of water from a decanter and took two capsules, smacking his lips mechanically, like a goldfish. Sitting back, he looked around the room in his usual blank, uninterested way. Then a puzzled expression came into his eyes.

"Why you cry then, George?"

George shook his head silently.

"I do something you no like?"

"You never talk. It's as though we're strangers." And he broke off with a sigh. "I've told you all that before—what's the use?"

"I got big worry, George. No time to talk."

"It would be better than to think and think. What do you think about all day?"

Giulio slowly raised his eyebrows, as though gazing down upon a scene. "Bones and worms."

"Giulio, Giulio."

"Big worry, George."

"You'll drive yourself mad that way."

"I no mad at you. Just him." He lay one thin finger on his heart, lightly, as though afraid of rousing it.

"I don't mean angry . . ."

But Giulio was already tired of talking, and was plucking at the quilt again, ill, annoyed, retreating into sleep.

"Giulio, please, you've talked a little. Talk a little more—stay."

With an effort, his eyes sick and distant, Giulio stayed.

But now that he had his attention, George did not know where to begin, what to say. His mind spun; his tongue formed a few tentative words; then, clubbed by an immense fatigue, he sank into a chair with his head in his hands.

"I'm sick man," Giulio explained tonelessly, closing his eyes. After a silence he opened them and looked over at George, painfully, as though from under a crushing weight. "Tonight I hold your hand in bed again, like always. Hold your hand every night, you know that."

"You hold *my* hand?" George asked softly, lifting his head.

"In daytime," Giulio said slowly, his eyes laboriously fixed on George's attentive face, "in daytime only the bones and worms. But in the night . . . in the night, I see other things, too . . ." He was silent for a moment until a twinge had passed, then spoke again. "See you, George. And I hold your hand. Make you feel better . . ." His eyes still fixed on George's face, he gave an apologetic twitch of the lip as his lids closed, and slowly he nodded off to sleep.

Diane Wakoski

Diane Wakoski (1937–   ), a native of Whittier, was educated at U.C. Berkeley. She is among the state's most prolific and honored poets, with eighteen collections to her credit, including such noteworthy volumes as Medea: The Sorceress *(1990) and* Emerald Ice: Selected Poems 1962–87 *(1988), which won the Poetry Society of America's William Carlos Williams Award. Her verse is noted for experience presented with compassionate wisdom, as in the following brief excerpt from "Moneylight":*

> *What middle-age brings*
>
> *is the knowledge you can never*
>
> *be young again. Oddly satisfying,*
>
> *once you stop being sad. . . .*

In 1980 the University of Michigan Press published a volume of her criticism, Toward a New Poetry. *The poems included here are from* Emerald Ice.

. . . .

THE RING

I carry it on my key chain, which itself
is a big brass ring
large enough for my wrist,
holding keys for safe-deposit box,
friends' apartments,
my house, office and faithless car.

I would like to wear it,
the only ornament on my plain body,
but it is a relic,
the husband gone to other wives,

and it could never be a symbol of sharing,
but like the gold it's made of, stands for possession, power,
the security of a throne.

So, on my key ring,
dull from resting in my dark purse,
it hangs, reminding me of failures, of beauty I once had,
of more ancient searches for an enchanted ring.

I understand, now, what that enchantment is, though.
It is being loved.
Or, conversely, loving so much that you feel loved.
And the ring hangs there
with my keys,
reminding of failure.

This vain head full of roses,
crystal,
bleeding lips,
a voice doomed to listen, forever,
to itself.

THE PHOTOS

My sister in her well-tailored silk blouse hands me
the photo of my father
in naval uniform and white hat.
I say, "Oh, this is the one which Mama used to have on her dresser."

My sister controls her face and furtively looks at my mother,
a sad rag bag of a woman, lumpy and sagging everywhere,
like a mattress at the Salvation Army, though with no holes or tears,
and says, "No."

I look again,
and see that my father is wearing a wedding ring,
which he never did
when he lived with my mother. And that there is a legend on it,
"To my dearest wife,
        Love
        Chief"
And I realize the photo must have belonged to his second wife,
whom he left our mother to marry.

My mother says, with her face as still as the whole unpopulated part of the
state of North Dakota,
"May I see it too?"
She looks at it.

I look at my tailored sister
and my own blue-jeaned self. Have we wanted to hurt our mother,
sharing these pictures on this, one of the few days I ever visit or
spend with family? For her face is curiously haunted,
not now with her usual viperish bitterness,
but with something so deep it could not be spoken.
I turn away and say I must go on, as I have a dinner engagement with
    friends.
But I drive all the way to Pasadena from Whittier,
thinking of my mother's face; how I could never love her; how my father

could not love her either. Yet knowing I have inherited
the rag-bag body,
stony face with bulldog jaws.

I drive, thinking of that face.
Jeffers' California Medea who inspired me to poetry.
I killed my children,
but there as I am changing lanes on the freeway, necessarily glancing in the
rearview mirror, I see the face,
not even a ghost, but always with me, like a photo in a beloved's wallet.

How I hate my destiny.

PRECISION

Walking, remembering,
In the grass, I see what I think is
a small *coprinus,*
but I look more closely and decide:
        broken soda cracker.
Of course,
            this Southern California lawn
probably wouldn't be growing mushrooms.

I have already catalogued
Icelandic poppies—flamingo, salmon, vermillion,
party dresses—on the lawn,
and purple flags on another,
a whole bed of tiny white irises
and nasturtiums spilling over the cement-banked edge
of another yard.

It is March, and camellias are crowding
the bushes at every house,
pink, white, deep rose frills,
china-like,
            perfect.

Behind me, the mockingbird is singing one of his best songs,
        piccolo
        oboe
        harp
        and squeaking door all combined.
The drama is only a memory;
I arrived yesterday at the Los Angeles airport
and could not help some part of me wishing / expecting to see you,
M.,
waiting for me to return.
I suppose that is what it means
to be haunted.

In my real life
I neither expect
nor want you. Yet, some rehearsal of the past
is always with me.
Even this morning,
walking before breakfast in Santa Barbara
when I saw an ugly ranch house
with the porch light still on,
presumably from the night before,
I thought, "He hasn't come home. She is asleep
on the couch
with her clothes on, exhausted from
waiting most of the night."
And when I walked past another house
with the shades still drawn
but rock music pouring out of the closed windows, so incongruously
at 8 a.m.
thought
of a young couple who have just
awakened to make love and don't want to do it
without the right music.
And I felt safe outside in the sunshine, just observing the flowers.
There is no way I can imagine
love, sex or romance
without pain,
the cutting, cutting
sharp knife of denials;
what I want now is an orderly world
where morning is
each beautiful object in place,
the sun pouring in the window like champagne,
the china-white egg cup
with its neat boiled egg,
a burst of tulips, or poppies or
camellias on the table
                          in crystal
or cut glass,
the hot teapot, scalded and then filled with a fine dark tea,

and the day stretching plain,
unadorned
      before me,
Mozart as companion,
a book,
a book,
about death
or life
but not about
love.

We must go beyond beauty
to find it.
Invisible,
I want to wait for it
wearing the cap of darkness.

Richard Rodriguez

Richard Rodriguez (1944–   ) was born of Mexican parents in San Francisco, raised in Sacramento, and educated at Stanford University, Columbia University, and the University of California. His Hunger of Memory *(1982) remains an exemplary, controversial autobiography tracing the cost of enculturation in a multi-ethnic society. Patricia Holt, book editor of* The San Francisco Chronicle, *summarized mainstream opinion this way: "Rodriguez has described the awesome struggle of Spanish-speaking children in America in a way that no other Hispanic has ever portrayed it." Chicano critics such as Arturo Islas decried the book, asserting, "Rodriguez's failure to come to terms with his dichotomies as well as his feelings of alienation from his family love are pitiable." Richard Rodriguez has, in any case, established himself as an important contemporary essayist—his work is published in many leading periodicals. Because he speaks for himself in sometimes unpopular, insistently complex and revealing terms, Rodriguez has undermined stereotypes. His work demonstrates that Mexican-Americans constitute a diverse community—no single perspective dominates, not his or anyone else's. Of late, Rodriguez has placed California itself under his microscope; the essay that follows was originally published in* This World.

. . . .

AMERICA'S WILD CHILD

Mexican kids stand on Sunset Boulevard in Beverly Hills beside sandwich boards advertising "Star Maps." They stare patiently toward private horizons as cars whiz past. If you stop, they will sell you a map of the homes of the stars.

There are two futures in California. There is the glamorous, the famous, the gaudy telling of time in California as possibility—new beginnings. There is also a tragic way of telling the future in California as limitation.

One future describes California as a series of problems—pesticide contamination; drugs; bad air—a future mired in the past. Tomorrow, when the new freeway opens, it will already be obsolete. In five years, the small farming towns in the Central Valley will be one suburban blur. By the end of the century, Californians will not be allowed to barbecue.

If California now entertains tragic possibilities, such was not always our way. For generations, since its American beginnings, California denied inevitability.

The point of this place was that it represented an escape from certainty. Go to California and find gold. Go to California and find a new life.

America seems the least tangible of countries in the world because it is built on expectation. You can start all over here. That is why people come to America—to become something new. Immigrant Americans put up with tenements and sweatshops and stoop labor not in resignation to tragedy but in the name of the future ("something better for my kids").

At the edge of geographic possibility and under a paradisaical sun, California traditionally has played America's wild child. America's America. To people in Tulsa or Como, Mississippi, as much as to pilgrims from Vietnam or from Ireland, California has been the most extreme version of America.

Who can be surprised that the world came to California and still wants to come?

Most immigrants in the world head for America, and most of those choose California. Or would. And not only foreigners; the restless come also from Pennsylvania and Michigan.

But Californians are not in the mood to be flattered. Californians, like many other Americans, are troubled by the suspicion that something is dying. Call it the American Century.

Americans have seen Japanese economic and scientific ascendancy. When the Japanese came to town a couple of months ago and bought Universal Pictures, the typical American response was worry, not flattery.

What on Earth do the Japanese think they are buying when they buy a Hollywood studio?

What the Japanese businessman knows is that the world goes to American movies. No one else in the world makes movies the world wants to see.

The Italian businessman and the British mogul know this, too—they also have recently purchased Hollywood studios.

Did America invent the movies? It doesn't matter. The movies invented America for the world. The movies have been our best advertisement. And, not coincidentally, the home of the movies was California.

The French make lovely films about couples who go on picnics. And the British make movies about detectives in cardigans. Bombay has her elephantine soaps. But only the Americans seem to have understood the implications of the size of the movie screen.

It was the Jewish immigrants to America from Eastern Europe who established the scale of the movies and thereby taught us that we could aspire to lives of scope and grandeur. Neal Gabler is too modest in the subtitle he selected for his recent and excellent book, "An Empire of Their Own: How the Jews Invented Hollywood." The haberdasher's son and the tobacconist's son in fact invented America at the movies. They gave the democratic yearnings of Americans adequate range on the screen. A chandelier and a long car in every life, yes. But lips that were 10 feet long and faces that were 40 feet high became our best metaphors of democracy. The exaggeration flattered our private ambitions.

Who needed kings in such a world? Movies belonged to their own palaces. And the people on the screen, the "stars," belonged uniquely to a place where you could become anything you wanted to be.

The divorcée on "Wheel of Fortune" who tells Pat Sajak that she's "originally" from North Carolina came to California last year to get away from the past, as did the Joad family before her and Guatemalans today. Restless lives are the point of California.

The newcomers embarrass those of us who are born here with the knowledge that restless lives are the point of life here. John Sutter and Lucille Ball, John Fremont and Walt Disney—they are the famous Californians. They came here from somewhere else. They recreated themselves.

As a native-born son of California, I am under no illusions. I do not imagine that an editorial-page essayist is more important to the vitality of this state than a Mexican illegal immigrant who is, this day, working the artichoke fields around Salinas with an intensity we mistake as resignation. I think something closer to the reverse.

We native-born Californians have been looking at movies all our lives, but with a knowledge different than that of people who saw those same movies in faraway theaters. We recognized the street pictured on the screen, and we measured the exaggeration. Our movies became a kind of family album for us, marking the changes around us. The earliest films made in Niles or in Santa Barbara or in the San Fernando Valley (in those days when it could pass for the Old West) we saw with irony and regret for our dry, lovely landscape lost.

You do not have to be an "old timer" (although, of course, in a state of much change you can easily become an old timer) to remember orchards in the Santa Clara Valley or orange groves before Disneyland or the two-lane road where now there is freeway or searching dry creeks on Saturday mornings for arrowheads—and finding them.

The native-born discovers consequence, fears change as pollution or congestion or loss, the loss of the oak trees. The native-born saw parents work and work to create paradise for their children. To the native-born, however, paradise reduces to a three-bedroom house, a mother who knew how to drive, endemic sun. All were givens, not the symbols of paradise.

The dilemma facing California in the coming years is that the state will be separated into two "time zones," two competing futures. Already, native-born Californians are, on average, older than the newcomers. One California speaks of conservation, the other needs space. One California votes, the other does not. One is thinking of retirement, the other of jobs.

The native-born Californian ends up saving grandpa's stucco bungalow, preserving as historical landmark what was for grandfather a symbol of progress.

The native-born Californian's best gift to this state is the wisdom of tragedy: We will be the ones who must speak of limits, of restrictions, of conservation. We will be the state's finger-waggers, problem-solvers—an elect.

I do not think, however, that from the native-born will come California's great visionaries. What the newcomer offers California is comic vision. The newcomer's gift to California has always been the audacity of optimism and the assurance that one can forget the past, put the feud between the Hatfields and the McCoys far behind. The newcomer has always taught California (as America taught the world) that you can reinvent history.

Each side must learn the wisdom of the other. California's destiny depends on the melding of tragic and comic sensibilities. The land cannot sustain the unalloyed traditional immigrant optimism. On the other hand, those of us who are native-born must know that we are an imposition on California.

All the time now one hears native-born Californians complain that they have had enough of this or that. Crowds. Prices. Traffic. They mean there are too many newcomers, too many immigrants. They tell you they are thinking of moving to Oregon or to Australia.

California is becoming as crowded with individual ambitions as 18th century London or Paris, but there is as yet no great satirist, no Jonathan Swift to note the ironies of our state. Swift's "Modest Proposal" was that the children of the poor could be sold to the rich as food. My own modest proposal for California is that there should be a limit to California. Every family in this state should be allowed no more than three generations here. When your time is up, you would have to move on—move to Australia or Argentina or your condo in Baja, move to Oregon. Is there, after all, any other way to "save" California for those newcomers who give California its dynamism?

The Japanese businessman perhaps does not understand that the movie company is now a second-generation affair. The Eastern European immigrant long ago passed away and has been succeeded by a committee of executive vice presidents. Hollywood is a second-generation affair. The actress is the daughter of the actress. The director is the son of the producer. Hollywood films are filled with allusions to other, earlier films. Or Hollywood films are stuttering repetitions of tried formulas. Lacking vision of its own, Hollywood buys options on other people's lives.

Lacking confidence in a narrative line, second-generation Hollywood offers technology. The technological effect is meant to approximate the immigrant stories of an earlier generation.

Thus does THX Sound or Dolby stereo attempt to offer today's moviegoer something of what we all once recognized on the great screen at the movie palace when Henry Fonda and the rest of the Joad family got out of their smoking truck, to stare in wonder—as though at paradise—at California's Central Valley.

James D. Houston
Jeanne Wakatsuki Houston
John Korty

James D. Houston (1933–) was born in San Francisco, raised in the Santa Clara Valley, and eventually became a student of Wallace Stegner's at Stanford. In volumes such as Gasoline: The Automotive Adventures of Charlie Bates *(1978) and* Continental Drift *(1978), as well as* Farewell to Manzanar *(1973), which he co-wrote with his wife Jeanne Wakatsuki Houston, he has established himself as a major fictionist and commentator on contemporary California. His nonfiction volume,* Californians: Searching for the Golden State *(1982), is another landmark work.*

Jeanne Wakatsuki Houston (1934–) was born in Inglewood and spent four years of her childhood in the Manzanar internment camp during World War II. She eventually graduated from San Jose State College and with her husband, James D. Houston, wrote the award-winning memoir Farewell to Manzanar. *Those two collaborated with Mill Valley resident and prominent film producer John Korty to produce the screenplay of the same name. Jeanne Houston is a free-lance writer whose other works include* Beyond Manzanar: Views of Asian-American Womanhood *(1985).*

John Korty (1936–), an award-winning film director and producer, collaborated with the Houstons in writing the screenplay for Farewell to Manzanar. *He both produced and directed the film, so he successfully guided the next, performed level of this story's realization. First shown as an "NBC World Premier Movie" in March of 1976,* Farewell to Manzanar *brought Korty and the Houstons the coveted Humanitas Prize, a Christopher Award, and an Emmy nomination. John Korty is a longtime resident of Mill Valley.*

FAREWELL TO MANZANAR (excerpt)

FADE IN

EXT. DESERTED HIGHWAY—DAY

1. A VW bus in the distance, heading toward the camera along a desert highway. It is a bright, crisp, windy morning in the Owens Valley of eastern California—a flat, sandy plain broken by low trees and scrub brush. The Inyo Mountains rise on one side and the spectacular, snow-laced eastern face of the Sierras are glimpsed to the west.

Various shots as the car speeds along this road, until we are close enough to see the occupants, a family of four: Caucasian father in his early forties, a Nisei mother in her early forties, girl age thirteen, boy age fifteen.

They pass a sign that says:

LONE PINE, CALIF.

pop. 2060 elev. 3700 ft.

2. EXT. LONE PINE MAIN STREET—DAY

As they drive through, we see Lone Pine at midday. Motels, diners, and shops of western clothes, all set against Mt. Whitney as a backdrop.

3. INT. VW BUS—DAY

Jeanne, the Nisei woman in the van, gazes reflectively at the landscape—remembering. She has long black hair, is pretty, intelligent, seasoned.

4. EXT. ROAD NEAR MANZANAR—DAY

From the road, what we see mostly is low brush and sand. A few clumps of cottonwoods rise in the distance. Suddenly however, two small gate houses appear faced with flagstones and topped with pagoda-like, curving roofs.

Credits begin.

5. EXT. MANZANAR CAMP RUINS—DAY

We follow the van a little farther along 395, and see it turn left, across a cattle guard, down a straight dirt road, bordered by sagebrush. In a cloud of dust they seem to be heading for the mountains directly ahead. Nothing else is to be seen.

The road makes a corner, so that the van moves parallel with the mountains. Jeanne is gazing out the window now, with mixed apprehension and expectancy.

We see the van stop in a cleared parking area near a clump of low trees. As the family climbs out, we don't yet see any of the ruins of the camp. But as they stretch and begin to look around we sense that this is a place to be treated reverently. All we hear is the heavy wind.

The children move off toward the trees, exploring. The husband accompanies them, leaving Jeanne alone, standing by herself in the empty valley between the two ranges.

> JEANNE (v.o.)
> My name is Jeanne Wakatsuki. This is where I grew up.

Her gaze moves from the brushy landscape to a small cemetery surrounded by barbed wire. A simple white shrine with Japanese characters carved into it rises above the wire in the morning light.

6. EXT. WAKATSUKI HOUSE, 1941—DAY

Cut to a small pagoda, standing on a lawn. Pan up to a one-story frame house, about thirty years old—with a front porch and ample space around the sides.

Jeanne, age 12, is gazing expectantly out the front room window. It is early afternoon.

> JEANNE (v.o.)
> Until I was 12, we lived near the ocean in a big frame house with a brick fireplace. We were the only Japanese-American family in the neighborhood. My father liked it that way. He didn't want to be labeled or grouped by anyone. . . .

7. EXT. WAKATSUKI'S STREET—DAY

While she speaks, we see the neighborhood street scene, a clean, but lower-income part of town. A resort town.

A car enters the frame. We follow it to the front of the house. Two other cars are already parked in the driveway.

A couple climbs out of the car. The man, Goosey, is fifty, Italian-American, a fisherman, dressed in his Sunday best—pin-striped suit, wing-tip shoes. His wife is dressed up too. They carry an elegantly wrapped box, white, with a big silver bow.

They climb the porch stairs, knock on the door. When it opens they are greeted by Jeanne, wearing her party dress, who has been given this duty as "greeter"—being youngest in the family.

8. INT. WAKATSUKI HOUSE—DAY

Jeanne takes the package, and we follow her as she leads the couple from the door into the main room, where some 20 people are drinking, shouting. Everyone is dressed up for this party, and about evenly mixed, Caucasian and Oriental. Some are dancing now, to music from a large old-time radio.

Jeanne places the new gift on the table, and we glimpse several other boxes, and a cake which bears the inscription,

HAPPY 25TH WEDDING ANNIVERSARY

Goosey and his wife move directly to Ko and Misa, the guests of honor, whose anniversary it is. They are beaming, as they stand near this table, in the middle of the throng.

Ko is fifty-two, well-tanned and healthy skinned, dressed now in a brand new double-breasted worsted suit, with vest and silk tie and stick pin. He is a dude and dandy. He sports a moustache.

Misa is forty-five, small, round, serene, supremely happy. She wears a crocheted, rose-colored, floor-length dress with a rhinestone pin on her bosom. Her hair is in an upsweep.

GOOSEY
(hugging Misa)

Happy anniversary.

MISA

Thank you, Goosey. We're so glad you could both come.

Warmly she embraces Goosey's wife, while Goosey grabs Ko's hand, pumps it, and gives him a comradely punch on the shoulder.

GOOSEY

And happy anniversary to you, Captain.

KO

Thank you, thank you, thank you.
(he sniffs conspiratorially)
You drunk already? I can smell it on your breath. You want some more?

Ko looks around, spots Teddy, his oldest son, who is pouring drinks at the punch bowl nearby. Teddy is twenty-four, stocky, and moustachioed. Next to him stands his brother, Richard, twenty-one, younger but taller, more slender.

KO

Hey, Teddy. Fix this fisherman a drink. Fix me another one too.

Teddy smiles with amusement at his father's loud, rowdy manner. He exchanges a grin with Richard.

MISA

Now, Papa, don't overdo.

KO

(hugging her shoulder)
What you talking about, little mama? This whiskey is what keeps me strong. Ask Goosey.

10. INT. WAKATSUKI LIVING ROOM—DAY

Ko and Misa are in the middle of opening the gifts laughing and thanking the people.

Ko enjoys the center of attention and now begins to unwrap Goosey's large box with a show of ceremony. Already open on the table are boxes of silver flatware, tureens, candlesticks, etc.

When Ko finally gets the box open we see that it contains a fine, silver-plated ship's compass. Half a dozen other guests gather to admire it.

KO

Hey, Goosey, you shouldn't have done that. It's too nice . . . But you wait, next year, I'm going to have a fifty-footer. I'll put this compass right up by the wheel.

> (pulling Goosey toward the food)

Hey, you hungry?

> (he calls to the others)

Everybody come here.

11. INT. WAKATSUKI DINING ROOM—DAY

We follow Ko and Goosey to a second table, heaped with food. The smorgasbord of food should catch the cultural mixing: chicken teriyaki, sushi, prawns, lobster, potato salad, jello molds, stuffed eggs, baked ham, cakes and pies. Lots of soda pop in bottles.

This pan ends just as Teddy and Richard, the two brothers, arrive from the kitchen with the piéce de resistance—a great, gleaming roast pig with a big fresh pineapple for a head.

They carry the pig on a cutting board, which they place at one end of the table next to a cleaver already waiting there.

Ko makes ready to carve the pig, revelling in this production. With his arms he directs his guests into a semicircle.

KO

Okay. Okay. Make room. Don't get too close. This thing can slice your finger off before you know it.

He picks up the cleaver. He tests its blade with his thumb. He settles himself in front of the pig.

KO

Rich. Teddy. Hold onto this board.

Trying to be serious, the sons each take one side of the board. When Ko knows everyone is watching, he lifts the cleaver high and with a Samurai grunt and much flourish he cuts the pig in half.

The men cheer. The women murmur. Ko lifts the cleaver again. Two more chops and the pig is split into quarters.

Then he sets the cleaver down, he reaches behind him without looking, and Alice, his pretty 16-year-old daughter, has a towel there waiting. While he wipes his hands, he speaks imperiously to his sons (while winking at Goosey).

KO

Cut it up. You girls, bring platters over here. Everybody wants to eat.

12. INT. LIVING ROOM—DAY

Everyone is eating. A dance tune of the period is on the victrola. Chopsticks and forks are equally busy as Teddy's wife, Chiyoko, is carrying a plate of food across the crowded room. She is pregnant, wearing an apron, already matronly at twenty-three. She brings this plate to Granny, who sits in a chair waiting, smiling. Granny is seventy-five, the mother of Misa, and half-blind. She smiles at Chiyoko and her rounded belly.

Teddy, in high spirits, comes along and tries to get his wife to dance, but she is embarrassed, so he gives her a quick hug and goes off for more food.

13. INT. LIVING ROOM—LATER AFTERNOON

The platters are empty now and Alice is singing a song as part of the after-dinner entertainment. She stands near a piano where Teddy plays a simple accompaniment. It is for Ko and Misa, who are pleased and deeply moved.

ALICE

Everybody loves my baby,
But my baby don't love nobody but me,
Nobody but me.

Everybody wants my baby,
But my baby don't want nobody but me,
That's plain to see . . .

15. EXT. WAKATSUKI HOUSE—DAY

It is a sunny morning, a few months later. Chiyoko and Teddy are putting the new baby in a second-hand buggy. The rest of the family gathers on the sidewalk to accompany the men to their boat—all but Granny, who is working a geranium bed with the help of Calvin, Jeanne's thirteen-year-old brother. They wave the others good-bye.

JEANNE (V.O.)

Even our weekends were busy then, because that was when the boats usually left. We loved to watch my father and the other men get ready to go out after sardines. Teddy and Richard were the crew on my father's boat. You never knew how long they'd be gone—a few days, a week, a month. It depended on the fish.

16. EXT. HARBOR—DAY

The women are now standing on the pier watching the men finish loading. There are only three boats going out but the men are in good spirits and eager to cast off.

On his boat, Ko is yelling a lot, giving orders to his sons. Today he wears knee-high rubber boots, a rust-colored turtleneck sweater, and a black skipper's cap.

Ko's boat is thirty feet long, white and low-slung, with a foredeck wheel cabin.

KO

Hey, Ted, you sure you got that net stacked tight?

TEDDY
(amused, but not disrespectful)

Yeah, Pop. We checked it twice.

KO

Richard, go down and make sure those spare tanks are shut!

RICHARD
(kidding back)

Why am *I* always the one who has to go below?

KO

Cause that kind of work is good for college boys. Keeps them smelling like fishermen.

Now from the family's viewpoint we see the first boat puttering out from the pier, into the channel, toward open water that is visible beyond. Teddy unties the final line and jumps aboard, while the women wave their good-byes. Ko's boat pulls into line among the others. He stands tall at the wheel, the proud skipper of his crew of two.

When we see the boats again they are outside the channel, moving off to the horizon.

On the dock we see Misa, squinting against the sun, her serenity cut by the first signs of worry. It is very quiet now, just water lapping at the pilings.

> MISA

They're not moving anymore.

> CHIYOKO

How can you tell?

> MISA

They're usually out of sight by now.

> CHIYOKO

Maybe they found the sardines already.

> MISA

No. Look. They're coming back. They're all turning around.

> CHIYOKO

Why would they be coming back?

> MISA

Something with the engines.

> CHIYOKO

Maybe somebody got hurt.

> MISA

But they wouldn't *all* be coming back.

> ALICE

Maybe it's bad weather, mama. Maybe a storm or something.

They all glance at the sky, scanning the unmarred horizon. Misa shakes her head. There is no explanation. Jeanne and Sarah look at each other frightened. The boats get closer, coming back into the harbor. The women run out to the far end of the pier.

> A MAN'S VOICE
> (far away, yelling)

Pearl Harbor! They've just bombed Pearl Harbor!

CHIYOKO
(to Misa)
What does he mean? What is Pearl Harbor!

The fear transmits to Jeanne.

JEANNE
What is a Pearl Harbor? What is a Pearl Harbor?

17. INT. WAKATSUKI HOUSE—NIGHT

Jeanne's face shows the same look, this time lit by flickering flames. We hear a fire, before we know its source.

Then we see Ko squatting in front of their front-room fireplace feeding papers into a small blaze.

His face is fixed in a firm, anguished resolve. The papers are old documents, in Japanese and English: letter, photos, books.

Misa comes in carrying more papers, painted scrolls and a folded flag, which he takes from her. He stands up and unfolds it for one final look— a beautifully-made emblem of the sun, a solid red circle on a pure white background.

KO
Pure silk, mama. Given to me by my Aunt Toyo when I sailed from Japan. That was thirty-five, forty years ago—and it was very old then.

Misa cannot speak. Her face is a mask. She and Jeanne watch him throw it into the fireplace, watch it catch and burn.

Granny comes shuffling into the room in time to make out the flag of her native country going up in flames. She cannot comprehend why Ko is doing this. She is frightened, alarmed. She rushes over to him, speaking in Japanese.

GRANNY
Ko-san, what are you doing?

Angry at everything, Ko shoves her gruffly aside.

KO
What a stupid waste!

Misa hurries to comfort her mother, and speaks both to Granny and Ko.

> MISA
>
> It must be done.
>
> (then to Granny)
>
> Shi kata ganai.

> KO
>
> (turning on Misa)
>
> Why? Why must it be done?

Violently, he kicks all the remaining papers into the fire.

Misa, stricken by what he's said, cannot speak, and knows better than to answer when he's in such a mood.

> KO
>
> I'll tell you why it must be done. I am a fisherman, Misa. I got a boat. I got a short wave. Even my tide tables will be suspected of being secret codes.

18. INT. FBI OFFICE—DAY

Cut to a large freckled hand holding a dozen deputy badges. It is an FBI agent who walks down a row of miscellaneous men, dealing out the badges like cards, talking in a low monotone as he goes. The men pin the badges on their coats, a few smile self-consciously, others are grimly serious.

> FBI AGENT
>
> . . . And remember, men, none of us know what we're getting into here. Some Japanese may be law-abiding citizens, but you got to be prepared for the worst. Keep a sharp eye out for anything looks suspicious: radios, maps. . . .

19. EXT. SCHOOL CROSSING—DAY

Two overnight lawmen are questioning a Japanese-American gardener on a street Jeanne and Calvin cross on their way to school. They watch from behind a crossing guard outfitted with shoulder straps and hand-held stop signs.

JEANNE (V.O.)

Twelve is a difficult age for anyone, but it was especially hard for me in 1941.

One of the lawmen is searching the gardener's truck while the other leads the man to an unmarked car. Calvin and Jeanne cross the street now with their heads down, not even looking at each other.

JEANNE (V.O.)

I had always thought of myself as more American than Japanese. I had said the Pledge of Allegiance since the first grade. What did it mean, 'Liberty and Justice for all'? Hadn't America pledged something to me in return?

20. EXT. ISERI DRUGSTORE WINDOW—DAY

Mr. Iseri, a druggist listens to a small radio as he looks out the front window of his store.

JEANNE (V.O.)

I also didn't realize that the first and most 'patriotic' calls for 'getting rid of the Japs' came from farmers and small businessmen.

20A. INT. WAKATSUKI HOUSE—DAY

RADIO COMMENTATOR
(harsh, but trying to sound reasonable)

The census bureau tells me there are some *ninety-thousand* Japs in California alone. Now some of these people would not cause us any trouble at all. But plenty of them *would* if they thought they would get away with it. Many of them are fine citizens. But others have been sent to Japan for schooling, *and* for military training. . . .

Twelve-year-old Jeanne is still trying to comprehend as she sits in the family living room, listening to the radio. The rest of the family listens too, scattered around the room: Ko, Misa, Granny, Ted, Chiyoko, Alice, Calvin. A solemn scene as they exchange glances, trying to foresee where this will lead:

RADIO COMMENTATOR

Most of them are under domination by Japan to some degree, which makes *all persons* of Japanese ancestry potentially dangerous—at least until we can find some *foolproof* way of distinguishing between the *wolves* and the *rabbits*. Do you think it's merely an *accident* a Jap farmer outside Ventura happens to have his strawberry field lined up right next to the Ventura airstrip, with one piece of land shaped like an arrowhead and pointing *directly toward the runway*?

Richard can take no more of this. He talks back to the radio.

> RICHARD
> A lot of public roads point to airports, too. Better investigate the highway commissioner!

20B. INT. KITCHEN—DAY

Cut to another "JAPANESE PROBLEM" headline just as Richard drops a pile of coffee grounds on it and wraps up the garbage.

Everyone seems to feel better. Misa and Chiyoko are organizing breakfast. The younger kids are still in pajamas, helping to set the table. Ko is sipping hot coffee at the head of the table, while Teddy burps the baby.

21. INT. HALLWAY—DAY

The doorbell rings. Jeanne runs to it in her bathrobe and swings the door open. Two strange men stand there, backlit by the low sun. Before they say anything, she backs away, shaking suddenly and staring at the gun one of the men wears under his coat. The room is still. Ko gets up, goes to the door.

> FIRST AGENT
> Are you Ko Wakatsuki?

> KO
> Yes.

Ko's direct look seems to embarrass the First Agent.

> FIRST AGENT
> (showing his ID card)
> We'd like you to come with us.

> KO
> What for? Where to?

> FIRST AGENT
> We want to ask you some questions.

KO

May I ask what about?

SECOND AGENT
(impatient with politeness)
You know what about.

KO

How long will it take?

SECOND AGENT
(grabbing for his arm)
C'mon, Mr. Wakeupski. We can't spend all day standing here.

Ko pulls his arm away, with a low grunt and a show of Samurai defiance that puts the agents on guard. Ko swells with offended dignity. He turns to his family. Misa and Ted have moved halfway across the living room where they stand watching warily, holding Jeanne, who is still shaking.

KO

I'll call you as soon as I can, Mama. Teddy, you take care of the family until I get back.

Misa watches this in disbelief, but knows she can't stop it. Ko takes his coat from Chiyoko who has run to get it. One of the agents takes it from him and searches the pockets and the lining. Alice fetches his hat. Ko puts the hat carefully on his head, then passes between the two agents, as he walks outside, leading them to the waiting car.

Amy Tan

Amy Tan's (1952–) success with The Joy Luck Club *(1989), her first novel from which the following vignettes are excerpted, is a publishing legend. She wrote the episodic novel about Chinese women and their Chinese-American daughters while studying writing with Molly Giles—perhaps the most successful class project ever.* The Joy Luck Club *is at once an immigrant saga and a series of vignettes, sketches, and stories that link uniquely American situations with an older culture. For the author, "1989 was an awesome leap. I went from being an unpublished writer to a published writer." Her book won many awards and was nominated for even more, and it propelled its author to national prominence. A graduate of San Jose State University, Tan published a second novel,* The Kitchen God's Wife, *in 1991. Elgy Gillespie, writing in* San Francisco Review of Books, *opined: "If anything,* The Kitchen God's Wife *is a more satisfying book than its predecessor"—high praise indeed.*

. . . .

THE JOY LUCK CLUB (excerpts)

"Do not ride your bicycle around the corner," the mother had told the daughter when she was seven.

"Why not!" protested the girl.

"Because then I cannot see you and you will fall down and cry and I will not hear you."

"How do you know I'll fall?" whined the girl.

"It is in a book, *The Twenty-Six Malignant Gates,* all the bad things that can happen to you outside the protection of this house."

"I don't believe you. Let me see the book."

"It is written in Chinese. You cannot understand it. That is why you must listen to me."

"What are they, then?" the girl demanded. "Tell me the twenty-six bad things."

But the mother sat knitting in silence.

"What twenty-six!" shouted the girl.

The mother still did not answer her.

"You can't tell me because you don't know! You don't know anything!" And the girl ran outside, jumped on her bicycle, and in her hurry to get away, she fell before she even reached the corner.

"Wah!" cried the mother upon seeing the mirrored armoire in the master suite of her daughter's new condominium. "You cannot put mirrors at the foot of the bed. All your marriage happiness will bounce back and turn the opposite way."

"Well, that's the only place it fits, so that's where it stays," said the daughter, irritated that her mother saw bad omens in everything. She had heard these warnings all her life.

The mother frowned, reaching into her twice-used Macy's bag. "Hunh, lucky I can fix it for you, then." And she pulled out the gilt-edged mirror she had bought at the Price Club last week. It was her housewarming present. She leaned it against the headboard, on top of the two pillows.

"You hang it here," said the mother, pointing to the wall above. "This mirror sees that mirror—*haule!*—multiply your peach-blossom luck."

"What is peach-blossom luck?"

The mother smiled, mischief in her eyes. "It is in here," she said, pointing to the mirror. "Look inside. Tell me, am I not right? In this mirror is my future grandchild, already sitting on my lap next spring."

And the daughter looked—and *haule!* There it was: her own reflection looking back at her.

The Fresno Poets

. . . .

The Fresno Poets consist of a creative cluster unlike any other in the state, which has developed at the state university in Fresno. Six of the poets who follow still reside in Fresno, and the seventh now lives in nearby Sanger. DeWayne Rail is a native of Oklahoma whose family migrated to the Fresno area in the 1950s; he teaches at Fresno City College. Dixie Salazar, another Fresno State graduate, was originally from Illinois. Jon Veinberg's widowed mother fled Estonia and he was born in Germany; he spent his early years in various cities in the eastern U.S. before arriving in Fresno, where he graduated from both high school and college. The late Ernesto Trejo, who also taught at Fresno City College, was born—ironically enough—in the small Mexican community of Fresnillo; his recent collection, *Entering a Life* (1990), has been widely praised. Roberta Spear, who earned her master's degree at Fresno State, was born and raised in nearby Hanford and her poems have appeared in many major periodicals. Charles W. Moulton, a native of Modesto and an ex-college football player, has been instrumental in sponsoring poetry readings in Fresno and in promoting the work of others. Luis Omar Salinas, born in Texas, has lived in various San Joaquin Valley communities (Bakersfield, Lindsay, Fresno, and now Sanger) and he, too, is a Fresno State alumnus. Their work—along with other noted graduates such as David St. John, Larry Levis, Sherley Anne Williams, and Gary Soto—illustrate why poetry from this city at the state's geographic center is special.

DeWayne Rail

DEATH OF A HOG

Water boiling in a drum,
Knives oiled and honed like razors,
Mean nothing to the hog.

It grunts and eats some corn
And moves a little.
The boy knows he must be steady

In front of women,
But the .22 grows heavy
Like it does in dreams.

He follows leaves falling in the wind,
Hears laughter, sees his sister
Swinging from the hook and chain.

Her scarf is bright against the sky.
Now his father's lips are moving
But sound is gone. He fires

Down the tunnel of the hog's eye.

Dixie Salazar

. . . .

SCARS

Tonight scars rise
on the moon, where once
I threw a shoe,
my mouth opened to the milky way
to scream, or to drown,
choking on the bitter stars.
The small vessel of my body
filled then, with a familiar brew
that made me haunt the night,
a mad, barefoot ghost
crying and tearing its wild fringe
of hair. My soul was a gecko
stuck to the wall,
my heart, a stone,
dark as fish blood.
No one saved me then,
but I didn't die,
and when I opened my eyes,
the earth was far below,
a maze of boiling lights,
and I was just a slip of air,
circling back to the center
of an old wound.

Jon Veinberg

· ·

LAST SHOT

     Before the game
Farnsworth had said
his heart felt on fire
and inside the heart
was trapped a small dark
horse kicking out
at the bolted door
of his body. Whether
he scored 33 or 34
no one seems to remember
but as for me there's
not enough beer and bean dip
in this county to save me
should the world erase
that clean pick and roll
in double-overtime and how
that orange globe of sun
rose from his fingers that night
to mount its peak three rims
above a landscape of smoke
and balded heads, swayed
and suspended itself
for what seemed a comet's lifetime,
until it finally left its arc
and descended as a ball on fire
travelling through a serene
and perfect net.
     It was the first

and only time some of us
cried out in joy so openly
and in public and he pumped
his fists toward and through
the rafters so grandly
that with my own eyes I saw
the glow his body took
until it too ignited into flame
and out of his chest exploded
a herd of wild dark horses
galloping so fast
they left permanent shadows
on the blurred faces
of all those who applauded him.

Ernesto Trejo

. . . .

SOME WOMEN

All week they toiled,
off to work early, to catch three busses.
The five retarded women sometimes hold hands
like schoolchildren who haven't yet become
embarrassed at the touch of flesh.
And like schoolchildren they carry lunch pails
graced with pictures of Bugs Bunny
and Betty Boop and their own names
in large uneven letters. They walk
assiduously, mostly looking at the ground,
their brows lined with worry
and resolve. A little gray
is sprouting on their heads and their arms
show the freckles of their age.
Someone taught them to praise Jesus
in song, to give thanks
for all the wonders in their lives.
And they sing, off key,
unashamed and rapturous as they bake
pies all day long, as they wipe
the sweat off their arms and faces,
as they count exactly 37 cherries,
19 sacks of flour, one teaspoon of salt . . .
They sing to the miracle of numbers,
busses, and egg sandwiches with Kool-Aid.
They remember other days in other years
when they gazed out of windows
from their tiny rooms and took
their pills on time, and their naps,

and tried hard to learn to read,
how every day was like a tunnel
and the night noises always so loud . . .
But now they are blessed
with a life in a house, on a street
lined with cedars that sway in the wind
and point skyward at the blue.
They have each other, five women
who play games and sing and argue
but who are mostly thankful for the work
at the pie factory
where they get real paychecks
and break their backs for Jesus Lord.

Roberta Spear

GRAFFITI

On a plank fence that faces 6th Street,
the scroll unwinds—
blackened words put down
in the darkness of the night before.
And all we know is what the stars
are willing to tell us
or what the wood beetle mutters
in its borings. The wind strokes
the splintered surface: the hearts and daggers,
bits of swiped oranges, charred
numbers, and the tears of revenge.
This trail should lead back
to the softened corners
where the young doze off
as the sun finally rises. Next door,
our neighbor stands to
tuck in his shirt and goes out
to check the fruit of this day.
With his bucket and brush,
he rants in Armenian, erasing
the message left just for him.
But I try to imagine the rage of Jaime
before it vanishes
and Carlos' courage and who
made Maria feel *that way*. Were you
the one I passed once at dawn
in an empty parking lot,
drawing her gently toward you
and into your leather jacket?

Or the one I saw strutting down
the middle of the street
one freezing night, combing back
your shiny hair with your fingers
as you followed the stars north?
The crows angle downward now,
heckling poor Nishon as he
gathers the last sweet oranges
off the ground. Those birds
drop their black feathers anywhere,
like the scars of old passions,
before the earth has a chance
to throw up its arms
and frighten them away.

Charles W. Moulton

CAPTAIN OWL

He used to navigate B-52's up into Nam
and he had a sympathy
for the down trodden.
"Life is Hard," he would say.
"Some don't make it."
One day his soul followed a bomb down
and remained there with the dead and suffering.
Even the doctors couldn't help
or anyone rotten enough to want to face life.
They kept him sedated
but sometimes they'd forget
and he'd perch in the bed
with eyes round like an owl
and feed on suffering.
Finally the shrinks saw
he was normal and discharged him.

Luis Omar Salinas

. . . .

MY FIFTY-PLUS YEARS CELEBRATE SPRING

On the road, the mountains
in the distance are at rest
in a wild blue silence.
On the sides of the highway
the grape orchards unfurl
deep and green again
like a pregnant woman
gathering strength
for the time to come.
And with the passing
of each season
human life knows little
change. Forty years
in this valley,
the wind, the sun
building its altars
of salt, the rain that
holds nothing back,
and with the crop
at its peak
packing houses burn
into morning,
their many diligent
Mexican workers stacking up
the trays and hard hours
that equal their living.

I've heard it said
hard work ennobles

the spirit—
If that is the case,
the road to heaven
must be crowded
beyond belief.

Recommended Readings

Twelve writers, scholars, and critics were contacted and asked to recommend books for an ideal reading list of California titles, plus a small selection of movies based upon this state's fiction. Their various recommendations—some of which appeared on virtually every list, others on only one—are cataloged without comment below.

ANTHOLOGIES

Baloian, James, and David Kherdian, *Down at the Santa Fe Depot*
Beck, Warren A., *The California Experience*
Caughey, John and Laree, *California Heritage*
Cuelho, Art, *Proud Harvest*
Eisen, Jonathan, and David Fine, *Unknown California*
Field, Edward, *A Geography of Poets*
———. *A New Geography of Poets*
Haslam, Gerald, and James D. Houston, *California Heartland*
Jackson, Joseph Henry, *Continent's End*
Lee, W. Storrs, *California: A Literary Chronicle*
Margolin, Malcolm, *The Way We Lived: California Indian
    Reminiscences, Stories and Songs*
Markham, Edwin, *Songs and Stories*
Michaels, Leonard, David Reid, and Raquel Scheer, *West of the West*
Miller, Adam David, *Dices, or Black Bones*
Soto, Gary, *California Childhood*
Veinberg, Jon, and Ernesto Trejo, *Piecework*
Watts, Jane, *Valley Light*
Webb, Charles Harper, and Suzanne Lummis, *Stand Up Poetry*

POETRY

Alurista, *Return*
Barnes, Dick, *Lake on the Earth*
Bidart, Frank, *Golden State*
Bogen, Laurel Ann, *The Projects*
Bromige, David, *Desire*
Bukowski, Charles, *War All the Time*
——— . *Love Is a Dog from Hell*
Carver, Raymond, *At Night the Salmon Move*
Corso, Gregory, *Gasoline*
——— . *The Vestal Lady on Brattle*
Cuelho, Art, *Selected Road Poems*
Di Prima, Diane, *Pieces of a Song*
Divakaruni, Chitra Banerjee, *the reason for nasturtiums*
Elder, Gary, *Hold Fire*
Everson, William, *Man-Fate: The Swan Song of Brother Antoninus*
——— . *The Masks of Drought*
——— . *The Residual Years*
——— . *The Veritable Years*
Ferlinghetti, Lawrence, *A Coney Island of the Mind*
——— . *Endless Life: Selected Poems*
——— . *Open Eye, Open Heart*
——— . *Who Are We Now?*
Flanner, Hildegarde, *Poems, Collected and Selected*
Freid, Elliot, *Man Talk*
Ginsberg, Allen, *Howl, and Other Poems*
Gonzales, N.V.M., *Mindoro and Beyond*
Gonzalez, Rafael Jesus, *El Hacedor de Juegos*
Grapes, Jack, *Trees, Coffee, and the Eyes of Deer*
Gunn, Thom, *The Passages of Joy*
——— . *To the Air*
Hass, Robert, *Human Wishes*
Hotchkiss, Bill, *Fever in the Earth*
——— . *The Graces of Fire and Other Poems*
Inada, Lawson, *Before the War*
Jeffers, Robinson, *Cawdor*
——— . *The Double Axe and Other Poems*

———. *The Selected Poetry of Robinson Jeffers*

———. *The Women at Point Sur*

Kaufman, Bob, *Solitudes Crowded with Loneliness*

Keithley, George, *The Donner Party*

Kizer, Carolyn, *Mermaids in the Basement*

———. *The Nearness of You*

Koertge, Ronald, *The Father-Poems*

Kyger, Joanne, *Going On*

Levis, Larry, *The Afterlife*

———. *Winter Stars*

Lewis, Janet, *The Invasion*

Lim, Genny, *Winter Place*

Linenthal, Mark, *Growing Light*

Locklin, Gerald, *The Criminal Mentality*

———. *Poop and Other Poems*

———. *The Toad Poems*

Luschei, Glenna, *Bare Roots: Seasons*

———. *Farewell to Winter*

Mailman, Leo, *The Handyman Poems*

Malone, Marvin, *Bucolics and Cheromanics*

Marcus, Morton, *The Santa Cruz Mountain Poems*

———. *Pages from a Scrapbook of Immigrants*

McClure, Michael, *Selected Poems*

———. *Fragments of Perseus*

McDaniel, Wilma Elizabeth, *A Primer for Buford*

———. *A Girl from Buttonwillow*

———. *The Red Coffee Can*

———. *Sister Vayda's Song*

McFerrin, Linda Watanabe, *The Impossibility of Redemption*

Micheline, Jack, *Poems of Fire & Light*

Miles, Josephine, *Coming to Terms*

Minasian, Khatchik, *Selected Poems*

Moser, Norman, *El Grito del Norte*

Nathan, Leonard, *Carrying On*

———. *With the Skin*

———. *Western Reaches*

Northsun, Nila, *Diet Pepsi and Nacho Cheese*

Norse, Harold, *The Love Poems, 1940–85*

Oandasan, William, *Moving Inland*
Parkinson, Thomas, *Poems, New and Selected*
Patchen, Kenneth, *Selected Poems*
Peters, Robert, *Shaker Light*
Raborg, Frederick, *Tule*
Ragan, James, *In the Talking Hours*
———. *Womb-Weary*
Rail, DeWayne, *The Water Witch*
Robertson, Kirk, *Driving to Vegas: Poems 1969–1987*
Rose, Dorothy, *Dustbowl: Thorns and Roses*
Rose, Wendy, *The Halfbreed Chronicles & Other Poems*
Rexroth, Kenneth, *The Complete Collected Shorter Poems*
———. *The Signature of All Things*
Ruggles, Eugene, *The Lifeguard in the Snow*
Salinas, Luis Omar, *Crazy Gypsy*
———. *The Sadness of Days*
Schmitz, Dennis, *Eden*
———. *We Weep for Our Strangeness*
Snyder, Gary, *Axe Handles*
———. *The Back Country*
———. *Left Out in the Rain*
———. *The Practice of the Wild*
———. *Turtle Island*
Soto, Gary, *The Elements of San Joaquin*
———. *Who Will Know Us?*
Spear, Roberta, *Taking to Water*
St. John, David, *Hush*
———. *No Heaven*
———. *The Shore*
Stetler, Charles, *Roger, Karl, Rick, and Shane Are Friends of Mine*
Stowell, Phyllis, *Who Is Alice?*
Swanger, David, *The Shape of Waters*
Sward, Robert, *Collected Poems 1957–91*
Swigart, Rob, *Toxin*
Tagami, Jeff, *October Light*
Tallent, Elizabeth, *In Constant Flight*
Thompson, Don, *Granite Station*
Thompson, Gary, *Hold Fast*

Trejo, Ernesto, *Entering a Life*
Wakoski, Diane, *Emerald Ice*
———. *Medea the Sorceress*
Webb, Charles, *Zinjanthropus Disease*
Welch, Lew, *Ring of Bone*
Williams, Sherley Anne, *The Peacock Poems*
———. *Some One Sweet Angel Chile*
Wong, Nellie, *Dreams in Harrison Railroad Park*

DRAMA

Bullins, Ed, *Salaam, Huey P. Newton Salaam*
Fulton, Len, *Headlines*
Keithley, George, *The Best Blood in the Country*
Lummis, Suzanne, *Night Owls*
Lynch, Michael, *San Joaquin Blues*
O'Neill, Eugene, *Long Day's Journey into Night*
Patchen, Kenneth, *Patchen's Lost Plays*
Saroyan, William, *Hello Out There*
———. *My Heart's in the Highlands*
———. *The Time of Your Life*
Shepard, Sam, *Angel City*
———. *Buried Child*
———. *True West*
Steinbeck, John, *Of Mice and Men*
Valdez, Luis, *Actos*
———. *The Shrunken Head of Pancho Villa*
———. *Zoot Suit*

FICTION

Angulo, Jaime de. *A Jaime de Angulo Reader*
Austin, Mary, *The Flock*
———. *Lost Borders*
Atherton, Gertrude, *The Californians*
———. *The Splendid, Idle Forties*
Barrio, Raymond, *The Plum, Plum Pickers*
Brautigan, Richard, *A Confederate General from Big Sur*

——— . *Trout Fishing in America*
Braverman, Kate, *Lithium for Medea*
——— . *Palm Latitudes*
Bryant, Dorothy, *A Day in San Francisco*
Bukowski, Charles, *Fire Station*
——— . *Hollywood*
——— . *Post Office*
——— . *South of No North*
Cain, James M., *Double Indemnity*
——— . *The Postman Always Rings Twice*
Cain, Paul, *Fast One*
Carver, Raymond, *Will You Please Be Quiet, Please?*
Chandler, Raymond, *The Big Sleep*
——— . *Farewell, My Lovely*
——— . *The Lady in the Lake*
——— . *The Little Sister*
Clark, Walter Van Tilburg, *The Track of the Cat*
Conner, K. Patrick, *Blood Moon*
Didion, Joan, *Play It as It Lays*
——— . *Run River*
Dokey, Richard, *August Heat*
Dunne, John Gregory, *True Confessions*
Easton, Robert, *The Happy Man*
Fante, John, *Ask the Dust*
——— . *Brotherhood of the Grape*
——— . *Dago Red*
——— . *The Road to Los Angeles*
——— . *The Wine of Youth*
Fitzgerald, F. Scott, *The Last Tycoon*
Gentry, Curt, *The Last Days of the Late, Great State of California*
Hammett, Dashiell, *The Maltese Falcon*
Harte, Bret, *The Best of Bret Harte*
Haslam, Gerald, *That Constant Coyote*
——— . *Okies*
——— . *Snapshots: Glimpses of the Other California*
——— . *The Wages of Sin*
Henningsen, Helene, *Anton and Louisa*
Houston, James D., *Continental Drift*

———. *Gasoline: The Automotive Adventures of Charlie Bates*
———. *Love Life*
———. *A Native Son of the Golden West*
Houston, Jeanne and James D., *Farewell to Manzanar*
Huxley, Aldous, *After Many a Summer Dies the Swan*
Jackson, Helen Hunt, *Ramona*
James, Dan (Danny Santiago), *Famous All Over Town*
Johnson, Diane, *Lying Low*
Kerouac, Jack, *Big Sur*
———. *The Dharma Bums*
———. *On the Road*
Kingston, Maxine Hong, *The Woman Warrior*
———. *China Men*
———. *Tripmaster Monkey*
Kroeber, Theodora, *The Inland Whale*
Lee, Hector, *The Bodega War*
———. *Heroes, Villains, and Ghosts*
———. *Tales of California*
Leffland, Ella, *Love Out of Season*
———. *Rumors of Peace*
Le Guin, Ursula, *Always Coming Home*
Locklin, Gerald, *The Gold Rush and Other Stories*
London, Jack, *The Valley of the Moon*
———. *Martin Eden*
Lurie, Alison, *The Nowhere City*
Macdonald, Elisabeth, *Watch for the Morning*
MacDonald, Ross, *The Moving Target*
———. *The Drowning Pool*
———. *The Underground Man*
———. *The Zebra-Striped Hearse*
Mailer, Norman, *The Deer Park*
Masumoto, David Mas, *Silent Strength*
McCoy, Horace, *They Shoot Horses, Don't They?*
McFadden, Cyra, *The Serial*
Michaels, Leonard, *The Men's Club*
Miller, Joaquín, *Life Amongst the Modocs*
Mori, Toshio, *Yokohama, California*
Mosley, Walter, *Devil in a Blue Dress*

Mowry, Jess, *Rats in the Trees*
Najarian, Peter, *Daughters of Memory*
Norris, Frank, *The Octopus*
———. *McTeague*
Olsen, Tillie, *Tell Me a Riddle*
Otto, Whitney, *How to Make an American Quilt*
Pynchon, Thomas, *The Crying of Lot 49*
———. *Vineland*
Reed, Ishmael, *The Last Days of Louisiana Red*
Ridge, John Rollin, *The Life and Adventures of Joaquín Murieta*
Rintoul, William, *Rig Nine*
———. *Roustabout*
Roper, Robert, *Royo County*
Salas, Floyd, *Tattoo the Wicked Cross*
Sanchez, Thomas, *Rabbit Boss*
Saroyan, William, *My Name Is Aram*
———. *The Daring Young Man on the Flying Trapeze*
———. *The Human Comedy*
See, Carolyn, *Golden Days*
Seth, Vikram, *The Golden Gate*
Sinclair, Upton, *Oil!*
Soto, Gary, *A Summer Life*
———. *Living Up the Street*
Stegner, Wallace, *All the Little Live Things*
———. *Angle of Repose*
Steinbeck, John, *Cannery Row*
———. *East of Eden*
———. *The Grapes of Wrath*
———. *In Dubious Battle*
———. *Of Mice and Men*
———. *The Pastures of Heaven*
———. *The Red Pony*
———. *Tortilla Flat*
Stewart, George, *Fire*
———. *Ordeal by Hunger*
———. *Storm*
Tan, Amy, *The Joy Luck Club*
Taylor, Ron, *Long Road Home*

Villareal, Jose Antonio, *Pocho*
Wallace, Pamela, *Small Town Girls*
Waugh, Evelyn, *The Loved One*
West, Nathaniel, *The Day of the Locust*
Wilson, Harry Leon, *Merton of the Movies*
Yamamoto, Hisaye, *Seventeen Syllables and Other Stories*
Zepeda, Rafael, *Horse Medicine*

FILMS BASED ON CALIFORNIA FICTION

Barfly
The Day of the Locust
East of Eden
Farewell My Lovely
Farewell to Manzanar
Fat City
The Grapes of Wrath
Greed (based on *McTeague*)
The Human Comedy
The Long Goodbye
The Loved One
The Maltese Falcon
The Men's Club
Merton of the Movies
Of Mice and Men
The Postman Always Rings Twice
The Serial
Tell Me a Riddle
They Shoot Horses, Don't They?
Two Years Before the Mast
Zoot Suit

NONFICTION

Austin, Mary, *The Land of Little Rain*
Bakker, Elna, *An Island Called California*
Bell, Horace, *Reminiscences of a Ranger*
Brewer, William Henry, *Up and Down California, 1860–64*

Carrighar, Sally, *One Day on Beetle Rock*

Clemens, Samuel (Mark Twain), *Roughing It*

Dana, Richard Henry, *Two Years Before the Mast*

Didion, Joan, *Slouching Toward Bethlehem*

———. *The White Album*

Dillon, Richard, *Humbugs and Heroes: A Gallery of California Pioneers*

Dunne, John Gregory, *Delano*

Everson, William, *Archetype West*

Ferlinghetti, Lawrence, *Literary San Francisco*

Fine, David (ed.), *Los Angeles in Fiction*

Galarza, Ernesto, *Spiders in the House & Workers in the Field*

Haslam, Gerald, *Coming of Age in California*

———. *The Other California*

———. *Voices of a Place*

Holliday, James S., *The World Rushed In*

Houston, James D., *Californians: Searching for the Golden State*

Kahrl, William L., *The California Water Atlas*

King, Clarence, *Mountaineering in the Sierra Nevada*

Kroeber, Theodora, *Ishi in Two Worlds*

Latta, Frank, *Black Gold in the Joaquin*

———. *Joaquín Murrieta and His Horse Gangs*

Longtin, Ray C., *Three Writers of the Far West*

Masumoto, David Mas, *Country Voices*

Matthiessen, Peter, *Sal Si Puedes*

McWilliams, Carey, *California: The Great Exception*

———. *Factories in the Field*

Miller, Henry, *Big Sur and the Oranges of Hieronymous Bosch*

Muir, John, *The Mountains of California*

———. *My First Summer in the Sierra*

———. *The Wilderness World of John Muir*

Powell, Lawrence Clark, *An Orange Grove Boyhood*

Rodriguez, Richard, *Hunger of Memory*

Rojas, Arnold R., *These Were the Vaqueros*

———. *Vaqueros and Buckaroos*

Rolfe, Lionel, *Literary L.A.*

Royce, Josiah, *California*

Starr, Kevin, *Americans and the California Dream*

Steinbeck, John, *The Harvest Gypsies*

Stevenson, Robert Louis, *From Scotland to Silverado*

Taylor, Bayard, *El Dorado*

Thompson, Hunter, *Hell's Angels*

Walker, Franklin, *A Literary History of Southern California*

———. *San Francisco's Literary Frontier*

Wallace, David Raines, *The Klamath Knot*

Western Writers Series (Booklets from Boise State University, each on an
individual author, that include Californians such as Muir, King,
Chandler, Saroyan, Haslam, Stegner, Jeffers, Powell, and Houston.)

Credits

· ·

"Atsugewi Lovers' Song" from Theodora Kroeber and Robert Heizer, *Almost Ancestors*.

"Beginning of the World" from Theodora Kroeber and Robert Heizer, *Almost Ancestors*.

"Birth of the Sacramento River" from Robert Pearson and Ursula Spier Erickson, *The Californians: Writings of Their Past and Present*, vol. 1.

Boyle, T. Coraghessan. "The Human Fly" from *If the River Was Whiskey* by T. Coraghessan Boyle. Copyright 1989 by T. Coraghessan Boyle. Reprinted by permission of Viking Penguin, a division of Penguin Books USA Inc.

Braverman, Kate. "10 PM," "You Ask About Madness," and "Softenings" from *Hurricane Warnings*. Copyright 1987 by Kate Braverman. Reprinted by permission of the author.

Bukowski, Charles. "A radio with guts" and "the red porsche" from *Play the Piano Drunk/Like a Percussion Instrument/Until the Fingers Begin to Bleed a Bit*. Copyright 1979 by Charles Bukowski. Reprinted by permission of Black Sparrow Press. "Eulogy to a hell of a dame—" from *War All the Time:*

Poems 1981–1984. Copyright 1984 by Charles Bukowski. Reprinted by permission of Black Sparrow Press.

Chandler, Raymond. "I'll Be Waiting" from *The Simple Art of Murder* by Raymond Chandler. Copyright 1950 by Raymond Chandler, copyright renewed 1978 by Helga Greene. Reprinted by permission of Houghton Mifflin Company.

Coleman, Wanda. "The Screamer" from *A War of Eyes and Other Stories*. Copyright 1988 by Wanda Coleman. Reprinted by permission of Black Sparrow Press.

Didion, Joan. "Notes from a Native Daughter" from *Slouching Towards Bethlehem*. Copyright 1965, 1968 by Joan Didion. Reprinted by permission of Farrar, Straus & Giroux, Inc.

Duncan, Robert. "My Mother Would Be a Falconress" from *Bending the Bow*. Copyright 1968 by Robert Duncan. Reprinted by permission of New Directions Publishing Corporation.

"Earth Diver" from Constance G. DuBois and D. Demetrocopoulous, *Wintun Myths*, University of California Publications in American Archeology and Ethnology, vol. 28, no. 5, 1931.

Everson, William. "The Residual

ABOUT THE EDITOR

Gerald W. Haslam has published six collections of short stories—most recently *That Constant Coyote: California Stories,* which was awarded a 1990 Josephine Miles Prize for Excellence in Literature. In 1990, he also published two essay collections, *The Other California: The Great Central Valley in Life and Letters* and *Coming of Age in California: Personal Essays.* He has published one other essay collection, a novel, and four books of various nonfiction.

Haslam's career as a writer has been marked by his use of California's rural and small-town areas, its poor and working-class people of all colors, to explore the human condition. He is a professor of English at Sonoma State University.